The Mistresses of King George IV

Mrs Mary Robinson ('Perdita') by Thomas Gainsborough (1781).
Mary was Geoge's first mistress.
(Reproduced by courtesy of the Wallace Collection)

M. J. LEVY

The Mistresses
of
King George IV

PETER OWEN
London & Chester Springs

To Rachel

PETER OWEN PUBLISHERS
73 Kenway Road London SW5 0RE
Peter Owen books are distributed in the USA by
Dufour Editions Inc. Chester Springs PA 19425–0007

First published in Great Britain 1996
© M.J. Levy 1996

A catalogue record for this book is available
from the British Library

ISBN 0–7206–0956–9

Printed and made in Great Britain by Biddles
of Guildford and King's Lynn

Contents

Preface *vii*

A Brief Chronology *ix*

Mrs Robinson *13*

Mrs Fitzherbert *44*

Lady Jersey *77*

Mrs Fitzherbert Again *104*

Lady Hertford *128*

Lady Conyngham *152*

Epilogue *182*

Appendix *192*

Sources *195*

Select Bibliography *202*

Index *204*

Is it not a world to consider the desire of wilful princes, when they fully be bent and inclined to fulfil their voluptuous appetites, against the which no reasonable persuasions will suffice; little or nothing weighing or regarding the dangerous sequel that doth ensue as well to themselves as to their realm and subjects. And above all things, there is no one thing that causeth them to be more wilful than carnal desire and voluptuous affection of foolish love.

George Cavendish,
The Life of Cardinal Wolsey, c. 1557

No woman was ever really attached to him – Mrs F[itzherbert] perhaps the most. He was too selfish.

The Duke of Wellington to the
Marchioness of Salisbury, 1835

Preface

History has not been kind to the mistresses of George IV. Who now, outside the ranks of biographers and historians, can even remember their names? Insulted and calumniated in their day, they have most of them fallen into an obscurity so profound that it is almost total. True, Mrs Fitzherbert is remembered, but then, as a Catholic and, as some still believe, the rightful wife of George IV, her case is special; as, for rather different reasons, is the first of George's mistresses, the talented and exhibitionistic Mary Robinson. Untramelled by the same conventions as her fellow royal mistresses, following her affair with the King, she enjoyed a career as a fashionable and prolific writer.

The Times, when George IV died, described him as a libertine and a wastrel, an 'inveterate voluptuary', who 'professed a species of philosophy far more gross than Epicurus would have acknowledged'. 'Never was an individual less regretted by his fellow–creatures', it wrote, 'than this deceased King. What eye has wept for him? What heart has heaved one throb of unmercenary sorrow . . . for that Leviathan of the *haut ton*, George IV'?

The court of his father George III had had a 'powerful influence in maintaining the decencies of social intercourse throughout England', while his mother Queen Charlotte, 'by her resolute contempt for vice, and rigorous exclusion of female profligates from her presence, did actually cover the cause of the adultress with authorized and merited scorn'. Yet, their son's court was ruled by a 'series of licentious favourites. . . .

The divorced of both sexes and of all ages were not afraid of meeting a favourable reception from congenial spirits near the British Throne'.

Lady Jersey, perhaps the most fascinating of the King's mistresses, arranged and then wrecked his 'official' marriage to Caroline of Brunswick, the Tory Lady Hertford guided his politics, while Lady Conyngham dominated his social life and alienated his friends. Like Mary Robinson and Mrs Fitzherbert, all were in their different ways striking and powerful figures, and as such very much a part of elite life in their age.

I am particularly grateful to the following individuals and organizations for allowing me to reproduce material: the Hertfordshire Record Office for the Capel MSS; Mr Peter Day and the Trustees of the Chatsworth Settlement; The British Library; Mr Paul Burns of Burns and Oates for Sir Shane Leslie's *Mrs Fitzherbert* and Mrs Fitzherbert's *Letters*; Mr D. Jones for material in the Richmond-upon-Thames Local Studies Library; Macmillan Publishers Ltd for *Wellington and His Friends*; and John Murray Ltd for the Duchess of Devonshire's *Correspondence*, Lady Palmerston's *Letters* and *The Private Letters of Princess Lieven to Prince Metternich*.

All quotations appear unaltered, except that contractions such as 'wd' and 'cd' have been expanded and the ampersand has been replaced by 'and'.

A Brief Chronology of the Life of King George IV

1762	12 August	George Augustus Frederick born at St James's Palace, Westminster
1763	16 August	Frederick (favourite brother) born
1776	May	Sparks 'Nursery Revolution' at the Dutch House (Kew Palace)
1779	April	Begins close friendship with Mary Hamilton (sisters' sub-governess)
	December	Falls 'over head and ears' in love with Mary Robinson
1780	Dec.–Jan. 1781	Loses friendship and support of Frederick and Lieutenant-Colonel Gerard Lake (First Equerry), both of whom leave London. Separates from Mrs Robinson
1781	1 January	Officially enters society
	January (c.)	Begins affair with Elizabeth Armistead
	July	Enjoys brief affair with Madame von Hardenburg
1782	July	Begins close friendship with Charles James Fox
	August	Resumes affair with Elizabeth Armistead
1783	April–Dec.	Supports Fox–North Coalition
	June	Income settled by King and Government
	Autumn	Initiates redevelopment of Carlton House
	September	Pays first visit to Brighton
	11 November	Takes seat in House of Lords
1784	March	Falls desperately in love with Maria Fitzherbert

	8 July	Attempts suicide; persuades Mrs Fitzherbert to promise to marry him
1785	10 December	Receives letter from Fox outlining arguments against marriage to Mrs Fitzherbert
	11 December	Gives Fox an undertaking not to marry Mrs Fitzherbert
	15 December	Marries Mrs Fitzherbert at 'illegal' ceremony in London
1786	July	Shuts up Carlton House
1787	April	Debts debated in Parliament. Fox refutes rumours that the Prince and Mrs Fitzherbert are married
	21 May	Debts settled by King and Parliament
1788	Oct.–Nov.	During the 'Regency Crisis' manoeuvres to seize power from sick father
1789	September	Tours Yorkshire
1791	October	Withdraws horses from Newmarket following betting scandal
1792	31 May	Attacks extreme reformers in maiden speech in Lords
1793	January	Appointed Colonel Commandant of the 10th Regiment of Dragoons
1794	Spring	Begins affair with Lady Jersey
	23 June	Separates officially from Mrs Fitzherbert
	August	Informs the King of his wish to marry Caroline of Brunswick
1795	4 April	Meets Caroline for the first time, in London
	8 April	Marries Caroline in the Chapel Royal, St James's
	June	New financial settlement; Commissioners appointed to oversee his debts
1796	7 January	Charlotte (only legitimate daughter) born
	10 January	Writes 'last will and testament', leaving almost his entire property to Mrs Fitzherbert
	April	Caroline calls for resignation of Lady Jersey from her position as Lady of the Bedchamber

	31 May	Asks King for formal separation from Caroline
	29 June	Lady Jersey resigns
1798	Summer	Separates from Lady Jersey
1799	Summer	Bullies Mrs Fitzherbert into returning to him
1800	16 June	Attends 'public breakfast', formally recognizing his reconciliation with Mrs Fitzherbert
	26 December	Mrs Robinson dies
1801	Feb.–April	Plans new administration during illness of King
	Winter	Begins custody battle over fate of 'Minney' Seymour
1803	March	Annuity Bill passed; income increased
1804	Feb.–June	Again plans new administration during illness of King
1806	January	Supports 'Ministry of all the Talents'
	14 June	Wins Seymour custody battle
	Summer	Agrees to formation of Commission of Enquiry in order to investigate Caroline's behaviour – the 'Delicate Investigation'
	Autumn	Begins intimacy with Lady Hertford
	13 September	Charles James Fox dies at Chiswick
1807	Spring	Relaxes connection with Whigs
1809	Winter	Attempts seduction of Lady Bessborough
1810	October	King incapacitated
1811	5 February	Embarks upon 'Restricted Regency'
	7 June	Breaks finally with Mrs Fitzherbert
	19 June	Hosts fête at Carlton House to celebrate the beginning of the Regency
1812	February	Breaks formally with Whigs; elects to keep Tories in power under Spencer Perceval; begins 'Unrestricted Regency'
1814	June	Hosts visits of victorious allies to London
	9 August	Caroline leaves England
1816	2 May	Princess Charlotte marries
1817	5 November	Princess Charlotte dies at Claremont
1818	August	Initiates official enquiry into Caroline's conduct abroad – the 'Milan Commission'

	17 November	Queen Charlotte (mother) dies at Kew
1819	December (c.)	Separates from Lady Hertford; begins affair with Lady Conyngham
1820	29 January	King George III dies at Kew
	5 June	Caroline returns to England
	17 Aug.–6 Nov.	Public Enquiry in the Lords into Caroline's behaviour – the 'Queen's Trial'
1821	19 July	Crowned in Westminster Abbey
	25 July	Lady Jersey dies
	8 August	Queen Caroline dies in London
	Aug.–Sept.	Visits Ireland
	24–c.27 August	Stays with Lady Conyngham at Slane Castle, Meath
	Sept.–Nov.	Pays state visit to Hanover
1822	August	Visits Scotland
1823	March	Proposes making Lady Conyngham a residuary legatee of will
1826	May	Attempts seduction of Madame de Lieven
1827	5 January	Frederick dies
1829	10 April	Reluctantly gives assent to Roman Catholic Relief Act
1830	7 June	Attempts to leave bulk of his property to Lady Conyngham
	26 June	Dies at Windsor

Mrs Robinson

Mary Robinson's affair with the Prince of Wales began shortly before a command performance of *The Winter's Tale* at Drury Lane on the evening of 3 December 1779.

As she stood in a side wing, dressed for the role of Perdita, Mary Robinson noticed that the young Prince was looking at her. He followed her movements as she exchanged a few words with his friend Viscount Malden, then stared at her fixedly when a few minutes later she took the stage. She had never performed before the royal family before, and, thrown by the Prince's attention, she hurried through her first scene, barely able to suppress her anxiety. 'Indeed some flattering remarks which were made by his Royal Highness met my ear as I stood near his box, and I was overwhelmed with confusion.'

Earlier, as she had waited in the Green Room William Smith, who was to play Leontes, had remarked: 'By Jove, Mrs Robinson, you will make a conquest of the Prince; for to-night you look handsomer than ever'. Apparently Mrs Robinson 'smiled at the unmerited compliment', little foreseeing the 'vast variety of events that would arise from that night's exhibition'.

Predictably, the Prince's attention did not go unremarked. As the curtain fell many people noticed him make a pass at her, and, later, when she returned home to a small party at her house in Covent Garden, the 'whole conversation centred in encomiums on the person, graces and amiable manners, of the illustrious heir apparent'.

For his part, the Prince could think or talk of little else but Mrs Robinson; and within days he had convinced himself that he was passionately and unalterably in love. 'Adieu, Adieu, Adieu, *toujours chère*', he added to one of his last letters to his confidante, the attractive but unassailable Mary Hamilton, 'Oh! Mrs Robinson.'

It was characteristic of Mary Robinson to hint that she was a natural daughter of the witty and aristocratic Robert Henley, first Earl of Northington, when in fact her real father was almost certainly an ambitious ship captain and merchant called Nicholas Darby. Nicholas, who was born about 1720, had grown up in the rough and inhospitable environment of Newfoundland. Then, falling in love with Mrs Robinson's mother Hester Vanacott, whom he married in the small Somerset village of Donyat in 1749, he had settled in the bustling west country port of Bristol.

Mary was born nine years later in the Minster House, an evocative, part-medieval building, which stood flush against what was then the west wall of Bristol Cathedral. The front garden faced the popular promenade of College Green, while the back of the house was supported by the north cloister of what had until Henry VIII's time been St Augustine's Monastery.

In her *Memoirs*, Mrs Robinson describes herself as a happy child, dreamy, self-obsessed, excessively pampered by her mother, and even fashionably melancholic, like the boy poet, her fellow Bristolian Thomas Chatterton. She had siblings, but saw little of them. They were 'fair and lusty' boys, with 'auburn hair, light blue eyes, and countenances peculiarly animated and lovely'; whereas her eyes were 'singularly large in proportion' to her face, and her skin was 'swarthy'.

Her education was not neglected. While the boys played on the College Green, she learnt melancholy stories, poems and epitaphs. The distinguished Edmund Broderip taught her music on a Kirkman harpsichord provided by her father 'as an incitement to emulation' and at about the age of six she became a pupil of the celebrated More sisters in nearby Park Street.

But then disaster struck. For years Nicholas Darby had been investing in a 'wild and romantic' scheme, a plan to establish a permanent fishery on the southern coast of Labrador. He knew the coastline well, he was on excellent terms with the Society of Merchant Venturers of Bristol; Sir Hugh Palliser, Newfoundland's governor, supported his proposals, as did Lord

Northington and 'several equally distinguished personages'. 'The prospect appeared full of promise,' his daughter wrote, 'and the Labrador whale fishery was expected to be equally productive with that of Greenland.' Unfortunately, Darby's relations with the local Inuit Indians were bad, his crews were untrained and he fell foul of a number of regulations; then, to cap it all, during the autumn of 1767, a band of Inuit killed three of his men and ransacked his settlement. Distraught and facing bankruptcy, he then gave a bill of sale for his whole property, forcing his wife and his young family to leave their house in Bristol.

Mary was sent to Chelsea where she boarded with a brilliant alcoholic called Meribah Lorrington, while her mother did her best to build a new life out of the remnants of her tattered marriage. Apparently, during his North American sojourn Nicholas Darby had taken up with a young woman known only as Elenor, whose 'resisting nerves', unlike those of Hester Darby, could 'brave the stormy ocean'. Mary applied herself rigidly to her books, and wrote poems, and she became her new teacher's 'little friend', sometimes spending half the night discussing Mrs Lorrington's 'domestic and confidential' affairs in her chamber. Ultimately, however, drink got the better of Mrs Lorrington; and that, coupled with the 'singularly disgusting' appearance of her father, who wore 'a kind of Persian robe', led to the closure of the school.

For several weeks afterwards Mary boarded with a 'Widow Leigh', until her mother had the good though compromising idea of opening her own school in Little Chelsea. She hired a small house at No. 5 Park Walk, advertised for staff and gave Mary, not yet a teenager, full responsibility for teaching English. Mary also supervised the infant pupils' wardrobes, making sure that they were properly dressed by the servants and half boarders. However, 'just at a period when an honourable independence promised to cheer the days of an unexampled parent', Nicholas Darby heard about the school; and considering his 'conjugal reputation tarnished' by 'the public mode which his wife had adopted of revealing to the world her unprotected situation', he insisted on its closure. The 'pride of his soul' was 'deeply

wounded', writes Mrs Robinson; he was 'offended even beyond
the bounds of reason'.

A prouder heart never palpitated in the breast of man
than that of my father: tenacious of fame, ardent in the
pursuit of visionary schemes, he could not endure the
exposure of his altered fortune; while hope still beguiled
him with her flattering promise, that time would favour
his projects, and fortune, at some future period, reward
him with success.

Aged about thirteen, Mary left Little Chelsea for Marylebone
High Street, where she enrolled at Oxford House, a kind of
finishing school, sited adjacent to the popular Marylebone
Gardens. She continued to write and on more than one occasion even attempted to compose a tragedy. She also rekindled
a girlish fascination with the stage, and hoped to become an
actress. John Hussey, the school's dancing master, arranged
an audition at Covent Garden Theatre, and she was afterwards
introduced to the manager of Drury Lane Theatre, the great
actor David Garrick.

For a time a stage career seemed very likely; Garrick was free with
his advice and very fond of her. Sometimes he would ask her to
dance a minuet; sometimes to sing a ballad; and he said that her
singing reminded him of his favourite Mrs Cibber. Mrs Robinson
was enthralled: 'Never', she later wrote, 'shall I forget the enchant-
ing hours which I passed in Mr Garrick's society.' But fate intervened in the form of an articled clerk; and just as she was about
to make her *début*, he persuaded her mother that she would be
better off safely married.

Mary's suitor was Thomas Robinson. He was young, plausible,
extremely handsome and he claimed to be the nephew and
heir of a rich, retired tailor called Thomas Harris. Mrs Robinson
first became aware of him when she caught him peering at
her from his employer's house in Chancery Lane. They played
a game of bo-peep, until Mrs Robinson's mother indignantly
closed the lower shutters of her drawing room. Robinson then

persuaded a mutual friend to invite the mother and daughter to make up a party of six for a day out at Greenwich. When Mary and her mother arrived at Greenwich, it was Robinson who was there to hand them down from their carriage. Soon Robinson was a regular visitor, often turning up laden with gifts on Mrs Darby's doorstep. He could see that Mrs Darby was still sad following the desertion of her husband and he recognized her need for consolation. He was always courteous, charming and, when the occasion demanded it, apparently selfless, even daring; when Mary's brother George went down with smallpox, it was Robinson who risked his good looks to nurse him. In fact, he was playing a shrewd game; recognizing that the shortest road to the daughter's hand lay through her mother's heart, he neglected nothing that could further entrench him in Mrs Darby's affections. Consequently, Mrs Darby idolized him; he was, she told her daughter, the 'most perfect of existing beings'.

Day after day, Mary's *début* was postponed; then she too fell ill with smallpox.

It was now that Mr Robinson exerted all his assiduity to win my affections; it was when a destructive disorder menaced my features and the few graces that nature had lent them, that he professed a disinterested fondness; every day he attended with the zeal of a brother; and that zeal made an impression of gratitude upon my heart, which was the source of all my succeeding sorrows.

Robinson so worked on the feelings of Mrs Darby at this point that she persuaded her daughter to promise her that if she recovered, she would give Robinson her hand. Robinson was, she said, the 'kindest, – the best of mortals! the least addicted to worldly follies'; in short, the 'man, of all others, who she should adore as a *son-in-law*'. Cajoled, bullied, 'repeatedly urged and hourly reminded' of some words of her father to the effect that he would hold his wife responsible if any harm came to his daughter, Mary took the road of least resistance, and consented.

Unfortunately, once the wedding was over, it turned out that
Robinson was not what he seemed. He had lied about his age,
lied about his income and, most of all, lied about the true
nature of his relationship with his 'uncle'. It now turned out
that he was not the nephew of Thomas Harris at all, but his
illegitimate son. They were on extremely bad terms. He also
owed a large sum of money.

Soon he plunged his not entirely unwilling wife into the glitter-
ing and fascinating world of masquerades and expensive living,
using her beauty as a bait to entrap any one foolish enough to
involve themselves in his financial transactions. For a while
she corresponded with an ambitious moneylender called John
King, apparently making absurd declarations of love in order
to inveigle money out of him. She visited the Pantheon and
Vauxhall Gardens and fell in with a psychotic dueller called
George Robert 'Fighting' Fitzgerald and a notorious libertine
known as Thomas 'the wicked' Lord Lyttelton.

Lyttelton, whom she describes as 'perhaps the most accomplished libertine that any age or country has produced'
was especially fond of her, and, used to getting his own way in
most things, he did everything he could to seduce her. He
flaunted his wealth, treated her with outward contempt in an
attempt to excite her interest, and, when that didn't work,
decided that his best policy was to bankrupt her husband.

On one occasion, finding none of these methods particularly successful, he turned up at the couple's house in Hatton
Garden and revealed to Mrs Robinson that her husband had
taken a mistress.

'Now,' said Lord Lyttelton, 'if you are a woman of spirit,
you will be *revenged!*' I shrunk with horror, and would
have quitted the room. 'Hear me,' said he. 'You cannot
be a stranger to my motives for thus cultivating the
friendship of your husband; my fortune is at your disposal.
Robinson is a ruined man; his debts are considerable, and
nothing but destruction can await you. Leave him!
Command my powers to serve you.'

Her sufferings 'undescribable', Mrs Robinson then went straight to an address in Princes Street, Soho, where she confronted Harriet Wilmot, the woman Lyttelton had named as her husband's mistress, and asked her whether or not she was acquainted with her husband? Miss Wilmot admitted that she was; 'He visits me frequently' she said, at the same time pulling off a glove and revealing a ring which Mrs Robinson recognized as belonging to her husband. 'I have nothing more to say,' remarked Mrs Robinson; who then rose from the chair where she had been sitting and departed.

On the following morning Mrs Robinson mentioned her talk with Harriet Wilmot to her husband. He did not deny the affair, but blamed Lord Lyttelton. 'He requested to know who had informed me of his conduct. I refused to tell; and he had too high an opinion of his false associate to suspect him of such treachery.'

Shortly after, Robinson's creditors caught up with him, as Lord Lyttelton had prophesied, and the couple spent fifteen months in the Fleet Prison.

It was a depressing period. Robinson, effectively deserted by his father, sunk into despondency, while Mrs Robinson, her health now 'considerably impaired', took on the legal work which her husband rejected, and even published a small volume of poems, entitled simply *Poems by Mrs Robinson*, to support them. By now, she had an infant daughter to support, her beloved Maria Elizabeth, though she was still pestered by libertines, including Lord Lyttelton.

But then someone mentioned that Georgiana, the young Duchess of Devonshire, was an 'admirer and patroness of literature', and with a 'mixture of timidity and hope' Mrs Robinson sent her a neatly bound volume of her poems. The Duchess liked what she read, and Mrs Robinson of the Fleet Prison was invited to visit the Duchess of Devonshire at Devonshire House, in Piccadilly.

'To describe the Duchess's look and manner', wrote Mrs Robinson of her first sight of the Duchess, 'would be impracticable; mildness and sensibility beamed in her eyes and irradiated her countenance.' The Duchess listened to her story, and expressed her surprise that at so young an age Mrs Robinson had already experienced 'such vicissitude of fortune', then with a 'tear of gentle sympathy' made her a present as a token of her 'good wishes'. Mrs Robinson was entranced; she 'had not words' to express her feelings, so overcome was she by the look and generosity of this 'best of women'. Soon, Mrs Robinson was a regular visitor.

The Robinsons emerged from the Fleet Prison during the summer of 1776, and once more the question of a theatrical career was mooted. This time Robinson did not object and before long a mutual friend, the actor William Brereton, introduced Mrs Robinson to Richard Brinsley Sheridan.

Sheridan had just taken over from David Garrick as manager of Drury Lane and, already a successful playwright, he was determined to make a powerful impression during his first season. He auditioned Mrs Robinson, and was suitably impressed. She was obviously talented, and he found her strikingly attractive. Thereupon he offered her a generous salary and sent her once more to David Garrick for further tuition.

Behind the scenes, much was made of Mrs Robinson's forthcoming début, which was set for 10 December 1776. Sheridan chose 'Juliet', a part that would be greeted with a flurry of encouraging criticism. A great deal was made of her background and 'superior' understanding, and the critics went to some lengths to make their notices helpful and reasonable. 'Her person is genteel,' noted the *Morning Post*, 'her voice harmonious . . . and her features, when properly animated, are striking and expressive.' She discovered a 'theatrical genius in the rough' which, when 'polished', would doubtless be 'brought to perfection'. 'Fly Flap', writing in the same paper, found her 'love-inspired Juliet' most 'truely and naturally depicted'. The *Morning Chronicle* was also impressed, though it did sometimes think she 'substituted rant for passion, and dealt in whispers where she evidently meant to be pathetic'.

For Mrs Robinson, her début was a frightening experience. On first appearing on the stage, she had been greeted with a round of applause so loud that it had almost 'overpowered

... [her] faculties'. She quickly gathered confidence, though, and the evening ended with 'peals of clamorous acclamation'.

She remained at Drury Lane until the spring of 1780, creating some roles and performing with some of the greatest actors and actresses of the age. She would have been the first 'Maria' in Sheridan's classic *School for Scandal* had she not been far advanced in her second pregnancy. She was not a great actress, but neither, as the reviewers suggested, was her acting entirely contemptible. She excelled as fashionable young women in light comedy roles, which were best able to make use of her beauty.

Within a few days of *The Winter's Tale* performance at which the Prince had been present, Mrs Robinson received a visit from a clearly embarrassed Lord Malden. Though a politician, he was diffident by nature and he seemed to Mrs Robinson on this occasion specially agitated. 'He attempted to speak,' she writes, '– paused, hesitated [and] apologized'; then 'hoped I would pardon him'. He had, he said, something to give her which he hoped she would not reveal to anyone else; then he handed her a letter.

Mrs Robinson did not recognize the writing, though the letter was addressed to her in her character as 'Perdita'. She smiled 'rather sarcastically', and as Malden stood by, opened the letter.

'It contained only a few words, but those expressive of more than common civility', and it was signed 'Florizel'.

'Well, my Lord, and what does this mean?' she asked. 'Can you not guess the writer?' Malden replied.

It was a love letter from the Prince of Wales.

'Astonished' and, as she later confessed, somewhat 'agitated' by Malden's remark, Mrs Robinson did not at first believe him. She wondered if he had written the letter himself as an 'experiment' either on her 'vanity or propriety of conduct'; and she returned him a 'formal and doubtful answer'. But Malden brought her a second letter along with a verbal message that the Prince was 'most unhappy' at the thought that he had offended her 'by his conduct'.

Henceforth, the Prince wrote Mrs Robinson dozens of letters; indiscreet and lovesick scrawls, which also contained slighting and damaging references to the royal family; he hated his life at Kew Palace, near Windsor, where he and his brother, the Duke of York, were kept virtual prisoners; the King, whom he did not like, was unkind to him; the Princess Royal, who was in poor health, was a '*bandy legged b– – –h*'. In happier letters, he spoke too of his 'inviolable affection'. 'There was a beautiful ingenuousness in his language', writes Mrs Robinson, and a warm and enthusiastic adoration, which 'charmed' her in almost every line.

Prevented from meeting privately by the watchfulness of the Prince's tutors, during February 1780 the couple did manage to communicate briefly at an oratorio, where Mrs Robinson behaved so outrageously that the King sent a message up to her seat in one of the upper boxes desiring the 'dart-dealing' actress to withdraw. 'Poor Perdita', remarked the *Morning Post*, quoting Shakespeare, on this ignominious occasion, 'Queen it not an inch further, but milk thy ewes and weep'.

Meanwhile Lord Malden acted as a kind of chaperon to Mrs Robinson, accompanying her and her 'cornuted' husband Thomas to Christie's the auctioneers and round other sights in London. Naturally, this gave rise to all sorts of rumours, and many people wondered if Lord Malden rather than the Prince was her lover.

The Prince had little money of his own at this time, but he offered to buy her jewels, an offer which, strangely, she refused. On one occasion he smuggled the King's official miniaturist Jeremiah Meyer into Kew Palace for a clandestine sitting. The miniature of the Prince was then carried to Mrs Robinson enclosed in a gold case in which he had also placed a small heart cut out in paper. On one side he wrote '*Je ne change qu'en mourant*'; on the other, '*Unalterable to my Perdita through life*'. This Mrs Robinson set round with diamonds, and carried everywhere.

It wasn't until June 1780 that the couple finally did manage to meet, and only then under conditions of the strictest secrecy. Malden hired a boat, possibly from an inn which then stood on an island between Kew and Brentford, and, under cover of night, he rowed Mrs Robinson over the river to the gates of Kew Palace.

Heaven can witness how many conflicts my agitated heart
endured at this most important moment! [writes Mrs
Robinson] I admired the Prince; I felt grateful for his
affection. He was the most engaging of created beings. I
had corresponded with him during many months, and his
eloquent letters, the exquisite sensibility which breathed   \
through every line, his ardent professions of adoration,
had combined to shake my feeble resolution.

Their meeting was but brief. 'A few words, and those scarcely
articulate, were uttered by the Prince, when a noise of people
approaching from the palace startled us', and Mrs Robinson
and Lord Malden returned to their boat, and thence to the
island.

This short meeting increased Mrs Robinson's ardour; and the
heart which before had been influenced merely by 'esteem'
was now 'awakened to the most enthusiastic admiration'. The
'graces' of the Prince, 'the irresistible sweetness of his smile,
the tenderness of his melodious yet manly voice', the fact that
she was no longer 'chilled into awe' by his rank, all contributed to increase her passion.

The Prince made her a number of foolish promises; having
already sent her a bond of the 'most solemn and binding nature', promising to pay her the stupendous sum of £20,000 as
soon as he came of age, he now said that he would set her up
in her own establishment. It wounded his dignity that she was
forced to earn a living on the stage, and he was desperate for
her to live apart from her husband. The bond was expressed
'in terms so liberal, so voluntary, so marked by true affection'
that when Mrs Robinson had received it she had scarcely had
'power' enough to read it. Now in a fatal moment, she gave in
to vanity, and succumbed to the Prince's wishes.

In the meantime, 'many and frequent' were her meetings
with the Prince in the grounds of Kew Palace. The Prince's
favourite brother, the Duke of York, was always of the party, as
was the stalwart Lord Malden. In spite of the constant risk of
discovery, the Prince would occasionally sing with 'exquisite

taste', and the 'tones of his voice, breaking on the silence of
the night' sometimes seemed to Mrs Robinson, like 'more than
mortal melody'. Indeed, in her version of the affair these meetings were almost trite; 'nothing could be more delightful or
rational' than their 'midnight perambulations'.*

In spite of some half-hearted attempts to keep the affair out
of the newspapers, by July news of the relationship could no
longer be suppressed. Most people in London society had some
opinion of the matter, while the newspapers, all of whom wrote
for a small élite readership, were always looking for spicy, gos-
sipy paragraphs. 'And so', wrote 'Ovid' from Windsor on 14
July 1780,

> the theatrical Perdita of Drury Lane is labouring night
> and day to insinuate to the world that an amour either
> has taken place or is about to take place, between her
> and a certain illustrious character. If the young gentleman
> really had any penchant for her, which, however, is not
> the case, her present system of vain-boasting must give his
> heart a very speedy quietus.

Many people made the standard comparison with Charles II
and his mistresses, wondering if Mrs Robinson was aiming at a
title like Barbara Villiers, whom Charles created Countess of
Castlemaine and Duchess of Cleveland. Was she a new Nell
Gwynn, mused others? while one paper published a quite vicious
poem addressed to Lord Malden on the *'report of Perditta's being created a countess'*. Some of the attacks were pornographic;
'Crop' for instance, hinted in one article that Mrs Robinson
was fond of flagellation. Such was the public interest that Mrs
Robinson was 'frequently obliged to quit Ranelagh, owing to

---

* Later, the Richmond librarian A.A. Barkas recorded a local tradition that
the couple met not in the grounds of Kew Palace but at a house occupied
by some of the Royal Family's servants. 'It was quite the usual thing', he
writes, 'to see the lights all over the house, and to hear sounds of revelry
until 3 and 4 in the morning. The house was called "Hell House" and is
said to have had a private entrance at the back from Kew Gardens.' (*Richmond Notes MSS*, vol. I, Local Studies Collection, Richmond Library, Surrey)

Mrs Robinson

the crowd which staring curiosity had assembled' round her box; and 'even in the streets of the metropolis', she 'scarcely ventured to enter a shop without experiencing the greatest inconvenience'. Then, during November an anonymous friend wrote a letter to the *Morning Post* warning the London papers that should they continue to persecute her with scandalous paragraphs but a little longer, then he was confident that they would have her 'blood to answer for'.

Naturally the King hated all this publicity; he read the papers, and was thus perfectly familiar with the most lurid accounts of his son's and Mrs Robinson's behaviour. 'Your own good sense must make you feel that you have not made that progress in your studies, which, from the ability and assiduity of those placed for that purpose about you, I might have had reason to expect,' he wrote to the Prince two days after his eighteenth birthday on 14 August.

> Whilst you have been out of the sight of the world that has been kept under a veil by all those who have cirrounded you, nay your foibles have been less perceived than I could have expected; yet your love of dissipation has for some months been with enough ill nature trumpeted in the public papers.

'God', the King told his son, had 'bequeathed' him 'quickness of conception'; why would he not then reflect on the truth that 'every one in this world has his peculiar duties to perform, and that the good or bad example set by those in the higher stations must have some effect on the general conduct of those in inferior ones'?

> I certainly shall think it right to make some new arrangement concerning you, but as it is a matter involved with difficulties, I trust you will rest contented when I say that I mean to do it with no greater delay than what must naturally arise from them. Believe me, I wish to make you happy, but a father must, with that object in view, not forget that it is his duty to guide his child to the best of

his ability through the rocks that cannot but naturally arise in the outset of youth.

This new arrangement was for the Prince to leave Kew Palace at the end of the year for Buckingham House (the site of the present Buckingham Palace), where he would enjoy his own establishment and some limited independence. He could go to plays and operas, provided he gave notice to the King and was accompanied by his regular attendants; he was not to go to balls, assemblies at private houses, and certainly not to masquerades, a popular form of entertainment and one which the King particularly reprobated. The King also reiterated a former command that the Prince would keep away from his wayward uncles, the Dukes of Gloucester and Cumberland. Unfortunately, the Prince rather enjoyed the latter's company; he liked Cumberland's *joie de vivre*, his lax attitudes and rather brutal sense of humour; and during the closing weeks of 1780 and the early months of 1781 he was frequently to be found in his uncle's company.

At the same time the Prince lost the company of the Duke of York and Lieutenant-Colonel Gerard Lake, his First Equerry and 'best friend' and a stabilizing influence, both among the few men he could confide in. The Duke, whose ascendancy over his brother was well known, was sent to Hanover to study the art of war, while Lake was posted to America. The Prince's parting from his brother was extremely moving; according to the *Annual Register*, he was 'so much affected with the misfortune of being deprived for so long a period of the sole companion of his youth, that he stood in a state of entire insensibility'.

Mrs Robinson in the meantime had moved out of the house she shared with her husband in Covent Garden and settled in a small house in wealthy Cork Street. She entertained lavishly, particularly the friends of the Prince, and became deeply indebted. She bought furniture, paintings, books and the latest Parisian fashions and took to driving round St James's and the royal parks in a succession of gaily coloured phaetons. At the theatre, where she could often be seen in a side box, she appeared with all the 'splendour of a Duchess'. She even took a side box at the Opera House, an almost unheard-of innovation for a woman of her background.

Robinson repeatedly pestered her for money; and there was an embarrassing incident when she caught him making love to a 'fillette' in one of the boxes at Covent Garden. 'Her jealousy instantly became ungovernable. . . . She flew to the box – seized the unhappy husband – dragged him by the hair of his head into the lobby, and there spent her violence in blows and reproaches', much to the amusement of a 'numerous auditory'. At length, she bore him away 'in triumph' to her house, where, 'we hope', a journalist remarked, 'from the mild mediations of the *patient* M[alden], harmony and concord will be shortly restored, and poor penitent *Tommy*, be again received in to her *princely* favour'. Later, when the couple were on slightly better terms, it was suggested that Robinson had stumbled across a 'few secrets' which Mrs Robinson was anxious to keep out of 'court circulation', and that that accounted for her 'condescending' behaviour towards him.

For his part, Robinson was as much ridiculed as any spurned husband, laughed at in the streets and pointed at in the papers as the 'King of Cuckolds'; during October readers of the *Morning Post* were slyly informed that the Revd Martin Madan, the author of a notorious volume on polygamy, was presently at work on a *Defence of Cuckoldom*, dedicated to Thomas Robinson.

Meanwhile, with the prospect of some degree of independence close at hand, the Prince began to have second thoughts about his connection with Mrs Robinson. It occurred to him that it was foolish to tie himself to one person; after all, Mrs Robinson was not the only beautiful and available woman. Moreover, the Duke of Cumberland was against the match, as were many of his friends, and they put it about that he had been deceived by Lord Malden. Indeed Malden himself gave some colour to this charge, when he told Mrs Robinson that he had himself conceived 'so violent a passion' for her that he was the 'most miserable and unfortunate of mortals'.

Rumours of a separation first emerged in the papers during

mid-December 1780, but then were swiftly denied in words
that apparently left no room for contradiction: 'On the contrary', declared a paragraph in the *Morning Post*, 'the happy
Perdita has gained so much ground' in the Prince's affections,
that her 'amazing success has given a mortal stab to the pride
of a certain young lady, who entertains so high an opinion of
her mother's double coronet, and of her own personal merit,
that she thinks herself a proper match for the Grand Mogul.'
This however was premature, for the Prince did indeed soon
switch his attentions, though not to an aristocrat, but to Lord
George Cavendish's mistress, the popular and alluring Elizabeth Armistead. Lord George discovered the liaison when, one
night returning drunk to Mrs Armistead's house, he was, un-
accountably, refused admittance. He searched one of her rooms,
'stretched out his arm with the candle in his hand' and discovered the Prince hiding behind a door. Fortunately, his
drunken condition did not predispose him to violence, but 'it
luckily had another effect – he burst out a laughing, made his
R.H. a low bow and retir'd'.

Mrs Robinson seems to have first become aware of the Prince's
new love on Houndslow Heath, where, having shortly before received a letter from the Prince briefly stating that they must
'meet no more', she bumped into Mrs Armistead, apparently
on her way back from a meeting with the Prince at Windsor.
'My foreboding soul instantly beheld a rival, and, with jealous
eagerness, interpreted the, hitherto, inexplicable conduct of
the Prince, from his having frequently expressed his wish to
know that lady.'

When the Prince refused to speak to her at the Castle, Mrs
Robinson wrote him a furiously worded letter, vehemently
complaining of the 'calumnies' her enemies had 'fabricated';
to which the Prince responded with a 'most eloquent' letter,
'disclaiming the causes alleged by a calumniating world', and
'fully acquitting' her of 'the charges which had been propagated to destroy' her. He agreed to see her, yet on meeting
her in Hyde Park on the *'very next day'* he turned his head away
from her, and 'even affected' not to know her. Overwhelmed

by this final blow, Mrs Robinson felt a distress which knew 'no limits'.

She subsequently sought other ways of regaining the Prince's affection, and when these failed to bring about a reconciliation or the promised establishment, she made it clear that she would stop at nothing, not even blackmail:

> A certain *amour royal* is now totally at an end [ran one warning paragraph in the *Morning Herald*]; a separation has taken place *a thoro* for more than three weeks, and a *settlement* worthy of such a *sultana* is the only thing now wanting to break off all intercourse whatever. Mrs Robinson thinking the adjustment of this part of the *divorce* too essential to be trifled with, has roundly written to her once *ardent lover*, 'That if her establishment is not duly arranged within the space of fourteen days from the commencement of the new year, his – – – – – – – – must not be surprised if he sees a full publication of all those *seductory epistles* which alone estranged her from *virtue* and the *marriage vow!*'

Galvanized by Mrs Robinson's threats, the Prince's friends then plotted to get his letters back, and on one occasion at least she was approached by the Duke of Cumberland. However, nothing they could offer was equal to the value of the letters. Mrs Robinson's friends attacked Mrs Armistead in the newpapers, ridiculing her charms and charging her with being little but the tool of the popular Opposition leader Charles James Fox and his colleagues, men who were desperate to influence the Prince's politics.

> There cannot be a stronger proof of the miserable shifts to which opposition are driven, than the reports they so industriously circulate, of a connection between that *High Priestess of Patriotism*, Mrs A– – –d and a certain heir apparent: the public, however … will not readily give into an account so foreign to the idea it entertains of his R– – – H – – – 's *taste*, as well as good *understanding*.

Consistent with the true idea that Mrs Armistead was connected to the Opposition, it was also suggested that somehow Mrs Robinson was hand in glove with the Government who would support her as long as her politics remained 'intirely ministerial'. Absurdly, even the Queen was said to be involved, smiling 'very graciously' upon the former object of her son's attentions.

The Prince, meanwhile, heady with the spirit of freedom, lost all control of himself; and, 'drinking and living too freely', he brought on a violent fever, which soon 'spent itself in a hideous humour' in his face. He was a month in the care of his physician Sir Richard Jebb, 'so ill that for two days', he told his brother, 'he was very much alarmed for me'. The Duke warned him from Hanover that he would permanently damage himself unless he changed, blaming his behaviour all on the 'Windsor Lodge Duke' (his term for the Duke of Cumberland):

> You know me, I hope, my dearest brother, too well to
> think me a preacher, but as you told me upon our
> dearest friend Lake's going away that you begged I would
> give you my advice, I could not refrain from saying so
> much, as my affection for you would not permit me to
> pass it over in silence.

The Prince had chosen for his friends Charles William Wyndham and Colonel Anthony St Leger, companions whom the King despised, rakes who were notorious for their recklessness, rudeness and outrageously drunken behaviour. One night at Lord Chesterfield's house on Blackheath they were so drunk that they released a 'large fierce house dog', which ripped open a servant's leg and savaged Wyndham's arm, after another guest, George Pitt, son of Lord Rivers, had attempted to tear the creature's tongue out. The Prince spoke of the King in the 'grossest' terms, 'even in his hearing', conduct which so alarmed his father that he confided to the Duke of Gloucester his fears that the Prince would refuse to obey him. Other nights the Prince spent in the 'lowest debaucheries'; he bragged publicly of his intrigues with 'women of quality'; he was duplicitous, disloyal, would draw in persons 'to abuse the King' and would then betray them. 'Examine yourself', the King wrote in one of his increasingly despairing letters, 'and see how far your conduct has been conformable [to my wishes] and then draw your conclusion whether you must not give me many an uneasy moment. I wish to live with you as a friend, but then by your behaviour you must deserve it.'

To Mrs Armistead, the Prince was only fitfully loyal, and so mean with his promises that during July 1781 she packed her bags and left London for Paris. By now, even the Prince had learnt to be a trifle more circumspect, and there was no compromising correspondence.

Two of his other affairs at this time were particularly unfortunate, one because it apparently terminated in the birth of a child, the other because it was politically damaging. He became attached to Grace Dalrymple Eliot during the early summer of 1781. A prominant demirep with aristocratic pretensions, she had recently returned from France, where Louis XVI's cousin, the profligate and immensely wealthy Duc de Chartres, had been among her most prominent admirers. The Prince and Mrs Eliot made love, and on 30 March 1782, Mrs Eliot gave birth to a daughter, whom she had christened Georgiana Augusta Frederica Seymour in honour of the girl's putative father. The Prince, though unconvinced that the child was his, was known to take a fatherly interest in her welfare.

The other affair was with the Countess von Hardenburg, the wife of an ambitious German diplomat, who had come to St James's in the hope of being appointed Hanoverian Minister in London. A capricious, 'very sensible, agreable, pleasant little woman, but devilish severe', she first made eyes at the Prince during a game of cards in the Queen's apartment at Buckingham House during the winter. She was something of a coquette, and when the Prince some months later suggested that they meet alone at her husband's house in London she affected to be shocked, forcing from him an apology. He then grew

still fonder of her 'and to so violent a degree' that even his
health was affected. Again Sir Richard Jebb was called for; the
Prince spat blood and lost weight and dropping 'every other
connexion of whatever sort or kind', devoted himself entirely
to 'this angelick little woman'. The couple then met at her
house in Old Windsor, where the Prince obtained from her a
fervent declaration of love; and two or three visits later, he
enjoyed the 'pleasures of Elyssium'. Unfortunately however the
Morning Herald then published a short paragraph stating that
the Countess had taken a house next to Mrs Robinson in Cork
Street and that she was the 'present rival of the Perdita'. Von
Hardenburg then approached his wife, forced her to confess
to some arrangement with the Prince and bullied her into
writing the Prince a letter, stating that she would never see or
write to him again. 'I almost fell into fits when I received the
packet,' wrote the Prince, 'but upon opening it I thought I
should have run distracted, as I conceived her to be guilty of
ye blackest ingratitude and cruelty.' However, he sat down and
wrote to both the Hardenburgs, conceding that though it was
true he was 'strongly attached' to the Countess, she was innocent of even the slightest impropriety, for she had 'always treated'
him with the 'utmost coolness'. At the same time he also sent
a separate note to Madame von Hardenburg, passionately re-
affirming his love. Thinking the affair at an end the Prince
contacted his Groom of the Stole, Lord Southampton, requesting
him to ask the King's permission for him to go abroad, as an
'unfortunate affair' had occurred which had left him 'excessively miserable'. Not surprisingly, the King refused.

A few hours later, however, the Prince received another note from
the Countess stating that her letter had been written under
duress, and suggesting that they elope. For a time the Prince
totally lost his head, consented to the plan, then 'stabbed to
the heart at the thought of what would probably turn out to
be her miserable situation', lost his resolution. He threw himself at his mother's feet, told her everything under 'ye promise of ye greatest secrecy'; she fainted. Distraught, he then sent
for Colonel Samuel Hulse, his Equerry, telling him to tell the

Countess that he would have been with her but for an 'unforeseen accident'. The Queen then informed the King, who sent for von Hardenburg, who within days packed his wife off to the Continent.

'By Heavens I shall go distracted: my brain will split!', wrote the Prince in his account of the affair to the Duke of York. 'You will perceive my agitation by ye horrid style and scrawl. You shall hear from me again almost immediately, as I have scarce any other satisfaction left than that of knowing I have a friend who will feel most truly for me.' The Duke, however, was not as impressed by Madame von Hardenburg's charms as his brother, and wrote the Prince some unpleasant revelations: 'If you knew her as well as I do, you would be completely cured of any particular affection for her.' It turned out, unbeknown to the Prince, that Madame von Hardenburg had been equally flirtatious with the Duke. 'I know also other stories of her', he later wrote, 'still worse than this, but I do not think it necessary to mention them to you as I think this is sufficient.' Nevertheless, although the Prince was soon consoling himself with the beautiful Lady Augusta Campbell, daughter of the fifth Duke of Argyll, he was still making enquiries about the Countess six months later.

Mrs Robinson, meanwhile, though still in a state of shock at the Prince's conduct and fearful that her creditors would foreclose on her, threw herself into yet another round of conspicuous consumption. She sat to George Romney, one of London's foremost portrait painters, sparked a new fashion for brimstone yellow phaetons, held increasingly wild parties at her house in Cork Street and, by way of contrast, rented an 'elegant villa' on the banks of the Thames in order to enjoy the 'rural sweets' of retirement. For a while it was rumoured that she had struck up a close relationship with the 'unusually handsome' Duke of Dorset, though by February it was pretty clear that she was indeed now having an affair with Malden. She thought too of returning to Drury Lane, now that she could no longer rely on the Prince, but this idea was scotched when it became clear that the audience would not tolerate it.

So she wrote self-referential puffs for the newspapers, with the intention, so it was said, of attracting the attention of 'some fool of fashion'.

The attacks on Mrs Robinson continued and, just as she was planning to expose the Prince, the same John King with whom she had been briefly acquainted shortly after her marriage took this opportunity to capitalize on some compromising letters she had written to him. King was a shrewd man and he knew how to make the most of a small amount of evidence.

He doctored some of Mrs Robinson's letters, added some of his own and put them together in a pamphlet with a rambling, though sporadically accurate, account of her life, ostensibly as a warning to the public for *'checking and prosecuting Swindlers'*. He then advertised the pamphlet in the newspapers, carefully stating that a selection of the original correspondence could be seen at his publishers in Paternoster Row.

Mrs Robinson and Lord Malden did attempt to retrieve Mrs Robinson's letters, though for some unexplained reason, Malden decided not to buy them. Consequently the letters were published, and scarcely a week went by 'for a considerable time, without the advertisement of a new edition'.*

The negotiations to end what the Prince was already describing as 'ye olde infernal cause Robinson' finally got underway during July. Although Mrs Robinson had returned some of the Prince's letters via the hands of Lieutenant-Colonel Lake, she did still possess the bulk of the correspondence. Already the Prince had received an undertaking from the King to help him out in the business, and Lieutenant-Colonel George Hotham, an extremely able officer, the Prince's Treasurer and the King's aide-de-camp had been despatched to Cork Street, where Mrs

---

* King (c. 1753–1823) never forgot Mrs Robinson, nor she him. In addition to his financial interests, he had a taste for politics and literature, and, though it is very unlikely that they ever subsequently met, they did move in the same social circles. For an interesting textual comparison, see her account of her first meeting with Lords Northington and Lyttelton (*Memoirs*, pp. 52–4) and King's version of the same event (*Letters from Perdita to a certain Israelite, and his Answers to them*, pp. 10–11).

Robinson gave him a figure of £4,000 to £5,000 as an estimate of her debts.

In conversation with Hotham, Mrs Robinson made it clear that she was not prepared to sell the Prince's letters, but she would return them if something was done about her debts. She did not believe she would have incurred such debts had the Prince not promised her wealth and an establishment. In fact, she declared, there was a moral obligation on his part to help her; after all, she had been a highly paid and successful actress. Hotham then reported back to the King, while Mrs Robinson gave responsibility for the negotiations to Lord Malden.

Hotham then made her an offer; he told Malden that 'in consideration of a past Connexion, which never more can be renewed, Mrs Robinson has it in Her Power to receive the sum of Five Thousand Pounds; which, on her Restitution of such Papers as passed during its Continuance, will instantly be paid her.' 'This sum,' he continued, 'on a strict Retrospect into every Part of Mrs Robinson's Conduct, during the Time the Attachment subsisted, is deemed a proper and sufficient Reward.' Nothing further would be offered; the proposal was final and, in case of Mrs Robinson's 'non-Acceptance' of the sum, Malden would receive 'no further Trouble on this Unpleasant Subject'.

This bureaucratically couched and rather heartless offer was not acceptable to Mrs Robinson. Five thousand pounds would hardly cover her debts and in any case she also hoped for an annuity. Thereupon she sent Malden to speak to the Prince, first at Buckingham House, then at the London home of Lord Southampton. Malden took away the impression that though the Prince did not think himself 'at liberty at present to make any direct and specific promise' relative to the extent of his 'future bounty' towards Mrs Robinson, there was not the 'smallest doubt' of the sincerity of his intentions.

'She says it is unnecessary', Malden later wrote, 'to assure your R.H. that she was led into a train of expences from the repeated assurances of yr R.H. to raise her above the frowns of fortune, Expences which have brought a load of debt upon her, that

she would not else have incurred'; that 'the idea of falling
from a state of splendor and independence (to which she always flattered herself she should be raised) to a level that must
at least be degrading to her, impresses her with feelings that
are hard to imagine'; 'she cannot bear', he continued, 'the
idea held out in Colonel Hotham's letter, that the money therein
mentioned is to be the consideration for the restitution' of
the letters, and 'that she is to be precluded all hope' of his
future bounty;

> the idea, she says, shocks her, as it not only carries the
> strongest appearance of a price put upon her conduct to
> yr R.H., . . . but gives her reason to fear that she will be
> left totally destitute and without an income hereafter. . . .
> Nothing she says can be more injurious to her feelings,
> nor will she bear the idea of having it supposed that she
> has sold papers so dear to her. . . . She does not wish you
> should think she has any desire of laying your R.H. under
> any obligation of doing for her hereafter any thing
> further than what yr R.H.'s honor and generosity would
> prompt you to.

Nevertheless, in consideration of the Prince's peace of mind,
she would surrender the letters.

Colonel Hotham, however, would have none of it. Whatever the
Prince might have said in conversation with Malden, he wrote, it
'never was intended to give Mrs Robinson any Expectation or
Hope, much less any Promise more than the Specifick sum'
mentioned in his original letter. Malden was aghast; and again
bypassing Hotham, he warned the Prince: 'If Mrs Robinson is
finally to conclude that it is your R.H's ultimate resolution to
limit your Bounty to the sum of £5000 only, and to refuse her
every reasonable expectation of your R.H's future assistance –
she cannot but consider the proposal as extremely circumscribed
and inadequate'.

Again this was stonewalled, so Malden tried a different approach; although Mrs Robinson still refused to give up all hope

of the Prince's future bounty, she had none the less authorized Malden to return the Prince's letters. In the meantime,
Malden wrote to Lord Southampton for clarification of what
the Prince actually said when he met him at Buckingham House.
Southampton reminded him of the Prince's exact words: 'I will
not say, what I will, or will not do in future. I will make no
promises, I will not bind himself. I owe it to the King not to do
it'. The meaning of the Prince's words, Southampton remarked,
was that 'neither your Lordship, nor any other Person should
have *a right* to form future pretentions, in Consequence of it.'

Unfortunately, from Malden's point of view, Southampton's
letter clarified nothing. He accepted that the Prince did not bind
himself to anything in particular; but surely at the same time
neither did he positively rule out any future 'hope or expectation'.

With a date fixed for the handover of the letters, and the
Prince becoming increasingly agitated, Mrs Robinson tried one
last desperate gambit: she wrote an angry, threatening letter
to Malden, which he forwarded to Hotham. She thought herself authorized to declare, she wrote, that the treatment she
had received from the Prince was 'so ungenerous and illib-
eral' that she would be 'sufficiently justified in any step' her
'necessities' might urge her to take. She had 'ever acted with
the strictest honour and candour' towards the Prince; she did
not now 'wish to do anything' which hereafter she might 'have
cause to repent'. She did not know what answer might 'be
thought sufficient' to Hotham's last letter; 'the only one I can
or ever will be induced to give, is that I am willing to return
every letter I have ever received from his R.H. bona fide, had
HRH fulfilled *every* promise he has heretofore made me'. She
never 'could or would have made him ampler restitution', as
she had always valued his letters as dearly as her existence and
nothing but her 'distressed situation' ever should have tempted
her to give them up at all. Hotham was unmoved, however,
and on 10 September Malden at last handed over the letters.

For Mrs Robinson, this was a disastrous outcome. Already
her debts exceeded £5,000 and her creditors were increasingly
restive. The only bright spot was that she still had the Prince's

bond for £2,000, a document which though it formed no part of the negotiations on this occasion could be bargained for later, and which would in the meantime be useful for gaining credit.

In royal circles the relief was palpable. The negotiation over the letters was common knowledge, and there was pleasure at the satisfactory outcome. During August the King had written to his Prime Minister Lord North about it as a subject which had 'long given' him 'much pain'; and one that he was loath to speak about in person. He admitted that the Prince had made Mrs Robinson some 'very foolish promises', but thought that due to her conduct any obligations he might have owed her were entirely cancelled. The £5,000 was 'undoubtedly an enormous sum', but he wished to get the Prince out of 'this shameful scrape. . . . I am happy at being able to say', he wrote, 'that I never was personally engaged in such a transaction which perhaps makes me feel this the stronger'. Lord North sympathized with the King; he admired his 'Paternal tenderness and wisdom', but that did not stop him reading the letters when Colonel Hotham returned them in triumph. They were, he later remarked, to his son-in-law, 'remarkably well written'.

Characteristically, and in spite of the appearance of confidentiality in Hotham's letters, the newspapers had a field day, commenting almost day by day on the negotiations. Most contributors to the *Morning Herald* took a favourable view of Mrs Robinson's part in the affair, while contributors to the *Morning Post* took the contrary view.

When such eminent persons as the parents of *Florizel* can be *threatened* into a compliance with the demand of a pr- - -te, what a defect is there in the laws of Britain? Surely it cannot escape the observation of those concerned in this ridiculous negotiation, that in case a sum was given to this woman in order to get possession of the original letters, that she would certainly preserve copies, and every use might be made of them that can possibly be made of the originals. It is certain had *Florizel*

debauched *Perdita*, he ought to have made her an ample
settlement for the loss of her honour; but as it is
notorious that was not the case, his family ought to treat
her menaces with a silent contempt. To negotiate with her
on any terms is only to make her impertinent, and if in
consequence of a disappointment, she dare to publish the
letters of a noble youth, betrayed into an indiscretion by
an artful woman, we may fairly say that her very existence
would be *apocryphal*.

'Shame', cried the *Morning Herald*, in response, even to hint
than an '*admired and illustrious young personage*' would break
any engagement he had entered into and then '*meanly banter*'
with a 'woman who he has exposed for many months past, to
every insult and injury'. The 'infamous writer' deserved 'chas-
tisement' for making the very suggestion.

Leaving Lord Malden to his own devices, Mrs Robinson left
London during October for Paris. Her fame had long outstripped
her, and when she first visited the Paris Opera House, the
audience immediately divided to form a passage for her to
pass through. The French Queen Marie-Antoinette expressed
an interest in seeing her, and she was pursued by the Duc de
Chartres and his 'gallant friend and associate', the equally libidinous Duc de Lauzun.

The Duc de Chartres entertained her at his splendid *jardin anglais*
at Mousseau, near the capital, held a vast rural fête resembling a
'beautiful *Pandæmonium*' on her birthday, but apparently failed
in his attempts to seduce her. More fortunate perhaps was the
Duc de Lauzun, who in his *Memoirs* describes Mrs Robinson as
'gay, lively, open, and a good creature. . . . I was an object to
excite her fancy,' he writes, 'a man who had brought home
great tidings, who came from the war [in America], who was
returning there immediately. . . . She felt that she could not
do too much for him; and so I enjoyed Perdita'.

She returned to London on Boxing Day 1781, dressed in the
latest Parisian fashions, and further in debt. Unwilling to economize, she fell still deeper into the hands of her creditors. On

25 January she attended the first of several sittings for a portrait at Sir Joshua Reynolds's studio, and in May threw over Lord Malden for the handsome and arrogant Colonel Banastre Tarleton. Colonel Tarleton, or 'Butcher' Tarleton as the Revolutionists liked to call him, had just returned from America where the notoriety of his bloody exploits on the plains of South Carolina had recently won him the friendship of the Prince and a private audience with his father.

That affair lasted for about two months, until July 1782, when Mrs Robinson temporarily dropped Tarleton for Charles James Fox, the brilliant and charismatic Whig politician. Fox had recently resigned his post as Foreign Secretary in Lord Shelburne's administration, and it was thought he was hoping to ingratiate himself with the Prince by relieving Mrs Robinson of the Prince's bond for £20,000. Probably he succeeded, for later it was widely believed that it was he who had negotiated its exchange as an 'equivalent' for a pension of £500 per annum.

Predictably, the newspapers made much of the affair, significantly contrasting Fox's behaviour with that of his young rival, the celibate William Pitt who, while Fox dissipated his 'time and talents on the turf, in gaming houses, and sacrifices to the Cyprian Goddess', was 'studiously' employed in qualifying himself for high office. Yet, according to George Selwyn, the 'connection' was 'perfectly right', for who else should the '*man of the people*' pass his time with but with the '*woman of the people*'?

'Now *Charles Fox* being dismissed from the Secretaryship of State', sermonized the *Morning Herald*, 'returned again to Gaming and Dissipation.'

And he resumed his Pharaoh Bank at *Brookes's*, and sojourned with Mrs Rob–s–n, the Harlot of the Day, and he drived her about in a Phaeton.

The rattling of the wheels filled the air of the streets, and the neighing, and trampling of the horses was heard afar off.

And the People turned, and gazed upon him, and said,

He driveth like *Jehu*, though not to the confusion of
Jezabel!

Fox claimed that the reason his friends saw him so often at
the window of Mrs Robinson's new house in Berkeley Square
was that it commanded a clear view of Lansdowne House, where
Lord Shelburne resided. 'You know, Sir, I have pledged myself to the *public* to have a strict eye on Lord S[helburn]e's
motions; this is my sole motive for residing in Berkeley-square,
and that you may tell my friends is the reason they have not
seen me at *Brookes's.*'
'I hear Charles saunters about the streets, and brags that he
has not taken a pen in hand since he was out of place', remarked Fox's aunt Lady Sarah Napier.

> *Pour se désennuyer* he *lives* with Mrs Robinson, goes to
> Sadler's Wells with her, and is all day figuring away with
> her. I long to tell him he does it to show that he is
> superior to Alcibiades, for *his* courtesan forsook him when
> he was unfortunate, and Mrs Robinson takes *him* up.

Mrs Robinson stayed with Fox until September 1782, when
Tarleton, again, succeeded in a blaze of nautical metaphor.
The '*Tarleton, armed ship*', according to the *Morning Post* after
a '*chase* of *some months*' had at last come '*along side*' the '*Perdita
frigate*' which had 'instantly surrendered *at discretion*'. 'The *Perdita*'
it wrote, was a 'fine *clean bottomed vessel*' that had taken 'many
prizes during her cruize, particularly the *Florizel*, a most valu-
able ship belonging to the *crown*, but which was immediately
released after taking out the cargo'. Fox consoled himself with
another of the Prince's former mistresses, Mrs Armistead (the
'dearest Liz' of his letters), eventually and surprisingly offering
her marriage.
    Yet Mrs Robinson remained a friend of Fox, as of the Prince
and, like the Prince, she became a convinced Foxite in politics. She sported the Fox-North colours during Fox's unpopular and controversial return to power during 1783, and offered

the new ministers the use of her house for their meetings.

When Fox bought her a splendid new *vis-à-vis* – the 'aggregate of a few stakes' at Brooks's – she produced a design for the door panels rich with political symbolism. It showed her cypher, half concealed by the rays of the rising sun; beneath a lion couchant. 'If this was the Perdita's own fancy', remarked one angry commentator, 'it might be pardoned, as the folly of a weak woman; but manners and decency should have whispered, that such puns as the *Rising Sun* and the *British Lion* humiliated under the curtain of a Courtezan's bed, were jokes unbecoming her fancy or her folly.'

Folly was very much to the fore during the summer, and at no time more so than when Mrs Robinson, having suffered a miscarriage, refused to take any proper rest, but apparently rushed down to Brighton overnight in an open chaise in order to save Tarleton who was threatened with an execution. Her errand was successful, but at the cost of her health; and by October it became apparent that she was going to be permanently paralysed.*

Her financial problems deepened. She gave up her box at the Opera, stopped going to masquerades and left off most of her servants. Then the famous *vis-à-vis* was briefly seized in execution for a debt of £500. Soon she was even too poor to puff herself in the newspapers. 'The *Cyprian divinity* of Berkley-square, is said to be *on her last legs*', quipped a writer in the *Morning Post*, gleefully. 'Thus the fate of the *Buff* and *Blue* [i.e., the Foxite Whigs] extends through all their connections.'

Rumour, in the meantime, having associated the Prince with Lady Clarges, Lady Jersey and Lady Salisbury, was soon to connect him with the attractive and illiterate Charlotte Fortescue, and a Mrs Hodges, though it was to Mrs Robinson's former patron, the Duchess of Devonshire, and to the yielding Lady Melbourne that his erotic energies were chiefly directed. Both

---

* It seems she had a stroke. 'Mrs Robinson is said to have lost the use of one side of her frail and lovely tenement, by a paralytic stroke' reported the *Morning Herald* on 22 October 1783; 'if that be true, alas poor PERDITA indeed'. Later, she was crippled with rheumatism.

were highly attractive and dissipated leaders of Whig society, doyennes of wit, intrigue and fashion.

The Prince took every opportunity to foist himself on the Duchess. He pestered her with unwanted advances, and slyly snatched the occasional kiss at Devonshire House. Yet, apparently, she was proof against his blandishments. In any case, he was 'too fat', she confided to a notebook, he looked 'much like a woman in men's cloaths' and though his face was 'very handsome', he was graceful, 'goodnatur'd' and undoubtedly intelligent, she also knew of his 'shabby' behaviour to his mistresses.

Mrs Fitzherbert

No one who watched Mrs Fitzherbert cradle her dying husband Thomas in her arms at Nice during the spring of 1781 would have predicted that within the space of five years she would become, by some accounts, the wife of the Prince of Wales.

For a start, she was religious and a Roman Catholic, moral, conventional in outlook, and entirely circumspect in all her relations with men. Then she was neither witty, outstandingly beautiful, nor exhibitionistic, preferring her own circle of wealthy and rather strait-laced recusant families to the glamour of princes or the rivalries of court. She spoke French fluently, but was not a gifted conversationalist; she was neither accomplished as a letter writer nor remarked upon as a musician. Her beauty was of the homely variety; until her relationship with the Prince, it was never said of her as it was, for instance, of Mrs Robinson, that she had transfixed an admirer at first glance or illuminated a room by her presence. Her best features were her golden hair and fine complexion, an asset that led one commentator to remark that even at sixty her skin was still like a child's. Yet the caricaturists predictably emphasized what were deemed her less attractive qualities, concentrating, almost obsessively, on her full breasts and large, aquiline nose.

Of her early days, we know that she was born on 26 July 1756 and that she was the first child of Walter and Mary Smythe, he a former soldier and a son of a baronet; and that at about the age of twelve she was sent from Brambridge, her father's estate near Winchester, to Paris, to be educated in the Faubourg

St Antoine at an English convent run by Conceptionist nuns. On one occasion her parents took her to Versailles, where she was childishly amused by the 'novelty' of seeing Louis XV pulling a chicken apart with his fingers. The King, however, amused by the novelty of *her* conduct, sent her a 'dish of sugarplums' by way of one of his courtiers, the Duc de Soubise. 'Attentions from Royalty', she later remarked in connection with this incident, 'commenced with her at a very early age.'

Thomas Fitzherbert was not her first husband; at the age of nineteen, following her return to England, she had married Edward Weld, the handsome and immensely rich owner of Lulworth Castle in Dorset. Barely three months after their wedding, he died after falling from his horse, having willed her his property; but unfortunately, he left the document unsigned.

She married Thomas Fitzherbert in 1777, dividing her time between his estate at Swynnerton in Staffordshire and Park Street, near Hyde Park, his town house in London.

Probably, she first met the Prince during March 1784, when she was a guest of her friend, Lady Anne Lindsay, at the Opera House; though there are other accounts, including one that it was shortly after the Prince had spotted her out riding. 'The Prince had seen her in her carriage in the Park and was greatly struck with her – ' reminisced the diarist John Wilson Croker, 'inquired who she was – heard the widow Fitzherbert, contrived to make her acquaintance and was really *mad* for love.'

The more the Prince begged her to give herself to him, the more reluctant she was to do so, for she recognized that not only would it be against her own moral code, but also that it was against the laws of her religion. The Prince was unable to offer her a legal marriage because of the Act of Settlement of 1701, which confirmed an earlier law that only a Protestant unencumbered with a Catholic wife could inherit the throne; and because of the Royal Marriage Act of 1772, which declared that 'no descendant of the body of his late majesty King *George* the Second, male or female [below the age of twenty six] . . . shall be capable of contracting matrimony without the previous consent of his Majesty, his heirs, or successors'.

That should have been the end of the matter, but for the Prince's childlike inability to accept the situation. He drank himself into a succession of stupors and threatened to commit suicide. Mrs Fitzherbert then made a decision to go abroad to avoid him.

On 6 July the Prince wrote to the Duke of York stating his intention to follow Maria abroad, though fearing that his letter might be read by the King, he did not mention Mrs Fitzherbert directly. Instead he mentioned the escalating cost of Carlton House, the prospect of 'dissipation' and the '*very, very unpleasant situation*' he found himself in at home. The King was so 'excessively unkind', he wrote. 'Sometimes not speaking to me when he sees me for three weeks together, and hardly ever at Court, speaking to people on each side of me and then missing me, and then if he does honor me with a word, 'tis merely " 'tis very hot or very cold".' The subject of Mrs Fitzherbert he thought was best preserved 'in petto' until he saw him.

Two days later, realizing that Mrs Fitzherbert was about to leave, and that he would have to do something quickly, he stabbed himself with his sword in a room in Carlton House, bluntly affirming to his horrified attendants that life without Mrs Fitzherbert was not worth living. He then sent Lord Southampton, Lord Onslow, the Hon. Edward Bouverie, and Keate, his surgeon, on a desperate errand to Park Street with the message that only Mrs Fitzherbert could save him. At first she suspected a trick, and rather than go with them, she treated them in a 'most peremptory manner'; only when she had wrested the concession that the Duchess of Devonshire might accompany her would she, at last, agree to go with them.

They found the Duchess in the midst of a party at Devonshire House and with 'frighten'd countenances' urgently begged her to accompany them. 'Having nobody to consult [the Duke was not then at home] I consented,' wrote the Duchess ruefully, and the party returned at once.

The state of the bleeding Prince so overpowered Mrs
Fitzherbert that on first seeing him, she very nearly collapsed.
By now the blood had washed all over his chest, and it really
did look as if he were dying. The Prince took advantage of
her obvious distress to tell her that 'nothing would induce him
to live unless she promised to become his wife'. Mrs Fitzherbert
meekly complied with this request, after which the Prince immediately placed a ring upon her finger.

Of course, she immediately regretted her decision; and
later, when the party returned to Devonshire House, the
Duchess drew up a memorandum, which both she and Mrs
Fitzherbert signed: 'We went there [Carlton House] and she
promis'd to marry him at her return, but she conceives as
well as myself that promises obtain'd in such a manner are
entirely void'.

Still shocked, on the following morning Mrs Fitzherbert sent
a bitter letter to Lord Southampton 'protesting against what
had taken place, as not being a free agent'.

She put her threat into action, and left London for the
Continent.

The Prince was not slow to take advantage of Mrs Fitzherbert's
promise; and on 17 July he sent her an inordinately long letter. Once again he threatened, in a tone that was both
'rhapsodical' and 'earnest', to end his life if he found that he
could not do without her; swore that he had broken with Lady
Melbourne and conjured her to accept some bracelets as a
further token of his ever-increasing affection. Convinced that
she was now his, he signed himself 'not only your most affectionate of Lovers, but the tenderest of Husbands'. Keate meanwhile recommended a period of quiet for the Prince, a plan
that was unfortunately spoilt by the Duchess, who sent an angry
letter to Onslow suggesting that the Prince had not stabbed
himself at all, but that he had been bloodied by Keate and
then merely ripped off his bandages. This was too much for
the Prince, who, more in sorrow than in anger, sent the Duchess
a long, self-justificatory letter in reply:

My dearest Friend, For such I shall still call you although
your letter to Mr Onslow last night makes me doubt
whether or not you wish me to look upon you any longer
in that light. Conscious as I am of my own innocence,
and of my having no intention even in the smallest
instance to deceive you or her that is dearer to me than
life, and having endeavoured to convince you throughout
the whole of my late proceedings, of the irreprochable
integrity which has ever actuated me (excepting in one
instance, for which you know I sufficiently suffered) and
which I flatter myself will ever be the principles of my
conduct through life, you will not I hope be surprized at
the feelings which so severely occupy my whole mind.

The Prince denied that it had ever been his intention to
involve the Duchess in any way in the affair, and assured her
that if she really believed that he had merely been bloodied
by Keate then he was quite willing to allow himself to be exam-
ined by another surgeon, 'if your want of confidence in a man
to whom you had ever expressed yourself as looking upon him
as your best and dearest friend, could make you wish to subject him to so mortifying as well as degrading a situation'.
  The Duchess's conduct, he thought, in conveying her doubts
as to his veracity through a letter to Onslow, was both 'unkind
and ungenerous'.

If you are not convinced of my innocence, say so to me.
Why did you fear writing to tell me so? Beleive me, I
have too much self regard and too much pride,
notwithstanding the true affection and great friendship I
bear you, to live in any society, where my character is in
the least degree suspected, but more particularly in one
where I have so long had the good fortune to be
esteemed and received upon a very different footing. . . .
You know that I frequently have told you, and especially
of late in moments which I not only thought but hoped
would be the last of my miserable existence, that

excepting her who was present, you was the next dearest object to me in life.

'Have I ever entertained even for an instant towards you a single sentiment which the tenderest of brothers might not entertain for a sister?' he wondered, conveniently forgetting that he had. He did not seek his 'acquittal' on the subject 'as a favor', but demanded it as a 'justice' due to him.

Mrs Fitzherbert meanwhile, in order to avoid the Prince's embraces, fled through France to the fashionable spa town of Aix-la-Chapelle, then on to Holland, back to Paris, on to Switzerland, back to Holland, before settling several months later at Plombières, where she was pursued by the optimistic and indefatigable Marquis de Bellois. Reputed the handsomest man in France (till he was shot in the face), the Marquis was also a rake; and ill-natured gossip was soon put around that Mrs Fitzherbert was pregnant by him.

Confused and often despairing, she rifled literature for themes relevant to her situation, copying into her commonplace book line after line of verse. 'Woman, Sense and Nature's easy fool', ran one quotation,

If poor weak woman swerve from Virtue's side,
Ruin ensues, contempt and endless shame
And one false step entirely damns her name.
In vain, with tears the loss she may deplore
In vain, look back to what she was before
She falls like Stars that set to rise no more*

These attempts to 'fight off' the prospect of marriage to the Prince were considerably impaired by the Prince's determination to keep in close touch with her through a network of spies and through a persistent and sometimes desperately maintained correspondence. Indeed, so many letters were carried

---

* One of the most eloquent statements on the sexual 'double standard' and a popular audition piece, the lines are spoken by Edward IV's mistress Jane Shore in Nicholas Rowe's play of that name (1714).

through France and at such a speed that the Government became extremely suspicious, and at various times three couriers were arrested and put in prison.

In Mrs Fitzherbert's absence, the Prince often got outrageously drunk to dull the pain of her departure, and wore himself out in frequent bursts of angry and increasingly uninhibited torrents of emotion. There were some particularly embarrassing moments at Mrs Armistead's house on St Anne's Hill, near Windsor, where to testify the 'sincerity and violence of his passion' he rolled on the floor, struck his forehead, tore his hair and fell into hysterics, 'swearing that he would abandon the country, forgo the crown, sell his jewels and plate, and scrape together a competence to fly with the object of his affections to America'. Not for the first time it was rumoured that he was mad. 'If the Young Man goes on so he must kill himself,' wrote Mary Noel to her niece on 28 December 1784, 'for he has been ill, and kept the house a fortnight.'

In addition to his obsession with Mrs Fitzherbert, he was also worn down by the magnitude of his debts which, contrary to his best intentions, were inexorably rising. His stables alone cost him £31,000 per annum, double Colonel Lake's estimate in 1783, and almost half his annual income. He was 'totally in the hands' of his builder, upholsterer, jeweller and tailor: 'In every . . . department, such fresh expence arises from one hour to another, from quarters in which it is so little to be expected, that it is utterly impossible for me to give more than a random guess for a week forward,' wrote Lieutenant-Colonel Hotham during October. The Prince spent some of this money on furnishings for Carlton House and on jewels for Mrs Fitzherbert. An undisclosed sum went to bankroll the Opposition. Often he was overcharged.

On 24 August, he again wrote to the King, once more informing him of his 'embarrassed situation' and of his intention 'of putting in full practice a system of economy' by leaving immediately for the Continent. The King's reply was bitter and indignant: the Prince was 'void of every degree of reflection and of those feelings which a good heart must experience';

his conduct had 'grown worse', not better, since his removal to Carlton House; and the King insisted on the Prince turning over a new leaf and acting like a 'rational being'; otherwise, 'he will in every sense be ruined and lose the affection and protection of him who as yet remains his very affectionate father'.

The Prince, unmoved, repeated his threat; he had taken 'every possible and respectful means' to inform the King of his wish to go abroad, and he saw no fresh reason for altering his decision. In addition it was pointless for him to make any retrenchments, for, as he told Lord Southampton, any savings that would accrue would be merely a 'drop of water in the sea'. The King then hinted that though he would not back down on his refusal to allow the Prince to go abroad, something might be done for him if Colonel Hotham would fully disclose the true nature of his liabilities. As the Prince was not prepared to do this, the matter was not settled until 1787.

The Prince now tried a different tack, and during the spring of 1785 sent for Sir James Harris, the urbane British Minister at The Hague, to sound him out about the possibility of a trip to Holland. Would he, he wondered, be received abroad if he travelled not as a prince, but in a 'private character'? Harris replied that he would not.

'But what am I to do? Am I to be refused the right of every individual? Cannot I travel legally, as a private man, without the King's consent? . . . I am ruined if I stay in England. I disgrace myself as a man.'

'Your Royal Highness,' responded Harris, 'give me leave to say, will find no relief in travelling the way you propose. You will either be slighted, or, what is worse, become the object of political intrigue at every Court you pass through. . . . Surely, Sir, the King could not object to any increase of income Parliament thought proper to allow Your Royal Highness?'

'I believe he would,' replied the Prince. 'He hates me; he always did, from seven years old.'

Harris did his best to compose the quarrel; and made some progress. But, surprisingly, some weeks later, the Prince himself temporarily provided a solution to the problem: 'If you are come, my dear Harris, to dissuade me again from travelling, let me anticipate your kind intentions by telling you I have dismissed that idea from my mind. I see all my other friends, as well as yourself, are against it, and I shall subscribe to their opinion'.

For her part, Mrs Fitzherbert, in an undated letter to the Duchess of Devonshire, gave the impression that even if the Prince did come abroad she, for the time being at least, would not return with him to England, for 'why should I appear to give into measures I can never consent to?' Her situation was 'unpleasant' and 'cruel'; she 'always spoke and acted very openly' to the Prince 'and I believe that no one can say but that my reasons are just and painted in their true Colors, that I have neither exagerated or diminush'd any thing'. At Carlton House she suspected the Foxites of meddling: 'Whatever Mr F[ox] or his friends say to him they know in their own breasts they cannot approve off [it]', and she was confident that there was 'not one of them that will take it upon themselves' to say that if she did not marry the Prince it would be

> a legal proceeding ... they may wish to please [the
> Prince] and to appear to forward his views which they
> know can never esentially hurt him, at least that can never
> bind him to anything. ... I don't speake with any want of
> regard or respect for his friends, but they are certainly not
> my Friends, it is very natural for them to say *such and such
> are the proposals, it is not our affair, and she is of an age to
> take care of herself.*

This apparent decisiveness was, however, an impression rather than a reality, and it masked a temperament that was, in Lady Anne Lindsay's words, becoming daily more 'irresolute and inconsequent'. Mrs Fitzherbert missed her family, she missed her friends and she was tired of the rudeness of her French servants. At one point she spoke of entering a convent, and actually wrote a letter to an abbess at Liège, but then ripped it up, having decided, after all, not to send it.

Still the Prince bombarded her with letters, cajoling her for her hardness of heart one minute, threatening suicide the next. Then, during October, she finally gave in. 'I have told him I will be his,' she ruefully told Lady Anne, who was already in England. 'I know I injure him and perhaps destroy for ever my own tranquillity.'

The Prince was ecstatic; and on 3 November he wrote her an extremely long letter, dense with professions of love and an extremely circumstantial account of a tangled attempt on the part of some Pittites to find a solution to the problem of his income; 'such a train of extraordinary and wonderful events' had recently taken place, he wrote, that he could hardly persuade himself that he had not been dreaming:

Come then, oh! come, dearest of wives, best and most adored of women, come and for ever crown with bliss him who will through life endeavour to convince you by his love and attention of his wishes to be the best of husbands and who will ever remain unto the latest moments of his existence, *unalterably thine.*

He had, he said, spoken to Mrs Fitzherbert's uncle Henry Errington, who, in view of Maria's father's constant ill health, was acting as her special adviser: his advice was for her to set out for England, 'the very next moment' after she received the Prince's letter; she was not to breathe a word of her intentions to any other member of her family; they would be married immediately on her arrival; Lady Anne Lindsay agreed with him in everything; she was almost every day at Carlton House, where she and her sister had discussed every detail of the forthcoming marriage with the Duke and Duchess of Cumberland. 'Everything will be done as private as possible;' he wrote, 'no one else besides the Duke and Dss will be present unless it is the Duke and Dss of Devonshire; in short, everything is settled. We want nothing but your arrival.' He would, he said, either meet her in a hackney chaise on the Rochester to London Road or wait till he heard of her arrival in Park

Street, to which place he would 'fly upon the wings of love'.
Romantically, he also enclosed a painting of one of his eyes by
the fashionable miniaturist Richard Cosway: 'If you have not
totally forgotten the whole countenance, I think the likeness
will strike you.'

The news that Mrs Fitzherbert was at last on her way back
to England threw Devonshire House into an uproar. She never
thought it would come to this, Georgiana told the Prince shortly
after Mrs Fitzherbert's arrival in early December. 'It is indeed
indeed madness in both.' She was 'quite wild with the horror
of it'. 'Pray see Charles Fox tomorrow', she counselled, 'or let
me write to him.' When she met the Prince in person they
had a 'warm and violent' quarrel.

Fox, in spite of what Mrs Fitzherbert might have thought,
was also against the marriage and, having presumably been
briefed by the Duchess of Devonshire, he sat down to write
the Prince a long admonitory letter. An illegal match would of
course be disastrous for the Whigs, not least because of its
potential effect on the succession:

> If such an idea be really in your mind, and it be not now
> too late, for God's sake let me call your attention to some
> considerations. . . . In the first place, you are aware that a
> marriage with a Catholic throws the Prince contracting
> such Marriage out of the succession of the Crown. Now,
> what change may have happened in Mrs Fitzherbert's
> sentiments upon religious matters I know not; but I do
> not understand that any public profession of change has
> been made. Surely, Sir, this is not a matter to be trifled
> with; . . . consider the circumstances in which you stand.
> The King not feeling for you as a father ought, the Duke
> of York professedly his favourite, and likely to be married
> agreeably to the King's wishes; the nation full of its old
> prejudices against Catholics; and justly dreading all
> disputes about succession;* – in all these circumstances

* The Protestants' hatred of Catholicism had erupted as recently as the

your enemies might take such advantage as I shudder to think of. . . . I have stated this danger upon the supposition that the Marriage would be a real one; but your Royal Highness knows as well as I, that according to the present law of the country it *cannot*; and I need not point out to your good sense, what a source of uneasiness it must be to you, to her [Mrs Fitzherbert], and above all to the nation. . . . If there should be children from the Marriage . . . will it not be said that we must look for future applications to legitimate them, and consequently be liable to disputes for the succession between the eldest son, and the eldest son after the legal Marriage?. . . . In the meanwhile, a mock Marriage (for it can be no other) is neither honourable for any of the parties, nor, with respect to your Royal Highness, even safe. This appears so clear to me, that if I were Mrs Fitzherbert's father or brother, I would advise her not by any means to agree to it, and to prefer any species of connection with you to one leading to so much misery and mischief.

The Prince's response to this was to retreat into a private world, where the truth had no more independent existence than whim or his latest selfish feeling. 'Make yourself easy, my dear friend,' he wrote to Fox. 'Believe me, the world will now soon be convinced, that there not only is, but never was, any grounds for these reports, which of late have been so malevolently circulated.'

At first it was thought that a military chaplain, the Revd Philip Rosenhagen, would conduct the marriage, but having perhaps reflected on the penalties under the Royal Marriage Act he became frightened. So the Prince sent for the Revd Samuel Johnes, a friend of Lord North and the Rector of Welwyn in

summer of 1780, when opposition to the Roman Catholic Relief Act had culminated in the 'Gordon Riots'. One victim was Mrs Fitzherbert's consumptive husband, Thomas, who, having exacerbated his illness combating the rioters, was carried over to the South of France in the hope that the climate would alleviate his condition.

Hertfordshire. However, he too dropped out, and instead his
place was taken by one of the Prince's four chaplains in ordinary, an impecunious cleric called the Revd Robert Burt, who
accepted on the condition that the Prince would pay his debts
for him and on coming to the throne make him a bishop.

All barriers then removed, at about six o'clock on the evening
of 15 December 1785, Mrs Fitzherbert and the Prince were
reunited in her Park Street drawing-room. Burt began the service
and the couple were finally joined according to the rites of
the Church of England. It had earlier been decided that her
parents would not be present in case the marriage ever came
to court, though they knew of their daughter's decision. Instead, one of her brothers, John Smythe, represented her immediate family, while she was given away by her uncle Henry
Errington.

Immediately afterwards the Prince wrote out a marriage cer-
tificate: 'We the undersigned do witness that George Augustus
Frederick, Prince of Wales, was married unto Maria Fitzherbert,
this 15th of December, 1785. John Smythe, Henry Errington,
George P., Maria Fitzherbert' and this was handed to Mrs
Fitzherbert for safe-keeping.* No one else was present except
for a mutual friend, Orlando Bridgeman, who kept watch for
intruders at the door.

Afterwards the couple set off for a brief honeymoon, apparently at a house on Ham Common near Richmond.

Soon the country was awash with rumour as speculation grew
that there either had been, or was about to be a marriage.
''Tis said is fact,' confided the soldier John Gabriel Stedman,
'and such if true, is a thousand pities.' 'I know very little of
her history', remarked the actress Sarah Siddons, 'more than
that it is agreed on all hands that she is a very ambitious and
clever woman . . . it seems everything goes on with the utmost
formality; provision made for children, and so on.' The question of children was also raised by the Revd Reginald Heber,

* Later, fearing that the document might be produced in a court of law,
Mrs Fitzherbert was persuaded to cut out the names of her witnesses. The
mutilated document is now in the Royal Archives at Windsor.

who feared that if Mrs Fitzherbert should prove a 'breeder', 'the national consequences may be very serious. The supplications of every loyal subject for the long, long life of the present King and Queen will now be offered up with more frequency than ever'.

More sceptical however was another commentator, Robert Hobart, who described all talk of the marriage as the 'Lie of the day', though even he quoted a report that the Prince had taken a box for Mrs Fitzherbert at the Opera House, and 'that he constantly passes the greater part of the night with her'.

The most fashionable members of society talked of little else: Mrs Fitzherbert was to move into Carlton House; she was married by a Roman Catholic priest; she was to have £6,000 a year; she was to be created a duchess.

Catholics, such as the Earl of Denbeigh and Lady Jerningham, naturally took the most considered view, concerned as they had to be with the consequences for themselves and their co-religionists. 'God knows how it will turn out – it may be to the Glory of our Belief, or it may be to the Great dismay and destruction of it!'

As for the Prince, when asked about the marriage he would neither confirm nor deny it.

Inevitably many families were rather wary of entertaining Mrs Fitzherbert in such ambiguous circumstances; and for a while her reception in society was not very encouraging. Her close friend and relative Lady Sefton dropped her, as did the Welds and the Fitzherberts; while the Duke of Portland advised his wife to have nothing more to do with her. The Duchess of Devonshire took a middle road; she would leave her name at her house, but she would not, she assured her mother, go with her to the opera. If she had a large assembly, she would ask her because she had done so before and because, officially, Mrs Fitzherbert was still an unmarried woman. 'But this is all I will do, and I will avoid the assembly if you like it, and indeed from my own choice I shall not have one.'

Meanwhile there was the outstanding problem of the Prince's debts, and during the following April he sent Lord Southampton to the King with a renewed plea for help. By now the debts were over four times his annual income – and rising. He still owed almost £80,000 on Carlton House, and the stupendous sum of £30,000 for 'incidental charges not yet come in, or to be ascertained exactly'. He was on all sides surrounded by a 'precipice' from which only the King could save him.

On 15 June he forwarded Colonel Hotham's latest estimate, a sum little short of £270,000. 'I confess the sum is large', he wrote,

> but what adds more to my distress is, that the longer it continues unpaid, so much the more it will continue to augment. I therefore have nothing to do but to throw myself upon your Majesty's benevolence, hoping for your gracious assistance, which if I am so unfortunate as not to meet with, will throw me into a situation below that of the lowest individual in the country.

Unswayed, the King merely asked his son for an explanation of his past expences and 'reasonable security against a continuation of his extravagance'. Only when these were complied with would he extricate him from the 'embarassment to which his own imprudence has subjected him'.

In a fit of pique, the Prince sent the King a lofty note in which he apologized for the trouble he had hitherto given him and assured him that he would hear no more from him as he was now convinced that he had no reason to 'expect at present or in future', even the 'smallest assistance'. In a later letter he added that it was not mere selfishness that had prompted his applications, but concern for his creditors and the threat of 'legal insults as humiliating to me as I am persuaded they would have been offensive to your Majesty'.

Having failed to convince the King, he took the extraordinary step of shutting up most of Carlton House, and dismissing almost every member of his household. On 7 July he wrote to Lord Southampton informing him of his decision, and asking him to pass on his sincere and grateful thanks to his staff for their past services. He still hoped to go abroad, if and when he could persuade the King; till then he had taken a 'firm determination' not to appear in public. He philosophized that his was not the 'worst of situations', for he had the consciousness of acting 'right and justly'.

Mrs Fitzherbert was also forced to economize, and following the Prince's lead she too closed up her London house, laid off most of her servants, and took to driving what was said to be a 'shabby old carriage' through the streets of Brighton. There were few people of note there, and it was clear that many people wanted to avoid her. Consequently, she went to few balls, and except for a brief trip to Bath to see her father, now dangerously ill, and the occasional journey to London or Richmond, her time passed almost quietly. She lived in a small villa, resplendent with green shutters, and separated by only a narrow strip of garden from the building which the Prince was in the process of metamorphosing into the Marine Pavilion.

Economy however was never one of the Prince's strongest points, and to those prepared to listen to him he made it clear that it was not meant as anything more than a temporary expedient. The plan was to shame the King, to bring him round, not to doom the Prince to comparative poverty. For a while, indeed, he was tempted to borrow money abroad, and there were rumours that the former Duc de Chartres, now Duc d'Orléans, had offered him a portion of his splendid fortune; then the politician Sir Ralph Payne came up with an offer, while Gloucester's MP offered him £2,000. All offers were politely but firmly rejected. Ultimately, the King stood firm, so there was nothing left to do but to have the matter raised in Parliament.

Accordingly, on 20 April 1787, Alderman Nathaniel Newnham, a man 'who possessed neither eloquence nor public consideration', an Independent MP for the City of London, rose from his seat and asked Pitt:

Whether it was the design of the Ministers to bring
forward any proposition to rescue the Prince of Wales

from his present very embarrassed condition? for though
he thought that His Royal Highness's conduct, during his
difficulties, had reflected greater honour and glory on his
character than the most splendid diadem in Europe had
upon the wearer of it, yet it must be very disagreeable to
His Royal Highness to be deprived of those comforts and
enjoyments which so properly belonged to his high rank.

Pitt's answer was brusque and to the point: it was not. Consequently Newnham gave notice that he would himself bring
forward such a motion on 4 May.

The possibility that the Prince's relationship with Mrs
Fitzherbert might be discussed in Parliament naturally caused
a great deal of commotion. With the exception of Fox and
Sheridan, few of his Whig friends were in favour of the Prince's
move, while Pitt had always doubted that the Prince would be
brave enough to go through with it. The Prince himself cam-
paigned in the House, wrote a stream of letters and attempted
to speak to most of the members. On 22 April, as the King
pondered his next move, he wrote to the Earl of Hertford in
an attempt to secure his powerful interest. He even went so
far as to show some members his accounts and his correspondence with the King, making some converts, particularly among
the independent-minded 'country gentlemen'.

Before the matter could be taken much further however
Pitt decided to see if he could call the Prince's bluff and on
24 April, addressing himself to Newnham, he asked him if he
would define in exact terms the 'scope and tendency' of his
coming motion. Newnham merely hedged: 'As to the particular parliamentary form which it would wear, it really had not
been decided upon by himself, but the object of it he had no
objection to state, as it was to rescue his Royal Highness from
his present embarrassed situation'.

Fox, who had not so far spoken, intervened, and addressing
himself to Pitt he told him that he 'entirely agreed' that the
Prince's parlous financial state was a 'subject of peculiar novelty,
but so were the circumstances' that had given rise to it; why

then could the business not be 'forestalled' and 'something done in the interim to render it unnecessary' for Newnham to proceed with his motion?

Pitt offered a threat to the Alderman: If Newnham was still determined to bring forward his motion then he, for his part, 'would, however distressing it might be to him, as an individual, discharge his duty to the public, and enter fully into the subject'.

There the matter stood for three days. But on 27 April, Newnham moved that an 'humble address be presented to his Majesty, praying him to take into his royal consideration the present embarrassed state of affairs of his Royal Highness the Prince of Wales', and the scenario which almost everyone feared happened. The massive, rough-looking figure of John Rolle rose from amongst the Tory squires sitting below the gangway on the ministerial side of the House, and before Pitt had a chance to reply, he caught the Speaker's attention:

> If ever there was a question which called particularly upon the attention of that class of persons, the country gentlemen, it would be the question which the honourable Alderman had declared his determination to agitate, because it was a question which went immediately to affect our Constitution in Church and State.

Immediately, a shudder of alarm ran through the House. For reasons which have never been satisfactorily explained, Fox was not in the House to answer Rolle, so Sheridan replied, feigning incomprehension of Rolle's meaning. But Rolle refused to back down: 'If a motion were urged, which he thought highly improper to be proposed, the honourable gentleman would find he would not flinch from it, but act as became an independent country gentleman to act upon such an occasion, and state without reserve his sentiments, according as the matter struck him. He would do his duty'.

Pitt made another attempt to persuade Newnham to withdraw, and against a background of mounting excitement stated that he, for his part, might with 'infinite reluctance' be forced to disclose 'circumstances which he should otherwise think it his duty to conceal'. This was too much for Sheridan: 'Some honourable gentlemen had thought proper to express their anxious wishes that the business should be deferred', but Pitt, he now argued, had 'erected an insuperable barrier to such a step. It would then seem to the country, to all Europe, that the Prince had yielded to terror what he had denied to argument'. And later that evening, a chastened Pitt withdrew his statement: 'The particulars' to which he had alluded, 'related only to the pecuniary embarrassments' of the Prince of Wales, and to his correspondence with the King, and not to any 'extraneous circumstances'.

When, later that evening, Sheridan met the Prince at Carlton House to discuss the day's parliamentary proceedings, he found him in such an agitated state that he was barely able to hold a coherent conversation. Clearly, the Prince was relieved that something had been done to counteract Pitt, but there was now the very real possibility that by raising the matter of his alleged marriage to Mrs Fitzherbert Rolle would provoke a potentially disastrous discussion. There was only one thing for it, and that was for someone to return to the House and, with the Prince's full authority, deny every rumour of the marriage. First though, unable to face Mrs Fitzherbert himself, he sent Sheridan to inform her vaguely that some explanation would 'probably' be required by Parliament.

Mrs Fitzherbert replied that she was 'like a dog with a log round its neck' and that she would therefore rely on Sheridan and the Prince's other friends to protect her. She obviously could not speak out, and while she understood that something would have to be done to relieve the Prince of his debts, she hoped that it would not be at the price of her honour. Sheridan was sympathetic; he liked Mrs Fitzherbert, and rather than tell her that this was precisely what the Prince had in mind, he chose to mollify her.

Fox, however, had no such scruples; he was not a friend of Mrs Fitzherbert, nor did she care for him: she disliked his influence on the Prince and she disliked his morals. Seeing that he could at one blow serve the Prince and put paid to the rumour that he had been present at the wedding, he decided that he would take it upon himself to make in Parliament an unambiguous speech denying the allegations. He had, after all, the Prince's letter of 11 December 1785 assuring him that there were no grounds for the allegations, and, moreover, when he had mentioned the rumours to him the Prince had dismissed them out of hand as '*ridiculous*' and '*nonsense*'. Fox therefore felt on safe ground, even if it meant offering extreme offence to Mrs Fitzherbert.

His opportunity came on 30 April. Rising from his seat, and quickly warming to his theme, he addressed a House fairly brimming over with curiosity and impatience.

> On a former occasion he had heard [Pitt] throw out
> certain hints which appeared to his mind extremely like a
> menace, and that of a very extraordinary nature, but those
> hints had, he understood, on Friday last been much
> narrowed by explanation, and confined to certain
> correspondence and letters which had passed on the
> subject without doors. . . . He desired it to be understood,
> not as speaking lightly but as speaking from the
> immediate authority of the Prince of Wales, when he
> assured the House that there was no part of his Royal
> Highness's conduct that he was either afraid or unwilling
> to have investigated in the most minute manner.

With respect to the Prince's correspondence with the King, he would like to have it put before the House, because it would 'prove' that the conduct of the Prince had been 'in the highest degree amiable'. As for Rolle's allusion to some 'danger to the Church and State', until 'that gentleman thought proper to explain himself' he was unable to say 'with any certainty' precisely to what he referred; 'but he supposed it must be meant in reference to that miserable calumny, that low, malicious falsehood, which had been propagated without doors, and made the wanton sport of the vulgar'.

'What species of party', he wondered, 'could have fabricated so base and scandalous a calumny. Had there existed in the Kingdom . . . an anti-Brunswick faction, to that faction he should have certainly imputed' it; for he 'knew not what other description of men could feel an interest in first forming, and then circulating with more than ordinary assiduity, a tale in every particular so unfounded, and for which there was not the shadow of anything like reality'.

Not only was it nonsense, but the Prince himself had 'authorised' him to declare that in the House of Lords he himself would submit to even the 'most pointed questions, which could be put to him respecting it, or to afford his Majesty or his Majesty's Ministers the fullest assurances of the utter falsehood of the fact in question, which never had, and common sense must see, never could have happened'.

It was, most people agreed, an extraordinary speech; either Fox was right, in which case Mrs Fitzherbert was after all merely the Prince's mistress, or he was wrong, in which case he had lied to the House, or been deliberately lied to by the Prince. After such a speech, there did not seem room for further discussion.

Rolle, however, was still not satisfied, and shortly after some other contributions he rose to his feet: Fox had said that it was 'impossible' the marriage had happened; and everyone knew that there were 'certain laws and Acts of Parliament' which forbade it:

> but though it could not be done under the formal
> sanction of the law, there were ways in which it might
> have taken place, and those laws in the minds of some
> persons might have been satisfactorily evaded, and yet the
> fact might be equally productive of the most alarming
> consequences.

He therefore begged for further clarification from Fox.

Fox responded with his most categorical statement yet: the marriage 'not only never could have happened legally, but never did happen in any way whatsoever'; it had from the 'beginning been a base and malicious falsehood'. Unfortunately, later that evening Fox bumped into Orlando Bridgeman, who told him he must have been 'misinformed', for he himself had been at the wedding.

While Fox's speech helped to bring round the King and Pitt, who soon after entered into negotiations on the Prince's debts, the effect on Mrs Fitzherbert was almost catastrophic. Fox, she later remarked, had 'rolled her in the kennel like a street walker'; he knew 'every word' he had uttered was 'a lie'; he had compromised her religion and deliberately and cold-heartedly destroyed her character.

The Prince, having plucked up the courage to meet her on the following day, apparently tracked her down to the house of one of her many relatives, the Hon. Mrs Butler. Adopting a look of pained innocence, he professed to be as shocked by Fox's speech as she was. 'Only conceive, Maria, what Fox did yesterday,' he is supposed to have said. 'He went down to the House and denied that you and I were man and wife! Did you ever hear of such a thing?' She turned pale, but did not reply to him.

Immediately she thought of breaking off every connection with the Prince altogether, a course from which she was only persuaded by his 'repeated assurances' that he had never authorized Fox to make such an unqualified declaration. Some of her friends believed the Prince, while others argued that even if she was not entirely convinced, she was 'bound to accept the word of her husband'. He then realized that if he was to save their relationship then somehow he would have to make amends; in the meantime, after their conversation at Mrs Butler's, she refused to see him.

At first, he sent for the ambitious and handsome Charles Grey, and, having admitted that some sort of ceremony had taken place, begged him to say something in the House. Grey would do no such thing; if a mistake had been made, then it was for the Prince to rectify it, and this could only be done if he spoke to Fox in person. The Prince refused. 'Well, then,' he said, clearly annoyed, if Grey would not go down to the House, 'Sheridan must say something'.

Sheridan's speech in Parliament on 4 May was a masterpiece of tact and equivocation, delivered to a House by turns amused and perplexed. Newnham had briefly announced that he would not now be presenting his motion, but Rolle was still there to harry him, threatening further trouble should the agreement with Pitt not be in accordance with the dignity of the House. Sheridan began by saying that he could not but believe 'that there existed ... but one feeling and one sentiment in the House, that of heartfelt satisfaction at the auspicious conclusion to which the business was understood to be brought'. However, though the Prince 'felt the most perfect satisfaction at the prospect before him ... yet did he also desire it to be distinctly remembered that no attempt had at any time been made to screen any part of his conduct, actions or situation' from the view of the House. He reminded them that the Prince had offered to respond himself to any questions put to him in the House of Lords; that no one had done so 'was a point which did credit to the decorum and dignity of Parliament'. He then turned to Mrs Fitzherbert:

> But while his Royal Highness's feelings had been doubtless considered on the occasion, he must take the liberty of saying, however much some might think it a subordinate consideration, that there was another Person entitled in every honourable and delicate mind to the same attention, whom he would not otherwise attempt to describe, or allude to, except to affirm that ignorance or vulgar malice alone could have persevered in attempting to injure one on whose conduct truth could fix no just reproach, and whose character claimed, and was entitled to, the truest and most general respect.

Unlike most members of Parliament who professed to be, at least on the surface, satisfied with the verbal contortions of Sheridan's speech, Mrs Fitzherbert was not; and contrary to the Prince's heartfelt wishes, she still refused to see him. She still felt desperately let down, and so hurt that she demanded more than a speech by Sheridan. Moreover, always a cautious woman, she felt it best to wait a while before making up her mind, in order to judge the effect on her reputation. So, the Prince adopted his old tactic, turned to drink, raised a fever, had himself bled copiously, and once more threatened suicide. Fortunately for his sanity, if not her happiness, she gradually allowed herself to soften towards him, and by 25 May, it was clear to almost everyone that she had indeed forgiven him.

Contrary to her worst expectations, the response of most society people was almost uniformly kind, and even those Catholic families who had dropped her when rumours of her marriage to the Prince first arose, welcomed her back: 'I do not know what rules the ladies govern themselves by', remarked the Shakespearian scholar Edmund Malone to Lord Charlemont, but 'She is courted and queens it as much as ever'.

Elizabeth Sheridan, following her husband's speech, was in 'high spirits'. 'Poor Mrs Fitzherbert', she wrote,

> is very much to be pitied and I am glad for the honour of
> the fine world that they have shown more good nature
> and attention to her than perhaps the outrageously
> virtuous would approve. Everybody has been to visit her
> since the debate in the House of Commons and all
> people are anxious to countenance and support her.

Indeed, in the words of the Archbishop of Canterbury, it was all 'very odd'; not only was she 'more received' than she had been, but she stood 'more forward' than ever.

In the country at large, it was a different matter, however, as the antics of the fanatical Lord George Gordon and the pamphleteering talents of the veteran radical John Horne Tooke testified.

Lord George Gordon, then being prosecuted for libelling Marie-Antoinette and the French Ambassador, took every opportunity of introducing Mrs Fitzherbert into his defence, with the deliberate object of inciting an outbreak of anti-Catholic feeling. He maintained that he had met Mrs Fitzherbert in Paris during her flight from the Prince and that they had discussed some court intrigue, the details of which he wanted her to substantiate. On 30 April, immediately following one of his court appearances, he called at her house in order to serve her with a subpoena. He was turned out of doors by her servants, and afterwards visited in turn by one of her brothers Walter Smythe and a friend, who threatened to call him to account if he went to Mrs Fitzherbert again or took any liberties with her name in future; to which Lord George replied that he would not rest until he received a written note establishing once and for all Mrs Fitzherbert's 'just title'.

A few days later, Lord George sent a pompous account of the affair to Pitt: 'I think it my duty to inform you, as Prime Minister, with this circumstance, that you may be apprized of, and communicate to the House of Commons, the overbearing disposition of the Papists.' Fortunately for Mrs Fitzherbert, few people of influence were impressed by Lord George's behaviour, and after he had again attacked the French Queen and Catherine of Russia, the Attorney-General was compelled to remark that he was a 'disgrace to the name of Briton'.

Horne Tooke, rightly, smelled an establishment cover-up, and with devastating irony he took the Prince, Mrs Fitzherbert and Fox to task. Fox's speech was an 'additional slander on a much misunderstood, and misrepresented young man' he argued.

I have no doubt (for he is young and a prince) that some things might possibly be changed for the better in his conduct. But I will not believe, that at any time, and least of all in the moment and manner as reported, such a disavowal (be the marriage true or false), or any thing tending to lessen the character of the lady could possibly be authorized by him. And, though extremely disgusted with his politics, yet I have too much personal respect for Mr Fox, to believe, upon the authority of a newspaper, that Mr Fox was either the adviser, or silent seeming approver, much less the medium of such a disavowal. If such a measure had been thought advisable, or even necessary, upon any important score; yet Mr Fox knows better how to time even his necessary measures. What! at the moment when the payment of debts and revenue were the questions, then to get up and make this disavowal; and thus give it the appearance of sacrificing, on compulsion, a defenceless woman's character (with whom, I suppose, at least there was friendship) for so mean a consideration as a paltry sum of money! No. I will never believe it!

He concluded the first part of his pamphlet with the statement that the Prince's marriage was 'neither *unusual,* nor *improper,* nor *impossible,* nor *illegal,* nor affected by the act of *exclusion* or the act of *settlement;* but such as does honour to his sentiments, and is highly beneficial to his country'.

There was also trouble for Mrs Fitzherbert when during early July she followed the Prince to Brighton. The Prince's arrival was much looked forward to, but her presence was not greeted with universal pleasure. Some scrupulous people immediately made plans to leave, and there were complaints when it was noticed that she had rented a splendid house on the North Row, close to the Marine Pavilion. There were consolations however; some of her friends were especially kind, and on 12 July the Countess of Talbot led a delegation of several ladies to her house on what was pointedly described in the newspapers as a 'formal visit'.

The Brighton people took her to their hearts. 'They honoured her, they almost worshipped her,' reminisced one beguiled resident. 'Proud was the aspirant of Fashion who succeeded in obtaining her notice in public; honoured the devotee of gentility who could boast the least acquaintance with her in private. To be invited to meet her at the palatial Pavilion was acknowledged to be a covetable distinction.'

The Prince drove Mrs Fitzherbert on the Steyne and

accompanied her to the theatre and to the races at Brighton and Lewes. Soon they were joined by Marie-Antoinette's intimate friend, the Princesse de Lamballe, and a large French contingent. Other visitors included the Duke of Bedford and the Duke and Duchess of Cumberland. There were several balls and, on one occasion, when the Prince returned to London to meet the Duke of York, who had just arrived back from Hanover, Mrs Fitzherbert presided over a 'grand concert of vocal and instrumental music' at the Pavilion.

Yet, if the people of Brighton were prepared to overlook some irregularities, Mrs Fitzherbert's enemies were not, and just as she had suffered for her connection with the Prince in the matter of his debts, so she also suffered when during the following year the King fell gravely ill, thus raising the possibility that the Prince might become Regent. To all intents and purposes, it looked as if the King had gone mad, such was the violent and uncharacteristic nature of his behaviour; he spoke obscenely, rambled for hours at a stretch, gave orders to imaginary individuals and, in his delirium, imagined that London was flooded.

Under Pitt's guiding hand, the Government played a shrewd, prevaricating game, moving for a committee to examine the journals of the House for precedents and introducing a series of resolutions which, if accepted, would bind the Prince to a number of restrictions. This was unacceptable to Fox who, to the surprise of many Parliamentarians, adopted the un-Whiggish position that all discussion was unnecessary as the Prince by virtue of his father's incapacity was already 'completely and legally' Regent. Hearing this and recognizing Fox's blunder, Pitt immediately slapped his thigh and whispered, 'I'll un-Whig the gentleman for the rest of his life.' Yes, he admitted, the Prince had a claim to the exercise of royal power, but to demand it as an inherent right independent of Parliament as Fox had done was little less than 'treason to the constitution of the country'.

The Prince behaved like a fool, jesting with his friends at Brookes's, and boldly cabinet-forming with Grey, Lord Loughborough and Sheridan. He was unable to contain his excitement at the prospect of power and, unhappily, rumours inevitably circulated that he was getting drunk and ridiculing his father. It was said he would spy on the King, and invite his friends to gaze at him at Windsor, as if he were an inmate of Bedlam; and that he and the Duke of York had drunkenly imitated his mad gestures in half the drawing-rooms of London. Mrs Fitzherbert, in the meantime, having, it was believed, allowed the Prince to convince her that if Regent he would at the very least make her a duchess, hobnobbed with the Prince's Private Secretary Captain 'Jacko' Payne, and even offered house room to the Prince's chief adviser in the affair, an impecunious Sheridan.

Her involvement alarmed the late Dr Johnson's volatile friend Mrs Thrale, who voiced the fear that if the Prince did become Regent he would 'pack' a parliament, and then use his majority to overturn the Act of Settlement and confirm his marriage. 'Our Hope' then, wrote Mrs Thrale mournfully, would be in the Prince's 'Profligacy'; for Mrs Fitzherbert would 'seize the first Moment of his Returning Virtue or decaying Powers to teach him the intolerant Principles of Popery'.

Time and again, Pittite journalists and pamphleteers played on this fear; on 10 December the *Morning Post* stated that Fox now had reason to believe that the Prince had lied to him about his alleged marriage. The Prince retaliated by sending his *maître d'hôtel*, Louis Weltje, to buy a controlling share in the paper – a not unusual example of news management. Other journalists were silenced with bribes, while Sheridan suppressed a pamphlet.

Of those who would not be silenced no one was more ingenious and persistent than the Revd Philip Withers, chaplain to the Dowager Lady Hereford. Taking his cue from Horne Tooke and a host of polemicists, he harried both the Prince and Mrs Fitzherbert in a flurry of best-selling pamphlets. Noting that 'considerable time' had elapsed since Horne Tooke had suggested that the Prince had married Mrs Fitzherbert in contempt of the Royal Marriage Act, he asked why the

'Chancellor, the Judges, and both Houses of Parliament' had still not investigated his charges:

> Every inhabitant of the realm is more or less interested in this mysterious business; Who can tell what dissentions may arise, what treasons may be expended, what blood may be shed, in future days, from disputable pretensions to the throne? NOW is the time for legal Investigation. It is a duty we owe to ourselves and posterity.

In another pamphlet he begged the Bishop of London to take action against 'The WIDOW FITZHERBERT of Pall Mall . . . for a loose disorderly course of life – namely for fornication with his ROYAL HIGHNESS GEORGE, PRINCE OF WALES'; and also against the Prince for 'aiding, abetting and comforting the said Widow Fitzherbert in her sinful practices'.

> Send your Citation, my Lord, to the suspected fair one. – If innocent – let her wipe off the foul aspersions of the PARTY. If guilty – let her receive the correction of the Church . . . compel the fair Delinquent to kneel and receive your spiritual reproof – Chasten also her body, for the good of her Soul. . . . But in the midst of Judgment, Holy Father, be mindful of Mercy.

In yet a further pamphlet he accused Mrs Fitzherbert of being party to a popish plot; part of a plan to introduce a number of Catholics into Parliament at the next election. 'She has correspondence in France through the Gros Abbe, the Duke of Orléans's bastard brother; and through Abbe Taylor, and some Irish Friars in many parts of Italy. There is no doubt a secret cabal is forming which will counteract the purposes of every wholesome administration.' Foolishly, he also repeated the rumour that she had had a child by the Marquis de Bellois; the slur gave Thomas Erskine, the Prince's Attorney-General and a man of 'terrifying eloquence', an opportunity of taking him to court for libel.

The Prince's friends tried to distance him from the entire issue by putting it about that in any case his interest in Mrs Fitzherbert was waning.

> I find it is a measure of the party to say that the Prince, from his amiable character, retains a friendship for Mrs Fitzherbert; but that she has not the least remaining influence; that he is quite tired of her, and in love elsewhere, therefore the public need have no further alarm on her account.

It was even said that the Prince, unable to stand the loss of popularity occasioned by his connection with a Catholic, had entreated Mrs Fitzherbert to go to France or anywhere else that might get her out of the country, and had offered her £10,000 per annum.

Meanwhile the egregious John Rolle again took the opportunity of raising the Fitzherbert question in Parliament. On 7 February, during a debate on a clause in the Regency Bill which provided that if the Prince either left the country or should 'at any time marry a Papist; then, in every case, all the powers and authorities vested in his said Royal Highness, by virtue of the Act, shall cease and determine', he moved an amendment to insert the words: 'or shall at any time be proved to be married, in fact, or in law, to a Papist'. By this, he said, 'he meant nothing personal or disrespectful, nothing injurious or hateful to the feelings of any individual'. He spoke only from the

> regard he had to the principles of the Constitution which were the bulwarks of our freedom, . . . Could he have brought himself to believe that, as the clause stood at present, it was sufficiently strong, he would not have proposed the amendment; or if any person would step forward and confirm the declaration solemnly made by [Fox] . . . he should be satisfied. That declaration had satisfied him at the time, nor did he mean to impeach its credibility, but as doubts and scruples had nevertheless

been still entertained without doors, he wished them to be effectually silenced, and that the question might be set at rest for ever.

Fox, perhaps predictably, was absent from the House on this occasion, so it was left to Grey and to a host of other Whigs to vindicate Fox, damn Mrs Fitzherbert and once more defend the Prince's long-tarnished reputation. There was no division on the amendment, but there was a furious debate, during which the Royal Marriage Act was read, and several allusions were made to Mrs Fitzherbert.

For the Prince, however, all this came too late; for by the time the Commons passed the Regency Bill on 12 February the King was very much better. The distressing symptoms which had so alarmed the country were no longer so apparent, and even the most sceptical Whig physicians were forced to accept that he was far on the road to recovery. Consequently on 19 February, when the Bill came before the Lords, the Lord Chancellor made a speech in which he stated that in view of the King's returning health, it would be 'indecent' to take the matter any further. Few people found it in their hearts to forgive the Prince for his behaviour during his father's illness, and it was clear that he was more hated than ever.

Disappointed in her hopes, Mrs Fitzherbert resigned herself to the continuation of her position as the Prince's unofficial wife, but with the additional burden that she was now actively disliked by the Government. The caricaturist James Gillray caught the national mood when he depicted her as the chief mourner in a funeral procession for 'Miss Regency', and it was mischievously hinted elsewhere that she did not care for the Prince at all, but had fallen madly in love with Sheridan. The Prince assuaged his grief by riotous living, drowning his sorrows with the disreputable Sir John and Lady Lade, and perpetrating sometimes gross practical jokes with the outrageous Barrymore family and the exquisitely accoutred Colonel George Hanger. Sir John, a former admirer of Mrs Robinson and an outstanding whip, fostered his liking for expensive phaetons and encouraged his long-standing interest in racing.

'Few were the happy hours' that Mrs Fitzherbert could number at this period, wrote the diarist Thomas Raikes. The Prince was

> young and impetuous and boisterous in his character, and very much addicted to the pleasures of the table . . . often when she heard the Prince and his drunken companions on the staircase, she would seek a refuge from their presence even under the sofa, when the Prince, finding the drawing room deserted, would draw his sword in joke, and searching about the room would at last draw forth the trembling victim from her place of concealment.

Naturally, their relationship suffered. Mrs Fitzherbert was often depressed; the Prince seemed aloof and uncaring. She had financial problems too. And, inevitably, there were arguments. As early as June 1791 the poet Edward Jerningham, a particular friend of the Prince, noted that the 'Tittle Tattle of the town' was the separation of the Prince and Mrs Fitzherbert; while the Duke of Gloucester gave it as his opinion to Lady Harcourt, that there was 'not much love between them'; that the Prince had his 'amusements' elsewhere; that he had 'much consideration' for Mrs Fitzherbert, but she was sometimes 'jealous and discontented'.

Some of these 'amusements' were provided by the singer Anna Maria Crouch. The Prince gave her a bond and money amounting to £12,000, and bought off her husband; and for a while he was clearly enchanted. Yet, despite these enticements, for some reason he only made love to her once, after which she returned to a former lover. However, that was not the end of the affair, for her 'profusion reducing her to want', she later determined to blackmail him. The Prince became alarmed and at last he sent Captain Payne to her with three bags each containing a thousand guineas, in the hope that he could buy her silence. Payne, however, decided that in view of her poverty she would probably be satisfied with a smaller sum, so he left two of the bags in his coach and handed her just one of them as all the relief the Prince was then able to offer. Unable to resist the 'fascinating contents', Mrs Crouch immediately accepted the bag and the affair was satisfactorily concluded.

On that occasion, Mrs Fitzherbert forgave the Prince. But then he fell for the handsome Lady Jersey and she was given no such opportunity.

During the summer of 1794, having arranged to meet the Prince for dinner at his brother the Duke of Clarence's house near Hampton Court, Mrs Fitzherbert received a note from the Prince briefly informing her that, though it was all 'exceptionally inconvenient', one of his sisters had asked him to go to Windsor. There was nothing unusual about this message, and she thought nothing more about it until later that day Payne brought her a further letter from the Prince, stating that he would never enter her house again.

Mrs Fitzherbert immediately recognized the influence of Lady Jersey. She felt devastated and betrayed and, when she next met the Prince, a few weeks later, she flew into an ungovernable temper. Having listened to her tirade, the Prince professed to be more 'hurt' than words could express. 'I really think myself too ill used,' he wrote to Captain Payne. 'God knows what I have done to merit it.'

With Payne, he discussed how best to manage their separation. He quickly settled on Mrs Fitzherbert an annuity of £3,000 and wrote her a painfully composed letter. He confessed to Payne:

> To tell you what it has cost me to write it, and to rip up every and the most distressing feelings of my heart and which have so long lodg'd there is impossible to express. God bless you my friend; which ever way this unpleasant affair now ends I have nothing to reproach myself with. I owe nothing to her family, whatever was due, was due to herself, but in either case this letter is a final answer.

For her part, Mrs Fitzherbert determined to avoid the Prince, and at the first opportunity she put her house up for sale and left London for Margate.

Lady Jersey

If Mrs Fitzherbert was the most moral of the Prince's mistresses, then Lady Jersey was certainly one of his most dissipated. She laughed, gossiped, danced and intrigued her way through life, devoting herself unashamedly to the pursuit of pleasure. She was an accomplished musician, she loved amateur theatricals, wit, poetry, politics, talent in all its forms and almost everything which either was or was likely to become the fashion. She was sarcastic and intelligent, a valetudinarian, yet ambitious and an excellent practitioner of the always cruel and sometimes dangerous art of malice.

Lady Bessborough, who often met her in society, once remarked that she always needed a rival to torment, and certainly Lady Jersey thrived on conflict. Her aristocratic hauteur saw her through most situations, and she was a master of repartee. Even her friends were not safe from her wit: the Countess of Mount Edgecumbe was a 'sea Cowcumber' and 'Do you know that Ly Melbourne has been mad?' she once wrote to the Duchess of Devonshire.

> She is quite well again now, the other day she found
> herself ill and was going up to her maid when she met
> her on the stairs and talk'd very wildly. She carry'd her
> into her room, and it was half an hour before she came
> to her senses. They call'd it an indigestion.

Though in her early forties, a doting mother of seven daughters and two sons, and a grandmother to boot, Lady Jersey had by no means lost her charms, and not even her enemies could deny that she was still an extremely beautiful woman. Tall, thin, elegant, dark-haired and often outrageously coiffured, she simply oozed sex appeal and self-confidence. Sir Nathaniel Wraxall, a considerable connoisseur of female beauty, once spoke of her 'irrestible seduction and fascination', while Robert Huish, a later biographer of the Prince, described her as 'the type of the serpent – beautiful, bright, and glossy in its exterior – in its interior, poisonous and pestiferous'. For many years, she had been closely involved with the fifth Earl of Carlisle, wit, politician, sometime playwright, poet and pamphleteer, and a man who later had the misfortune to offend his kinsman Lord Byron; another of her lovers, the diplomat William Augustus Fawkener, was said to be the father of one of her daughters.

Her relations with her husband, the fourth Earl, were cordial yet distant. He shared her taste for amateur theatricals, she mocked his lack of a sense of humour, though there was no doubting his looks, urbanity or the exquisitely polished appearance which had led the bluestocking Mrs Montagu to refer to him as the 'Prince of Maccaronies'. Following a career as an MP, he had held a number of appointments at court, including Master of the Buckhounds and Captain of the Gentlemen Pensioners.

The Prince had known Lady Jersey since the 1770s* and, later, finding her much like Mrs Armistead, had even taken a 'great fancy' to her. Yet, during 1782 when he first approached her, he was unambiguously balked. 'If he is in love with me I cannot help it,' she remarked. 'It is impossible for anyone to give another less encouragement than I have.' By 1794, however, she had had enough of the Earl of Carlisle and, bringing her considerable charms into play, she determined to make a conquest of the Prince.

Sensing that her best line of attack on the Prince was to

---

* During the spring of 1796 the Prince described Lady Jersey as one of his 'oldest acquaintances' (George, Prince of Wales, *Correspondence*, III, 169).

undermine Mrs Fitzherbert, she represented her as self-seeking and duplicitous. She blamed her Catholicism for his unpopularity, and stated that in any case the marriage of 1785 was invalid. Without Mrs Fitzherbert he would be free to marry a Protestant princess, and secure a considerable addition to his income. With considerable artifice, she suggested as a suitable bride the Prince's unattractive cousin, Princess Caroline of Brunswick, correctly surmising that such a woman would not threaten her own position at court.

Lady Jersey's words were music to the Prince's ears, matching, as they did, his own intentions. Perhaps after all he was still only a bachelor; and though he was not able to shed entirely his affection for Mrs Fitzherbert, by Lady Jersey he was infatuated.

Consequently, during August 1794, the Prince had a meeting with his father, who was then holidaying at Weymouth. He told the King that he had now 'broken off all connection' with Mrs Fitzherbert and was desirous of 'entering into a more creditable line of life by marrying' his twenty-four-year-old cousin, Princess Caroline of Brunswick.

The Prince's choice pleased the King, and on 24 August he sent to the Prime Minister William Pitt a brief account of the meeting: 'Undoubtedly she is the person who naturally must be most agreeable to me,' he wrote. 'I expressed my approbation of the idea, provided his plan was to lead a life that would make him appear respectable, and consequently render the Princess happy.'

The woman chosen by Lady Jersey to be the Prince's bride was, in every sense, monumentally unsuitable. She was not dull, but eccentric, stubborn, thoughtless, full of energy, impulsive, careless, wilful and unencumbered by conventional notions of decorum. On one occasion when she was told she couldn't go to a ball, she whipped herself up into a frenzy and convinced her startled mother that she was about to give birth. She liked sex too, and there was more than one rumour of a lover; while one diplomat spoke darkly of some 'stain' upon her character. 'They say that her passions are so strong', wrote the Queen, privately aghast at the possibility of having such a woman as a daughter-in-law, 'that the Duke himself [Caroline's father] said that she was not to be allowed even to go from one room to another without her Governess, and that when she dances, this Lady is obliged to follow her for the whole of the dance to prevent her from making an exhibition of herself by making indecent conversations.'

However, the Prince, who quite possibly didn't know of these rumours, liked the idea of marriage to his rumbustious cousin. It would, after all, be only a marriage of convenience, putting no other obligation upon him than that he should produce an heir and that he should be civil to her.

At Brunswick, Lord Malmesbury (the former Sir James Harris) settled the details of the proposed match, while Lady Jersey consolidated her position by distancing the Prince from those of his circle who remained loyal to Mrs Fitzherbert. Two of the first to go were his old friends Lord Hugh and Lady Horatia or 'Racey' Seymour. Lord Hugh, who had since served as the Prince's First Groom of the Bedchamber was made a Lord of the Bedchamber, a higher position than the one he had formerly occupied but incompatable with the position he really wanted, a seat on the Board of Admiralty. The news of the appointment provoked an outcry from his Hertford relatives, and even a flurry of letters from the Marquis, his brother:

> I appeal to your candor and to the personal knowledge which you have of his feelings, whether an arrangement made for him in his absence [he was then at sea] and without his knowledge, even though it raised him in an official light, would not appear to him (as it has done to the world at large) a departure from that favor on your part which it has been his ambition both to possess and deserve.

To which the Prince replied with admirable nonchalance that it was too late, as Lord Hugh had already been superseded. Lord Hugh for his part hated Lady Jersey; writing to Captain Payne, he remarked that the Prince was 'so thoroughly' under Lady Jersey's influence, that there was every chance she would 'compleat his ruin. I understand that she is working hard to separate you from him'. 'Is he really anxious to turn me out of his family,' he asked Payne in a later letter, or is it 'only the object of that bitch under whose influence he is at present to remove from him those that the world has approv'd of being about him?' Meanwhile, the Prince advanced Lord Jersey to the position of Master of the Horse.

Lady Jersey engineered her own appointment to one of the Princess's three Ladies of the Bedchamber, alongside the Countesses of Carnarvon and Cholmondeley, a key position which would give her unparalleled opportunities to torment her rival. She also named the Princess's Bedchamber Women, making sure to include her intimate friends Mrs Pelham and the wife of another of the Prince's Grooms of the Bedchamber, Mrs Hervey Aston.

She was quite shameless about this, and naturally rumours of her machinations arrived at Brunswick. In particular, one anonymous letter, perhaps the work of 'some disappointed milliner or angry maid-servant', arrived addressed to Caroline's mother, the Duchess. Its writer attacked the Prince and portrayed Lady Jersey as the 'worst and most dangerous of profligate women', whose intention was to lead Caroline into an 'affair of gallantry', for which purpose she would be willing to find her a lover.

Though evidently designed to shock Caroline, the letter did not even move her, so Malmesbury decided to see if he could frighten her. He told her that not only would Lady Jersey be 'more cautious than to risk such an audacious measure', but that it was '*death* to presume to approach a Princess of Wales, and no man would be daring enough to think of it'. Caroline then asked him whether he was 'in earnest'; to which he replied that English law was such 'that anybody who presumed to *love* her was guilty of *high treason*, and punished with *death*, if she was weak enough to listen to him; so also would *she*'. This, he noted with satisfaction, 'startled her'.

As the Princess, accompanied by Malmesbury and a small retinue, made her way across a war-torn Europe, Lady Jersey plagued the Prince with questions about protocol and how she and the other ladies should receive Caroline. She wanted to know exactly what they were to wear, and then what precautions would be taken should the yachts in which she and the other ladies were to travel out from Sheerness to meet the Princess fall in with a French squadron. Caroline, she noticed, was travelling in a fifty-gun warship; would not a warship be safer? The delays occasioned by her continual questions enraged even the Prince: 'I cannot express to you', he wrote to the Queen during January, 'the vexation I feel at all the contradictions and plagues that have successively follow'd each other since first the business came upon the tapis'. Had his wishes been followed, he declared, the Princess would have been in London 'at latest... six *weeks ago*'. In the event bad weather kept the ladies in port, and after further delays, at last Caroline arrived at Greenwich on 5 April 1795.

Lady Jersey was not there to receive her. After having made Caroline wait an hour, she did everything possible to make her first day on English soil as unpleasant as possible. First she complained that the Princess's dress was wrong, though Mrs Harcourt, who had travelled with Captain Payne from Sheerness, 'had taken great pains about it'. Lady Jersey preferred a white satin dress which, though more elegant than the Princess's muslin gown, obviously didn't suit her fuller figure. Then she said that the Princess's already rubescent cheeks were in need of rouge to give them colour. As Lord Malmesbury looked on, Lady Jersey insisted that if she travelled with her back to the horses in the Princess's coach on their journey to London, she would likely feel sick; could she not in spite of every precedent sit next to Caroline? This was too much for Malmesbury, who brusquely remarked that if Lady Jersey was unable to sit opposite the Princess, then she should not have accepted the appointment of Lady of the Bedchamber in the first place.

The Prince was even more unwelcoming. He met his future

Lady Jersey   83

bride at St James's Palace, where took place a scene of striking
awfulness. Caroline, introduced by Malmesbury, knelt to the
Prince and he greeted her politely enough, but then instead
of engaging her in small talk he withdrew to a corner of the
room and, motioning Lord Malmesbury over, remarked, 'Harris,
I am not well; pray get me a glass of brandy.' 'Sir, had you not
better have a glass of water?' asked Malmesbury, to which the
Prince responded with a curt, 'No!' and stalked off to see his
mother. If it had been an act of calculated rudeness it could
not have been more offensive. Caroline, naturally puzzled by
the Prince's behaviour, asked Malmesbury if he was always so
odd, at the same time observing with characteristic lack of tact
that he was 'very fat' and 'nothing like as handsome as his
portrait'. Malmesbury offered the rather lame excuse that the
Prince was naturally a 'good deal affected and flurried' from
his sense of the occasion, but 'she certainly would find him
different at dinner'.

Unfortunately she did not. Lady Jersey had prepared him
with an account of the Princess's conversation on their way
from Greenwich to London, during which she had foolishly
boasted of an earlier lover; the Prince sat down, 'evidently disgusted'. He listened, horrified, as his future wife rattled on,
praising Mrs Fitzherbert, 'affecting raillery and wit', and even
'throwing out coarse vulgar hints about Lady [Jersey], who was
present, and though mute, *le diable n'en perdait rien*'.

The wedding took place three days later on 8 April in a
stiflingly hot Chapel Royal at about seven o'clock in the evening.
Most of the royal family were there, and it was packed with
courtiers, some of whom were horrified that the Prince was
actually going to go through with the marriage. Lady Jersey
arrived in good time, and taking her position in sight of the
Prince, she kept her eyes on him, willing her support throughout
the service. The Prince arrived drunk, having filled himself
with brandy, though even this was not enough to fortify him
entirely, and some of those who looked on noticed he seemed
agitated and nervous. At least twice, seeming about to faint,
he was saved by the Duke of Bedford. Only Caroline seemed

unaffected by the mounting tension in the building, appearing even cheerful and collected.

As the ceremony proceeded the Prince became increasingly alarmed, and at one point there was an audible 'tush' when, suddenly, he got up from his bended knees, and looked imploringly at Lady Jersey.

Many people's thoughts were obviously with Mrs Fitzherbert, however, and when the Archbishop of Canterbury, Dr John Moore, asked the congregation if anyone knew of any 'lawful impediment' to the marriage, he put down his Bible and 'looked earnestly' first at the King, then at the Prince, who burst into tears in the painful silence. The Archbishop twice repeated the passage enjoining the husband to live in 'nuptial fidelity' with his wife for the rest of his life.

At the reception which followed the Prince sobered up slightly, though as night came on, he started to drink heavily again at the thought of what awaited him. Caroline, on the other hand, remained calm and even philosophical. 'Judge', she later remarked, 'what it was to have a drunken husband on one's wedding day, and who passed the greater part of his bridal night under the grate, where I left him.' Yet, the Prince did at last brace his nerves and, emerging from the grate, he consummated the marriage in the morning.

After spending a few days at Windsor, the couple went to Kempshot near Basingstoke for their honeymoon, where they stayed in a house which was a favourite of the Prince and Lady Jersey. Taking advantage of her position of Lady of the Bedchamber, Lady Jersey accompanied them. The other guests were 'blackguard companions' of the Prince, men who were 'constantly drunk and filthy, sleeping and snoring in boots on the sofas'. Here too, Lady Jersey took every opportunity to humiliate Caroline, tormenting her so successfully that at one point Caroline, in a fit of frustration, actually swiped up a pipe from a neighbour at dinner and blew smoke at both the Prince and her rival.

Naturally many people resented Lady Jersey's behaviour, particularly when it was accompanied by reports that on their return to Carlton House, the Prince had 'shut' Caroline up, and was only allowing her to see those people of whom he approved. On 13 May, one commentator, Lady Palmerston, wrote to her husband that she quite lamented 'our poor captive Princess', adding that she was unable to 'comprehend the motive which induces Lady Jersey to behave so injudiciously ill and what advantage she can derive by making the Prince behave not only like a fool but as a complete brute'.

> I thought Lady Jersey was as cunning as a serpent, though not quite as harmless as a dove, and that she would have done everything to conciliate not to disgust the wife and the world. Her worst enemy cannot wish her to pursue a line of conduct so destructive to the stability of her empire. She must feel like her cousin Robespierre* (for I am sure they are related) and that ere long she may not be murdered but she will be driven from society. How silly not to be content with cajoling and dressing Lord Carlisle. She might have gone out to the end of their days in a quiet respectable attachment.

Caroline, under the circumstances, coped as best she could, seeking solace where it was offered and sending desperate, sometimes pitiful letters to friends in Germany. 'I do not know how I shall be able to bear the hours of loneliness only I trust in the Almighty. The Queen seldom visits me, and my sisters-in-law show me the same sympathy. . . . The Countess is still here. I hate her and I know she feels the same towards me. My husband is wholly given up to her and so you can easily guess the rest. . . . I am so afraid of what is coming.'

Not for the first time, it was rumoured that one reason for the Prince's cruelty to Caroline was that he was jealous of her popularity, for from the first she had the happy knack of pleasing the 'gaping multitude'. This talent was remarked upon by Mrs Thrale, who noted during the summer that the 'Town' does

* The French revolutionary leader; overthrown by the Convention and guillotined on 28 July 1794.

nothing but rave about the Prince of Wales and Lady
Jersey and how she ridicules the Princess, and how Mrs
Pelham sets her Baby to hoot the Princess, and to take
her off, and I don't know what – Our honest King and his
honest Populace join to support the Foreign suffering
Wife, but there are those who abet the Countess and her
Royal Paramour – many say the Queen encourages Lady
Jersey. – What Times! What Wonders! What horrors!

Such was Lady Jersey's unpopularity that she was unable to
travel in the streets without being 'hissed and insulted'; *no Lady
Jersey'* was scrawled on walls in and around London. It was noticed
that the Prince had bought her a house. 'What a pitiful fellow
Lord J[ersey] must be,' observed Mrs Scott in a letter to her
sister Mrs Montagu. 'I hope his H – – – ss leaves his slippers at
her Chamber Door on proper occasions.'

The Prince was shocked to learn that, due to what he described as the '*infamous deceit of Pitt*', he would not after all
become financially solvent, even though the only reason why
he had entered into marriage with Caroline was for money.
Pitt proposed increasing his income by £65,000 to £138,000
per annum, adding £25,000 for finishing Carlton House and
£27,000 to cover the cost of the wedding. The Commons, however, were outraged when it was revealed that since 1787 the
Prince had accrued debts of £630,000. Consequently, Pitt's
proposals were badly received, and only when he suggested
deducting the enormous sum of £65,000 in addition to the
£13,000 which he had already suggested deducting on an annual basis from the Prince's income, did the Commons pass
the measure. On this occasion even the Prince's old friends
amongst the Whigs had been lukewarm. Fox supported the
more extravagant of Pitt's proposals, but suggested that the
Prince's debts would best be paid by the immediate sale of the
Duchy of Cornwall, a proposal which the King described as
'insidious and democratical'. Others sat on their hands, and
Charles Grey was widely applauded when he suggested limit-
ing any increase to £40,000.

The result was that the Prince was placed, in Sir Gilbert Elliot's words, in a 'worse situation than before he applied for relief, with the addition of having been made the butt of the whole ill humour of both Houses during a period of five years'. Voicing a common sentiment he went on to say,

> It is unfortunate both for him and for the cause of Royalty that he did not possess strength and resource of mind sufficient to decide for himself, to live respectably on twenty or thirty thousand a year, and apply the whole residue to a regular discharge of his debt without suffering the subject to be discussed in Parliament.

Furious that his wishes had been so flagrantly thwarted, the Prince once more shut up Carlton House and set about the dismal task of dismissing his servants, none of whom were spared except Generals Hulse and Lake, the Earls of Jersey and Cholmondeley and Caroline's four Ladies of the Bedchamber, including of course Lady Jersey. 'I have ordered letters of dismission to be written to [the staff]', he wrote to the Queen on 3 July, 'till I am enabled to resume the appearance due to my birth, and which I am deprived of.' He begged his mother to let it be widely known that she approved of his plan, 'as there is nothing that will afix so deadly a blow to all the attacks that are aimed in every shape and from every quarter at me, as the knowledge of what my conduct is, and that it meets with your approbation.' Then, leaving London behind him, he took his hated wife and Lady Jersey to Brighton.

In the meantime Caroline, by an extreme stroke of good luck, had fallen pregnant, and on 7 January 1796 she provided the Prince with an heir in the shape of an 'immense' girl, much to the delight of the King and Queen, after whom she was named, and most of their subjects. The *Morning Chronicle* salaciously noted that she arrived 'exactly nine calendar months wanting one day' after the wedding. The Prince, though extremely fatigued by the event, having stayed up for two nights, even allowed himself to feel slightly pleased with himself, going so far as to pen the following joke to his mother: 'The little girl is as well as possible and would if she could speak send her humble duty with her *papa's*'. However, it seemed he was more interested in the child born to Lady Jersey, who, coincidently, had also been pregnant, giving birth to a 'very fine little boy' during the previous October.

Now that the Prince had in a sense done his duty to the country, he considered his relations with his wife to be in large part at an end. He ignored Caroline as far as possible, ate at his friends' houses, and contrived never to be alone with her. When in London, he spent as much time as he could with Lady Jersey, whose presence was often noted at the Queen's card parties: 'The Prince of Wales in the course of the evening repeatedly came up to her table, and publicly squeezed her hand', wrote Charles Abbot of one occasion. Then, by way of diversion, he gave up Kempshot Park and took Northington Grange, a 'convenient and elegant' mansion situated close to the Portsmouth Road near Alresford.

During March the Prince's attitude to Caroline was so cold and dismissive that Malmesbury, following one interview, took away the clear and frightening impression that the Prince was set on an immediate separation. He reminded him that in his 'exalted situation' it was not his 'private feelings alone, whatever they may be' that the Prince had to consult upon such a measure, but the public, too, would 'claim a right to form a judgement and expect that a very considerable degree of deference should be paid to it'. A separation, he warned, 'could not at any time fail to excite a very strong sensation throughout the country', and he asked the Prince to ponder what might be the likely effect on his reputation.

Fortunately, the Prince was able to disabuse him; while the Princess 'continued quiet' and she did not 'attempt to give false impressions' of him to the public and to 'raise herself' at his 'expense', he would not 'expose her to the world', nor would he subject himself to those 'discussions which any other man, under similar circumstances' to himself in 'private life, would be certain of making'.

However, things did not continue quiet. Furious with Lady Jersey, tired of her company and frustrated at the lack of a private moment with her husband, Caroline sent the Prince a most disagreeable letter. She wanted to be excused from dining alone with 'Lady Jerser', a woman she could 'neither like nor respect, and who in her eccentric French she described as the Prince's 'mistress. . . . Forgive me, dear Prince if I express myself too strongly, consider that it is a heart pierced by the sharpest pain and the most mortal sorrow that begs your assistance; consider that it is the mother of your child that implores you thus the child that you love so greatly'.

Her letter drew from the Prince a long, carefully constructed response, angrily rebutting what he called the 'unwise, groundless and most injurious' imputations, which Caroline had cast upon him.

He begged Caroline to recollect that he had already described to her the 'peculiar circumstances' that forced him to dine 'abroad' so that she would not misinterpret his absence as deliberate neglect; and he confessed himself to be bewildered at the charge that he forced her to dine alone with Lady Jersey. He warned Caroline not to take at face value the many calumnies that had been circulated against Lady Jersey, as they were 'propagated' by persons 'no less seriously' Caroline's enemies than his own. 'They hope to further their private malignant views by fomenting discord between you and me, at the expense of *us both*', he wrote, and he would feel nothing but self-disgust if her objections to Lady Jersey forced him to 'meanly and dishonourably sacrifice in the eyes of the publick' a woman who, he had declared to her upon her arrival, was not his '*mistress*', as she had so 'indecorously' termed her, but a 'friend' to whom he was 'attached by the strong ties of habitude, esteem and respect'. In any case, he went on, were his relationship with Lady Jersey of a 'different nature', it was singular that she should express any 'repugnance'. Had she not, he reminded her, once launched out in praise of Mrs Fitzherbert, a woman 'whose character could never have been known' to her, but 'through the interested or vindictive suggestions of designing individuals'?

He continued:

You will recollect, Madam, that you have seven Ladies
in your family besides Lady Jersey, any, or everyone, of
whom it is in your power to summon either for dinner
or company at any hour of the day. Lady Willoughby, as
sister to Lady Cholmondeley, you know to be likewise
admitted to obey your invitation.

It was not his fault that the choice was not 'more extensive',
he wrote, but simply the consequence of long-standing etiquette.

But perhaps, the 'insinuation' that he forced her to dine
alone with Lady Jersey was not meant for him, but for the
public to whom she might hereafter appeal, citing her letter
in order to 'prove to others not so well inform'd' as himself
the grounds for her dissatisfaction. This he the more suspected
from the 'forc'd and insidious' compliment she had paid in
her letter to the nation at large, urging him to be as 'generous' and as truthful as his countrymen. 'If, Madam, such a
purpose has been indistinctly floating in your mind, I recom-
mend to you to ascertain to yourself exactly what result you
expect from it. What improvement does your situation admit
which does not depend wholly on the prudence and propriety
of your own private conduct?'

They had 'unfortunately' been 'oblig'd to acknowledge' to
each other that they could not find 'happiness' in their marriage; it now remained for them to make their 'situation as
little uncomfortable to each other' as possible.

Unfortunately, Caroline was not satisfied with the Prince's
response. She felt that her letter had been deliberately mis-
construed, and it goaded her into making further attacks on
Lady Jersey. Perhaps, she accepted, it had been thoughtless of
her to describe Lady Jersey as the Prince's mistress, but then
again, had he not told her at 'Breyton' when introducing the
subject that she should be happy to see him attached to an
'attraction of ancient date rather than to a young and beautiful woman'?

This latter charge the Prince denied; she had, he wrote, 'completely misapprehended' the meaning of the words which he had used to her at Brighton; it was 'impossible' that he could have begun the conversation; and to 'prove' to her that she had deceived herself, he then mentioned the only three occasions he could recollect during which words on the subject of Lady Jersey had passed between them: the first, when shortly after her arrival in the country she had mentioned the anonymous letters her mother had received at Brunswick; next, in the garden at Carlton House when she had mysteriously mentioned a 'circumstance respecting' Captain Payne which 'nobody' could have known but herself; and finally during a conversation he had had with her 'but a few weeks since'.

He insisted that he had never 'intimated the most distant desire' for her to show any special regard for Lady Jersey; but, on the contrary, his wish had always been 'that there would not be any distinction' in her behaviour to any of her ladies 'unless any of them should fail in respect or personal attention' to her, of which he could not but assure himself they were all 'equally incapable'. 'Without such a reason', he went on, 'you ought to feel that it must be at least a striking incivility to me to shew a wanton distaste towards any of your ladies', all of whom with 'solicitous attention' to her 'dignity' had been chosen to form her household. 'And if this spleen were exercised against one whom I had mentioned to you in terms of that particular esteem and friendship which long acquaintance had established, would it not be towards me the most offensive and revolting conduct that could be adopted?' He concluded:

Let me hope that this painful contest will now be closed. If you wish for more of my company it must strike you that the natural mode of obtaining it is to make my own house not obnoxious to me, and you will judge whether a captious tone towards me, or indirect managements against my tranquillity, are well calculated to make me feel at ease in your society.

But Caroline sent the Prince another letter, causing him to complain to his Chamberlain, the Earl of Cholmondeley, that he was 'tired to death of this silly altercation'. He also wrote to the Earl's wife, one of Caroline's Ladies of the Bedchamber, imploring her as a matter of some urgency to speak to the Princess about her personal cleanliness, a subject which so far he had only been able to allude to 'obscurely'.

As she presses me upon the subject in so strange a way I must conjure you to be perfectly explicit with her. Explain to her the indelicacy of bringing to anything like a public discussion circumstances which can with decorum hardly be mention'd between man and woman. If she shall still persist in this infatuation and will not open her eyes, make her understand that the indelicacy of the discussion and the consequences of it must be chargeable to herself and not to me, for I must meet it if such be her deter-mination. What must the King feel if he shall find me forc'd, and by the Princess too, to impart circumstances of so indelicate a nature to him?

In response to a message from Caroline, the Prince sent her a brief note defining the precise terms upon which they would in future live. In particular, he wanted to reassure her that should their daughter die, he would not propose a 'connec-tion' of a 'particular nature. . . . Our inclinations are not in our power,' he wrote. 'Tranquil and comfortable society is . . . let our intercourse therefore be restricted to that, and I will distinctly subscribe to [your] condition'. He hoped that that would be the end of the matter, yet a week later Caroline returned to the subject by sending him another one of her oddly worded letters. This time, she not only wanted him to make it clear that the idea of a separation originated with him, but she told him that she had also decided to send copies of their correspondence to the King.

This really was too much for the Prince. It was more than 'human nature' could bear, he told his mother; Caroline's

behaviour was 'so excessively wicked'. He could see 'no drift
in it, unless to try to create and make general mischief and
noise', which he would 'endeavour to prevent' by, if necessary,
exposing her. He was both 'shock'd and hurt to death that
the King should be plagued' with his and Caroline's letters.

There were more letters. Caroline wrote to the Prince again
a month later on 26 and 30 May, once more returning to the
old subject of Lady Jersey. Finally the Prince's patience snapped,
and on 31 May he wrote the King a long exculpatory letter,
formally supplicating a public and irrevocable separation. Hitherto, he wrote, 'motives of publick policy' had 'recommended
a suppression' of his private feelings; therefore, he had formerly 'aim'd at such an arrangement as might enable' him to
pass his life with the Princess 'upon such terms of civility as
might satisfy all outward appearances'. However, her 'insidious practices' had now 'totally frustrated this hope', as the
purpose of her last letters was obviously to avoid an 'accommodation'.

The King, unfortunately, was not as sanguine as the Prince.
He thought the Prince's letter was written more in 'warmth'
than in a 'cool state of mind'; and that it would put his case
in the 'worst possible light' were it 'produced as the grounds
for a separation'. Echoing the same words that Lord Malmesbury
had used to the Prince during March, he pointed out that the
Prince appeared to believe that his marital affairs were only a
private matter, as if a separation could be granted 'by the mere
interference of relations'. Rather, the public would have to be
informed, and 'being already certainly not prejudiced' in his
favour, the 'auspices in the first outset would not be promising'. Parliament too must needs be consulted and as 'no criminal
accusation' could be brought against the Princess, it would
'certainly' feel itself obliged to secure for her a large part of
his income. He did not think that the Princess's behaviour
had been exactly blameless, but on the other hand, the Prince
should have taken more trouble to guide her. He counselled
his son not to persist 'in an idea that may lead to evils without
bounds', but to have such a command of himself that might,

'by keeping up appearances, by degrees render' his life with the Princess 'more respectable and at the same time less unpleasant'.

Following this letter, and an incident at the Opera House where the Princess was wildly applauded, the Prince whipped himself up into a terrible state of frenzy, writing a barely rational letter to his 'dearest, dearest, dearest mother':

> If the King does not now manage to throw some stigma, and one very strong mark of disapprobation upon the Princess, this worthless wretch will prove the ruin of him, of you, of me, of every one of us. The King must be resolute and firm, or everything is at an end. Let him recall to his mind the want of firmness of Louis 16. This is the only opportunity for him to stemm the torrent.

The Princess, he wrote, was the 'vilest wretch' the world 'was ever curs'd with', for whom he could not 'feel more disgust ... from her personal nastiness' than he did 'from her entire want of all principle'. She was a 'very monster of iniquity'. 'God bless you, ever dearest Mother', he concluded. He was 'so overpower'd with unhappiness' that he felt 'quite light headed'. He knew not where else to turn 'for a friend', but to his mother.

The incident at the Opera House had occurred on 28 May, when, following Caroline's arrival, almost the entire audience spontaneously rose to their feet 'as if electrified by her presence'. Some men in the pit then 'jumped on the benches and waved their hats, crying out *Huzza!*' as *God Save the King* was called for. Clearly agitated, Caroline then repeatedly curtsied to the audience, remarking to the Duke of Leeds, who hurried to her box, that she supposed after such a performance she 'should be guillotined'. Had the Prince, Lady Jersey or indeed the Queen been there, according to Horace Walpole, they would have been publicly insulted.*

* The Queen always denied that there was any particular collusion between herself and Lady Jersey; rather, that she was the innocent victim of newspaper allegations. She had, she told the King on 22 January 1797, been so

A few days later, *The Times* commented loftily:

> When high personages, placed in the most exalted ranks
> of society, discard all the respect they owe to themselves;
> when they stoop to the most disgraceful connexions, and
> above all when their vices, disorders and impudence raise
> just apprehensions for the welfare of the State, if through
> some unfortunate event they should be placed on the
> highest point of the political and social State, it is then
> that the liberty of the Press ought to resume its dignity
> and denounce and point out to the public opinion him
> whom public justice cannot attaint.

The Prince was 'incorrigible', according to the *True Briton*. 'We
have long looked upon his conduct as favouring the cause of
Jacobinism and democracy in this country more than all the
speeches of HORNE TOOKE, or all the labours of the *Corresponding
Society*.'

As Caroline's character hourly rose in the public's estima-
tion, Lady Jersey became a hunted woman, and, having attempted but failed to brave the storm, she left her house in
Pall Mall and took temporary refuge in Berkeley Square, at
the London home of one of her daughters, Lady Anne Lambton.
When not in actual danger from the mob, she was snubbed by
society and, earlier, when she had appeared in public at an
assembly at the Duchess of Gordon's, not one person would
talk to her.

Fox's friend James Hare wittily summed up her situation
when he remarked that her appearances were 'more to the
credit of her personal courage than to the delicacy of her
feelings'.

'thoroughly wounded' by the affair that 'nothing ever could' make it up to
her, and she had become misanthropical. Like the Prince, she was convinced that she was surrounded by 'spye's', who reported every word she
spoke to the newspapers (Aspinall, *The Later Correspondence of George III*, vol.
II, p 536).

Her remaining friends left her in droves; and even her old friend Lord Harcourt at last concluded that she was the 'vilest, most artful of Women'. She had, he said, deceived him 'by her Deceit and pretended Goodness' for 'many, many Months'; now he forbade his wife to see her.

Cruelly, her ostracism coincided with the loss of her new-born son, whose death on 28 May initiated a brief period of mourning. She rented a house in Hammersmith where, daily visited by the Prince, she plotted, so it was said, an '*éclaircissement*' that would entirely alter the public's view of her.

On 4 June, from Northington Grange, the Prince sent an urgent, agitated note to the Earl of Moira, begging him to take Lady Jersey under his protection. 'I am sure she will be happy to see you', he wrote, as 'she stands in need of much consolation'. He had tried too, but often failed, to get the many inflammatory newspaper paragraphs about himself and Lady Jersey stopped, and he added to the bottom of the same note: 'For God's sake, press Erskine [his former Attorney General] respecting prosecutions.'

In the meantime, Lord Jersey did what he could to aid his wife, and though it went against his temperament, he even wrote a patently absurd letter to the King begging the monarch's 'most gracious condescension'. He was 'proud' to assert both his and his wife's 'honor'; they had been appointed to their posts by the Prince; and 'no invidious malice or the most designing artifices' would induce them to resign them. 'It would have been as abhorrent from all his just principles and feelings for his Royal Highness to offer the situations we hold', he wrote, 'except upon the strictest sentiments of honor, as, I trust, it is known to your Majesty to have been equally incompatible with our feelings to have accepted them.' It was therefore a 'duty' incumbent upon them to 'disappoint the wishes' of their 'secret enemies'. He requested a 'private audience'.

The King agreed to the meeting and heard Lord Jersey with 'great attention', till the Earl, warming to his subject, assured the King that Lady Jersey had always been 'a most faithful and virtuous wife'. Then, even the King's habitual reserve left him, and he broke out into a succession of 'whats', delivered in his odd staccato manner. The newspapers sneered: 'Lord JERSEY , wrote the *True Briton*, 'is said to have asked an audience of the KING, to assure HIS MAJESTY that Lady JERSEY was the most pure and virtuous woman living!!!'

Perhaps the most offensive of the paragraphs which the Prince objected to concerned an old accusation that during the summer of 1795, Lady Jersey had stolen, then handed to the Queen, some alarmingly candid letters from Caroline to her mother in Brunswick. It was said they contained some insulting references to the Queen and a description of Lady Jersey's character, no better than she merited. Caroline had first entrusted them to her English tutor, the Revd Dr Randolph, who was about to visit Germany; when his wife fell ill, he deferred his journey and sent the letters back to Caroline wrapped up in a parcel addressed to Lady Jersey at the Pavilion. According to Lady Jersey, the parcel never arrived, and though a thorough search was then made for the letters Caroline never received them.

'*To those whom it may concern*' thundered the *Sun*:

There are few crimes, which in the eye of morality, are more atrocious; few, which in the eye of the law, are more seriously deserving of punishment, than the CONCEALMENT AND OPENING OF PRIVATE LETTERS. If by chance, any letter so opened, should contain a single note, even for £5. the punishment annexed by law to the commission of such a crime, is nothing less than DEATH. In the eye of morality, the nature of its contents can neither aggravate nor diminish the crime, which is the violation of virtue, of decency, and of honour, so gross, so scandalous, so offensive, as to excite the most marked and general indignation, and to effect the exclusion of the culprit from all societies in which vice is detested and virtue cherished. ... If this hint be not taken, we shall discharge our duty; and speak more plainly.

And speak they did; as did satirist Isaac Cruikshank, who, having already depicted Lady Jersey as a predatory, snuff-taking hag, now featured her holding an open letter in 'Confidence Betrayed', one of a series of caricature 'Sketches from Nature!!! ... Lady [Jersey] is said to be one of the most adroit hands in England', remarked another paper – that is, 'at opening [someone else's] letter'.

She tried to defend herself, but it was far too late for words; so that when she wrote a coy letter to Dr Randolph in an attempt to exculpate herself from the substantive charge, there were many who thought that having already proved herself a thief, she was now about to show herself a liar. Adopting a tone of mock bemusement, she told Randolph that she could not 'in any way account' for the allegations in the newspapers, unless they referred to the loss of Caroline's letters. 'I think you will agree with me', she went on, 'that defending myself from the charge of opening a letter, is pretty much the same thing as if I was to prove that I had not picked a pocket'. She then threatened to show upon 'what grounds' so '*extraordinary* a calumny' was founded.

Unfortunately, Randolph was unable to shed much light; writing in response to another letter, this time from Lord Jersey, he stated that it was astonishing that he should after almost a year be asked to 'recur to dates, and state facts'; yet in view of the seriousness of the charges he agreed that he would lay an account of the business before Lady Jersey. He had a clear recollection of having left the parcel containing the letters for the Brighton Post Coach at the Golden Cross, Charing Cross, yet it was as much a mystery to him as it evidently was to Lady Jersey that it did not arrive safely in Brighton.

Subsequently, Lord Jersey put all the correspondence between himself, his wife and Dr Randolph together in pamphlet form, providing a very brief preface in which he asserted 'unequivocally, and without a possibility of contradiction', that every allegation was 'founded solely in malice and not in truth, and fabricated for the most wicked purposes'. No one was convinced. *The Times* commented acidly: 'We think her Ladyship has proved nothing by the correspondence'.

The Prince's mood lightened slightly when the Earl of Moira, who was acting as a kind of mediator, brought him a message from the Princess implying that she would at last accommodate herself to the Prince's wishes on the question of Lady Jersey. But this too foundered at first. The Prince conceded that in two to three months' time Lady Jersey would offer her resignation; now Caroline wanted an undertaking that she would not return to London during the interim. This was too much for the Prince, who stated in a letter to Moira that it was entirely contrary to the terms she had formerly agreed to. Her intention, he later added, was obviously to play 'foul' with them and, if they did not guard against it, would only lead to further 'mischief'. Yet in the face of mounting pressure – particularly from the King – for some sort of reconciliation, it was becoming increasingly clear that he and not the Princess was effectively beaten.

On 25 June Caroline wrote a short letter to the Prince confirming that their 'misunderstanding' was now at an end, and asking the Prince for his forgiveness. The Prince then sent her an even briefer reply. He thanked her for her letter; she would see him at Carlton House 'some time in the course of Monday'.

On 29 June, Lady Jersey wrote her resignation letter; in it, she informed the Princess that she had obtained the Prince's permission to resign 'into his hands' her position of Lady of the Bedchamber:

> The same duty and attachment which I shall ever be proud to profess for H.R.H. and which induced me to accept of that appointment, urged me to obey his commands in retaining it long after the infamous and unjustifiable paragraphs in the public papers rendered it impossible for a person of the rank and situation which I hold in this country (indeed for anyone possessing the honest pride and spirit of an Englishwoman) to submit to hold a situation which was to make her the object of deep and designing calumny.

The Prince had earnestly desired her not to resign as 'such a step would not only be regarded as a confirmation of every absurd and abominable falsehood that had been so industriously fabricated for the *present purpose*', and also used as a handle to attack the Royal Family itself, but the moment had at last arrived when she could 'with propriety' withdraw herself from 'such persecution and injustice'. She had at least the 'conscious satisfaction of *knowing*' that she had by her '*silence* and forebearance' given the 'strongest proofs' of her duty to the Royal Family, and of her 'attachment and gratitude' to the Prince, which could never end but with her life.

Already, on the previous day, Lady Jersey had been spotted '*modestly*' riding out of the gate of Carlton House, attended pointedly by a 'Servant in the Prince's livery'; on reading this letter, *The Times* was simply amazed at this further instance of her effrontery. No letter, it wrote, was more 'disrespectful. . . . Throughout the letter there is not one word of respect towards her Royal Highness'.

Beaten, but still partially unbowed, Lady Jersey stole out of London for Brighton where, having now abandoned her rooms with the Prince, she took a house next to the Duke of Marlborough's but still close to the Pavilion. The Prince arrived on 29 July, but she returned to Pall Mall very early on the following morning. For two days, a mob had carried through Brighton's streets a 'stuffed mawkin' with 'Lady J[ersey] written at full length upon it', and conscious of her unpopularity she was only too pleased to leave.

From Pall Mall she wrote an anguished letter to Edward Jerningham. Not only was her life 'more than insipid to describe' but it was also 'intolerable'. Her nights were 'sleepless and weary', she had lost her appetite, and every day was producing 'fresh proofs of treachery' from every quarter. Although the conduct of the Prince was 'perfect' and some people in Brighton had apologized to her, it seemed 'but in vain' and she concluded 'their recantation will deter others from running into the same error'. Not surprisingly, she felt trapped in London; the house in Pall Mall was 'accursed'.

The Prince joined her at Bognor Rocks on the south coast during early September where Lady Jersey, having taken a 'delightful' house, found a friend in Sir Richard Hotham, a 'clean old man, with white hair, white eyes, and white hands' who, desperate for the glister of royal patronage, was only too keen to offer her and her children his protection. She found the sea air 'delicious' and the countryside around Bognor 'beautiful. . . . The state of my poor mind requires dissipation and hurry,' she told Edward Jerningham; and she was never 'so well' as the day she left for Bognor from London. 'Pray write to me instantly,' she conjured him. Her house was too small to offer him a room, but she and the Prince 'would very much like to see' him.

When the Prince did arrive, she felt giddy with 'something which I suppose is joy', as she described it in one of a series of letters to Jerningham. The Prince was in 'great beauty, and spirits', and so 'delighted with the quiet life and with the place', that he did not appear to have the least 'desire to change it'. He was 'going to fly round Dorsetshire, make a nest' for her and her 'young ones' at Critchell House (an estate he had just rented near Wimborne), where she hoped to spend Christmas with him. She and her husband would then take possession of a new house in London, which the Prince had decided to provide for them in Warwick Street, adjoining Carlton House. 'The Dorsetshire part of my project you must keep to yourself;' she told Jerningham, 'but the house may be talk'd of.'

The house project shocked the public. Following Lady Jersey's resignation and her removal from Carlton House, many people were amazed that so soon afterward she should live in such a sensitive location. Not only was it against the public's wishes, but it was also a further slap in the face for Caroline. The Queen, when she heard about the proposed move, was amazed. Were it true, she wrote to her son, the possible consequences for him and Lady Jersey of such a 'public insult' made her 'shudder. . . . This is not cowardice, believe me, but your honor is at stake and indeed the honor of the whole family.' Unfortunately the Prince was unconvinced. 'As to the word, INSULT, my angelick mother,' he wrote, 'I think you know me too well not to know that I would not insult or ill treat anyone'; indeed, he was 'totally incapable' of it. 'However', he went on, 'it may very possibly be worked up into that, for I am well aware that the same pack of blood hounds, or hell hounds, which open'd upon me this last summer, is equal to the saying or doing anything that can hurt me.' Consequently, he stood firm, and when Lady Jersey took up residence, made sure that she was invited by the Queen to her drawing-room. This was not much relished by the Queen's other guests, however, who immediately turned their backs on her.

The Prince stood by Lady Jersey during 1797, but during the summer of 1798 observers began to notice a sea change in his sentiments. Perhaps tired of Lady Jersey now that she was more dependent on him, perhaps moved by the violent rekindling of his old affection for Mrs Fitzherbert, he abandoned Lady Jersey for a short series of affairs with other women. During August his friend Colonel McMahon struggled to suppress reports of the Prince and a mysterious Miss Fox, who sometimes went by the name of Crole and had been involved with Lord Egremont; her late father had once managed the theatre at Brighton. 'Some say she is youngish and pretty,' Lady Stafford told Lord Granville Leveson Gower, 'others that she is oldish, fat, and looks like a good House-Keeper.'

Now that he had secretly married Mrs Armistead, Fox, too, became alarmed at the possibility that the Prince might take advantage of his wife, and from Holkham in Norfolk he sent a pained letter to Mrs Armistead counselling her to be careful. Not that he was afraid of his 'Angel's doing anything wrong', but he had recollected from what Mrs Armistead had formerly told him that the Prince's 'way of persuading' her was to invent things about him; 'and though I should think Liz knows him too well to believe him, yet I have observed that the next time I have seen my Liz after the P[rince] has been with her she has had one of those *coldish* looks that make kins so *mis*.'.

For her part, Lady Jersey refused to take the Prince's hints, but cropped her hair within an inch of her head, and decided

that her best policy was to feign incomprehension, which embarrassed the Prince 'exceedingly'. She knew too much to be
brutally pushed to one side, so the Prince was forced to 'let
her down gently and to separate amicably'. He fell back on
his friends, and both Colonel Henry Norton Willis and Edward
Jerningham were sent to her to announce his determination.
However, both were repulsed, Willis with the significant words
that he had brought her a 'gilded dagger'.

Indeed, some sort of settlement was very much on the Prince's
mind, especially once he had contrived Lord and Lady Jersey's removal from Warwick Street to a house further afield in
Stratford Place, which had formerly belonged to Lord Talbot.
Probably, Lady Jersey was offered a bribe big enough for her
to go abroad, and for her husband to accept without too much
of a fuss the inevitable loss of his position. She never received
a pension, however, and during the winter of 1801–02 she was
so short of money that her husband was threatened with a
spell in debtors' prison.

Mrs Fitzherbert Again

In spite of the Prince's infatuation with Lady Jersey, he was never quite able to forget – even at the best of times – what he owed Mrs Fitzherbert. Not only had she made the huge sacrifice of going through a doubtful marriage ceremony with him, but she had also suffered the indignity of then seeing herself officially supplanted as his wife. He often worried himself with the thought that she might be unhappy and, on one occasion reflecting that he might actually predecease her, he sent Lord Loughborough to the King with the request that he would guarantee her annuity for the rest of her life. It was even later reported that her uncle Henry Errington had been sent to her days before the Prince's wedding to Caroline with the promise that the Prince would give up the match if she would come back to him – a request which, if in any way true, was certainly denied.

For her part, Mrs Fitzherbert was 'deeply distressed and depressed' when the Prince married Caroline, not least because she believed, incorrectly, that it might affect her reputation. Yet she in no way interfered in the affair and, helped by an intimate friend, Lady Clermont, she struggled to rise above her feelings. She spent the day of the wedding not in London, but close to the Thames-side village of Twickenham, in Marble Hill Hall, a Palladian villa that had once belonged to George II's mistress, the Countess of Suffolk, and which she rented from a Miss Hotham. Meanwhile, she gave her servants instructions to illuminate her town house in Pall Mall in celebration of the Prince's marriage.

On one occasion, the Prince, ill, hypochondriacal and clearly
overwrought after the birth of his daughter Charlotte, wrote a
long and oddly passionate will, leaving almost everything he
owned 'of every description, denomination and sort, personal
and other' to Mrs Fitzherbert, *'my wife, the wife of my heart and
soul,* and though by the laws of this country *she could not avail
herself publicly of that name, still such she is in the eyes of Heaven,
was, is, and ever will be such in mine',* for the truth of which
assertion he appealed to God. It was not her fault, he generously asserted, that they had separated. They had both, he said,
been *'calumniated'* by *'base, vile and scandalous wretches',* who
had represented him *'in lights and in a manner'* he *'never deserved'* and who had imposed *'the most infamous and basest of
calumnies'* on his *'too credulous and perceptible heart'.* Otherwise,
he wrote, she *'never could or would have persevered with such an
apparent cruelty and obduracy so foreign to the generous feelings of
her soul, in rejecting for so great a length of time every explanation,
every submission, every step'* his *'tortured heart frequently offer'd and
was most ready and anxious to make'.*

He then listed all the estates, property and personalities of
every kind she would inherit, including his bank account, all
the property he owned in Pall Mall and, as they had all been
bought with his own money, the fabulous contents of Carlton
House and the Marine Pavilion.

He hoped that when Mrs Fitzherbert was acquainted with
the will, she would no longer withhold her 'forgiveness' from
him but accompany it with her blessing,

> assuring her as I now do and calling God to witness at the
> same time, that I shall die blessing her as *my only true and
> real wife* with my parting breath and praying the Almighty
> and all-merciful Being to whom in this paper I have
> open'd the innermost recesses of my heart and of my soul
> to bless, protect and guard her through this life, looking
> forward with confidence to the blessed moment when our
> souls in a better world may again be united, never again
> to part.

He also sent his 'blessings and prayers' to his 'much-loved' brothers and sisters and asked his parents for their forgiveness for any faults he may have 'ignorantly and unguardedly' been guilty of, begging them that 'if there have been such' then they would ascribe them to the 'errors of judgment and of youth'.

His daughter Charlotte he put under the 'whole and sole' management of the King, until she should come of age, as he was desperate to keep her out of the hands of Caroline; for though he forgave her the 'falsehood and treachery' of her conduct towards him,

> *still the convincing and repeated proofs I have received of her*
> *entire want of judgment and of feeling, make me deem it*
> *incumbent upon me and a duty, both as a parent and a man,*
> *to prevent by all means possible the child's falling into such*
> *improper and bad hands as hers.*

As for his burial, he requested as simple an affair as possible, desiring only that his '*constant companion*', a miniature of Mrs Fitzherbert, might be placed next his heart and that when she in her turn died, his coffin might be taken up and 'souder'd' on to hers, so that their ashes might mingle in death. He did not forget an old servant called Santague, and there were kind words for one of Mrs Fitzherbert's friends, Isabella Pigot; the Earl of Moira, whom he had 'ever affectionately loved'; and for Captain Payne, whose enmity to Lady Jersey was now forgiven him.

There was talk too of a mysterious box, marked 'private', the contents of which he insisted on being published, such as they were, 'without any mutilation or ejection of any paper of whatever kind or sort', so that should anyone object to his wishes with regard to Charlotte, his reasons might then be known.

Turning his eyes inward towards his 'own heart' and invoking God, the Prince made the extraordinary claim that as far as he was aware, he had never hurt 'any human being, man or woman, either intentionally or premeditatedly':

that if there is anyone who either is or conceives
themselves to be under such circumstances, and of which
I am quite ignorant, I must freely and undisguisedly ask
their forgiveness, assuring Heaven that whatever faults or
weaknesses I may have been guilty of, they have never
arisen (after the closest inspection of my own heart and
of the principles by which it has ever been actuated) from
the most distant propensity to vice, or vicious inclination,

but only from 'those foibles which but too often fall to the lot
of those who are born to fame' and from the 'heedlessness
and thoughtlessness of youth'. After which, he expressed his
'fullest forgiveness' to everyone who had either 'publicly or
privately' injured him.

Having thus concluded a life *'most full of trouble and misery'*,
the Prince then addressed a 'last farewell' to Mrs Fitzherbert,
'to *her who whilst she and I were one did contribute the sole and only
happiness*' of his life. He had not had one moment of happiness since they had separated, and could expect none unless
they were once more united.

> To thee therefore my Maria, my wife, my life, my soul, do I bid
> my last adieu; round thee shall my soul for ever hover as thy
> guardian angel, for as I never ceased to adore thee whilst living,
> so shall I ever be watchful over thee and protect thee against every
> evil. Farewell, dearest angel, if I must quit thee and the whole
> world in thee by the decrees of Almighty Providence, be it so and
> the will of Heaven be obeyed, but think of thy DEPARTED HUSBAND,
> shed a tear o'er his memory and his grave, and then recollect that
> no woman ever yet was so loved or adored by man as you were
> and are by him.

He added half a dozen other sentences, including the following exquisitely malicious lines about the Princess of Wales:

> I forgot however to mention that the jewells which she
> who is call'd the Princess of Wales wears *are mine, having*

been bought with my own money, and therefore those every one and the whole of them I bequeathe to my infant daughter as her own property, and to her who is call'd the Princess of Wales I leave one shilling.

Mrs Fitzherbert did not see this extraordinary document for almost four years, until following a period of intense introspection the Prince, unable to resist the temptation any longer, finally gave her a copy. He claimed it was written as a kind of therapy, as a way of restoring his health after a debilitating and life-threatening illness and that besides himself, Payne, and one of his favourite sisters, Princess Elizabeth, no one else even knew of its existence. There was little doubt that it was sincere, in the sense that at the time the Prince wrote it, he certainly did love Mrs Fitzherbert, but it was also duplicitous, inasmuch as he was still infatuated with Lady Jersey. None the less, it wasn't the only expression of his returning affection; for four months later, at the height of the public's fury with Lady Jersey, he sent one of his brothers, the Duke of Cumberland, to Mrs Fitzherbert with a letter suggesting a full reconciliation. The Duke's visit caught her off her guard, and not knowing how to respond properly to such a proposal, she was unable to offer the Prince much in the way of a coherent answer. She admitted she still liked the Prince, but she thought that if they did get back together, they would quickly part again. She did, however, arrange to meet the Duke at Captain Payne's during the following day, where, the Duke optimistically wrote, he hoped to be more fortunate.

The Prince also drafted in the resourceful Colonel John McMahon, his future vice-treasurer, to help him in his pursuit of Mrs Fitzherbert, detailing him to keep a close eye on her at Cheltenham, where she spent three weeks during the summer of 1798. McMahon found her in high spirits and 'uniformly gracious and civil' even to him, though it had long been clear that she didn't like him. 'I know Mrs Fitzherbert classes me among the particular friends of Lady J[ersey]' he wrote, and he complained that he had been represented to her as a 'strong

partizan' in Lady Jersey's interest. He had, however, taken care
to do the Prince 'ample justice' by a 'side wind' through a
couple of Mrs Fitzherbert's friends; 'there does not', he boasted,
'exist a suspicion of anything like preconcertment'. A few weeks
later, Princess Mary also wrote to the Prince from Weymouth
to say that although Mrs Fitzherbert had recently been ill, she
was now 'in *greater beauty than ever*'. 'As for your amiable *left
hand* (as you call her)', she wrote, 'I have received two letters
from her and *have* given *your* message in one I wrote to her
this morning.'

During December an invitation from the widowed Duchess
of Rutland to spend a few days at Belvoir Castle to celebrate
the coming of age of her son the Duke, gave the Prince an
opportunity to do his own matchmaking. Finding the Duchess
as depressed for love of his absent friend the diplomat Arthur
Paget as he was for Mrs Fitzherbert, they put together a plan
by which each would aid the other. The Prince wrote to Paget
telling him that the Duchess was pining away for love of him;
indeed, he 'never did see any creature . . . so perfectly attached
as she is'. Meanwhile the Duchess and a mysterious 'friend'
worked behind the scenes to bring about a reconciliation with
Mrs Fitzherbert.

The Prince was extremely grateful to the Duchess for this
arrangement, thanking her again and again for the care she
took in

'the most *essential* circumstance, really the *only one* that can
ever give me *a taste again for life*, and if I do not express
myself as strongly as I ought to you for all your kindness,
beleive me, it is not from want of the just and due sense I
entertain of it, but from being totally inadequate to the
expressing myself as I could wish. Much and great I am
aware will be the difficulties I shall have to rencounter in
the accomplishment of *that object* that is *nearest and dearest*
to my heart, but nevertheless it is a duty I owe myself to
endeavour to *levy every obstacle however great* and to *convince*
you as well as every relation and friend of *hers* of *my*

sincerity and *attachment for her*, and that *at no period, however misrepresented*, there *never was an instant in which I did not feel for her*, as I am afraid she *never* felt for me.

He begged the Duchess to convey to him everything she could learn about Mrs Fitzherbert, even down to the 'smallest scrape of intelligence', for she knew as well as he that in affairs of the heart, 'even the *merest trifle*' could potentially become of the highest importance. '*Our friend*', he added,

I trust likewise will continue her good offices, and not cease either by word of mouth through you or by letter to afford me such intelligence as she may pick up, for it is of the utmost consequence to me to know everything in order not to get upon wrong grounds, not even for an instant.

Having already received some 'hints' from this source concerning his behaviour towards Mrs Fitzherbert's mother, Mrs Smythe (who was then with her daughter at Bath), the Prince thought it was essential that the 'friend' should write to Mrs Smythe telling her that he had enquired after her at Belvoir and that should he intimate a desire to call on her, 'which she did not doubt I should *wish* to do, it would be extremely unkind' not to see him. He also mentioned one other circumstance which the Duchess and her 'friend' might likewise 'hint at' or even 'assert' if they wished: 'everything' was '*finally at an end*' with Lady Jersey.

Though Mrs Fitzherbert was certainly aware that she was surrounded by spies, she did not draw the obvious conclusion. She still thought of herself as the Prince's wife, while it flattered her self-esteem to be the object of such an extraordinary wooing. Those of her friends who were against a reconciliation could only influence her so much and, sometimes, though she must have known that it was in her true interest to stay clear of the Prince, she allowed herself to weaken. After all, if she did not return to the Prince, at some stage he might well admit to all the world that they were married, and that would mean ruin for both of them.

Often Mrs Fitzherbert fell back on the support of Lord Hugh and Lady Horatia Seymour, both of whom were strongly against a reconciliation. She might have deceived herself formerly 'as to the nature of their connection', thought Lady Horatia, but if she reunited herself with the Prince, 'she would now be guilty . . . with her eyes open'. Both were shocked at the 'cruel trials' to which the Prince put Mrs Fitzherbert, and which would never have been used 'where a pretension to sentiment or morality existed'. Unfortunately, 'loving her' as he did, Lord Hugh did not feel able to broach the subject in the manner which it demanded, and both were soon called out of England.

When it was reported that Mrs Fitzherbert had died, the Prince totally lost control of himself; he could neither 'feel, think [nor] speak', and had he not been 'bereft of all sense' he would, he thought, certainly have committed suicide. He first read the story in a morning paper (all of which were sent to Carlton House); then, as if that were not shocking enough, three 'horrid' letters arrived for him 'from different people', as well as another to his and Mrs Fitzherbert's attorney, all of which confirmed it. Fortunately, the Duke of Cumberland, who had also seen the paragraph, thought of racing over to Mrs Fitzherbert's cousin Elizabeth Butler in Portman Square, where he found that the news was less cataclysmic. Soon after this, Mrs Butler sent the Prince a letter which she had received from Mrs Smythe, assuring her that Mrs Fitzherbert was still alive, and a few days later, the Prince himself received a letter from the '*old lady*', 'though rather short, still civil and kind', assuring him that though Mrs Fitzherbert had been very ill, she was not only 'quite out of danger, but every hour visibly mending'.

Still, such was the shock that he remained, as he told the Duchess of Rutland, in a dreadful state, and so agitated that he could hardly write two lines to Mrs Smythe to thank her for her letter. A week or so later, he went to Critchell House for a few days to 'collect his thoughts and ideas a little and to quiet in some degree' his nerves, which were, not surprisingly, 'shattered from the continued state of irritation' they had been in.

Finally, the Prince could bear the uncertainty no more. At about one o'clock on the morning of 12 June, in a state bordering on madness (for he certainly was not entirely sane), he began work on a last desperate attempt to win Mrs Fitzherbert back to him. 'Save me, save me, on my knees', he wrote,

I conjure you from myself whether, after a SOLEMN PROMISE GIVEN, PLEDGED TO MY BROTHER TO BE MINE AGAIN, *is there truth, is there honor in this world,* AND YET NOT INHERENT IN YOU.... IF YOU WISH MY LIFE YOU SHALL HAVE IT. If you BREAK YOUR SACRED PROMISE, RECOLLECT I AM FREED FROM ALL TIES OF ATTACHMENT TO THIS WORLD, *as there is no reliance, no more faith existing,* I THEN HAVE NO FEARS LEFT, NOTHING BUT HONOR IN A WORLD IN WHICH I HAVE EXPERIENCED NOTHING BUT MISERY AND DECEIT, *in return for* THE FINEST FEELINGS OF THE HONESTEST OF HEARTS, NOTWITHSTANDING ALL APPEARANCE MINE HAS EVER BEEN TO ME: REITERATE YOUR PROMISE OR RECOLLECT YOU SIGN YOURSELF MY DOOM. OH, GOD! OH, GOD! WHO HAS SEEN THE AGONY OF MY SOUL AND KNOWEST THE PURITY OF MY INTENTIONS, HAVE MERCY, HAVE MERCY ON ME: TURN ONCE MORE I CONJURE THEE, THE HEART OF MY MARIA, TO ME, FOR WHOM I HAVE LIVED AND FOR WHOM I WILL DIE. You know not what you will drive me to FROM DESPAIR, YOU KNOW YOU ARE MY WIFE, THE WIFE OF MY HEART AND SOUL, MY WIFE IN THE PRESENCE OF MY GOD: 'TIS THE ONLY ONLY REPRIEVE LEFT.

Should she not return to him, he would, he said, '*CLAIM*' her as such, '*PROVE*' their marriage to the King and his family and 'RELINQUISH EVERYTHING' for her; then should she still remain obdurate, he would commit suicide: 'IT IS THE ONLY THING LEFT ME; I SHALL AT LEAST FEEL MYSELF AN HONEST MAN AGAIN: SO HELP ME GOD, 'TIS MY FINAL DETERMINATION.'

Apparently, Mrs Fitzherbert received this latest crude attempt at emotional blackmail on the following morning, when, agitated and confused, she sent back a letter designed at the very least to stall him. She may or may not have been convinced by the Prince's interminable threats to commit suicide, but she must have been shocked at his idea of admitting their marriage to his father, and thus quite callously exposing her brother John Smythe and her uncle Henry Errington to prosecution. Nevertheless, she was by now more receptive to the Prince's pleading and when, within days, it was intimated that the Queen herself would not be averse to their reunion, she seems to have indicated that she would not much longer prolong their separation. First, however, she would need to appeal to Rome; since her marriage to the Prince had been followed by his marriage to Caroline, she wanted papal confirmation that the step she was about to make would be in every sense the right one.

Consequently, during the summer, while Mrs Fitzherbert stayed with her uncle at Red Rice, his house in Hampshire, the Revd William Nassau, one of the chaplains of the Warwick Street Chapel where she worshipped, began a secret journey to Rome with instructions to lay her case before the Pope, upon the 'express understanding, that, if the answer should be favourable, she would again join the Prince; if otherwise, she . . . [would] abandon the country' for ever. Fortunately for the Prince, the Vatican's judgement was that his marriage to Mrs Fitzherbert was the true one, so Mrs Fitzherbert was at liberty to rejoin him.

However, there was to be no formal reconciliation until the following June, leaving ample time for wit and speculation. No one seemed to know precisely what was going on, whether they were reunited or still separated. To Lady Jerningham, it was 'incomprehensible' that at one moment Mrs Fitzherbert and the Prince were apart, and at the next they were deep in conversation in a high box at the opera. She had thought Mrs Fitzherbert a 'woman of principle', she wrote, now she could 'comprehend it no longer'. To Madame de Coigny, on the

other hand, their relationship was like 'a *rondeau*, in which
variations are made *ad libitum*, but the return is to the first
air'. The strain told on the Prince, and many people remarked
on how ill he looked; how the 'stout, athletic figure, fat and
high-spirited, full of laugh and talk' had at last become thin
and quiet. He was plagued by hypochondria too; he had a
spastic bladder and he spoke of leaving the inhospitable English climate for Lisbon or Madeira. There was also the question of his debts, a running sore, which would in themselves
make any man miserable. Unfortunately, Mrs Fitzherbert was
not as sympathetic here as he would have liked, as her own
friend the banker Thomas Coutts had been a loser.

On 2 February 1800 she wrote to Coutts from Tusmore, near
Brackley, where 'tormented' with a 'rheumatism' in her head,
she begged him to leave 'that odious place Bath' for London.
'No one has or can feel more for the unjustifiable treatment
you have met with,' she wrote. 'Some time ago I had an opportunity of expressing my resentment on your account. The
answer was: I am very sorry for it, it was not either my fault or
intention. I wish not to blame but it is impossible to defend. . . .
Excuse this horrid scrawl', she added to the bottom of her
letter, 'I fear you will scarcely be able to read it.'

When at last the Prince and Mrs Fitzherbert were officially
reunited, it was in a magnificent style at a 'public breakfast' at
Mrs Fitzherbert's house on 16 June 1800. She 'hardly knew
how she could summon resolution to pass that severe ordeal',
she later reported, 'but she thanked God she had the courage
to do so'. The company, which numbered close to four hundred, arrived at about two o'clock in the afternoon, then settled
down to dinner at seven in three marquees which were
erected at enormous expense in the garden; they did not leave
until five o'clock on the following morning. The Prince, his
health now almost fully re-established, was in festive mood. He
was feeling better all the time, he wrote to Arthur Paget, such
was Mrs Fitzherbert's reviving effect upon him. He felt
reinvigorated, better able than he had been for months to
cope with the stresses and strains of a further outbreak of his

father's illness, the demands of his tailors, his debts and Pitt's resignation.

Mrs Fitzherbert did her best to steer clear of public contro- versy. As it was, the public mind was agitated on the question of a Catholic Relief Bill and she did not want to endanger her position by irritating it further. Although some people con- tinued to believe that she was the agent of a Catholic con- spiracy, and now and again it was rumoured that she was influencing the Prince's mind against her old enemy Fox, she did her best to avoid politics altogether; only on the question of Fox's return to office was she said to be implacable. Mean- while, away from the rough and tumble of public life, she told Lady Anne Lindsay that the Prince was 'much improved . . . all that was boyish and troublesome before is now become respectful and considerate' and they lived together 'like brother and sister'. The Prince showed his affection in tangible ways too; during October, he increased her income from £3,000 to £4,000 per annum.

One of the many shared interests that brought them together at this period was their mutual affection for Mary or 'Minney' Seymour, the infant daughter of Lord Hugh and his ailing wife Lady Horatia Seymour, who had been left in Mrs Fitzher- bert's care while Lord Hugh pursued his naval career and Lady Horatia convalesced in Madeira. The Prince, who was gener- ally very fond of children, loved to play with the child and was overjoyed when she learnt how to talk and called him 'Prinney'. Mrs Fitzherbert had often longed for a child of her own, and treated her more like a daughter than a ward, becoming on one occasion extremely alarmed when Lady Waldegrave, one of Minney's aunts, took the child and her nurse out for an airing without telling her. She was thus extremely shattered when during May 1801 Lady Horatia returned to England to take charge of her daughter. Fortunately for Mrs Fitzherbert, Lady Horatia's state of health still left much to be desired, and touched by Mrs Fitzherbert's obvious distress, she allowed herself to be persuaded that it was in Minney's best interests to remain with Mrs Fitzherbert a little longer. 'Do you think I

could be so unfeeling as to take her away from you immediately, when you have been so kind to her', she remarked, 'and
in fact more her mother than I have had it in my power to
be?' None the less, she was clearly relieved that Mrs Fitzherbert
had not so monopolized Minney's affections that, though she
called Mrs Fitzherbert 'Mama', she was unaware that she was
not her real mother.

There matters stood for about two months until during the
summer both parents died, Lady Horatia from tuberculosis, at
Bristol, and Lord Hugh some nine weeks later in Jamaica.
Henceforth, it wasn't entirely clear who was responsible for
Minney, whether Mrs Fitzherbert or, as was strongly urged,
Lord Hugh's executors and his children's guardians, his wife's
sister's husband the Earl of Euston and his brother Lord Henry
Seymour. The executors argued that though Minney was not
mentioned in Lord Hugh's will by name (it had been drafted
before her birth), when Lord Hugh had appointed them as
his children's guardians, he had clearly meant all his children,
born or unborn. Moreover, though they admired Mrs Fitzherbert
as a woman, they were fearful of her Catholic influence on
Minney's religious education. However, a compromise of sorts
was again reached, and Mrs Fitzherbert won a reprieve, under
the terms of which it was agreed that she would not lose Minney
immediately. Then, the Prince himself forcefully intervened,
offering his own, more solid, proposal for Minney's future.

'Fully convinced', that Minney's 'welfare and hapiness' were
'essentially dependant' on her living with Mrs Fitzherbert, he
told Lord Euston that 'nothing short of a stipulation' that she
should remain with her until she was of an age to choose for
herself would satisfy him. His 'ultimate view' was to raise Minney
up as a 'companion' and as a 'bosom friend' for his daughter
Charlotte, to which end it was 'absolutely necessary' that she
should be educated in Mrs Fitzherbert's house, under his watchful
inspection. Both he and Mrs Fitzherbert were, he said, keen
that the 'freest intercourse' should be kept up between Minney
and her relations, who should also, if they pleased, be eye-
witnesses of the course of her education as well as the forma-

tion of her mind and manners'. Minney's financial prospects would be good as he would invest £10,000 on her behalf in the funds. He then proposed himself, the elderly lawyer Lord Thurlow, the Bishop of Winchester and Lord Henry's brothers, Lord Robert Seymour and the Marquis of Hertford, as joint guardians, on the understanding that should 'anything arise with reference to her religion which, in the judgment of the guardians, shall render it proper to remove her', Mrs Fitzherbert would indeed give up the child. 'If this arrangement shall be approved, the contest will be put an end to, and the infant will be bred up in harmony with her family and with every protection to her spiritual and temporal welfare they can reasonably desire, but should Lord Euston and Lord Henry persevere' in their intransigence he would 'resist their efforts to the utmost of his power'.

While Lord Euston duly appreciated the Prince's proposal to settle £10,000 on Minney, neither he nor Lord Henry Seymour was intimidated by the Prince's bluster. 'As guardians to the children of our deceased friend', Lord Euston wrote in a letter to Captain Payne, 'we feel bound to act for them according to the dictates of our consciences, a principle which we are sure H.R.H. cannot disapprove, even though in this instance the observance of it has led us to decline H.R.H.'s most liberal offer.'

The Prince and Mrs Fitzherbert then lobbied other members of the Hertford family. The Prince pressurized Lord Hertford and Mrs Fitzherbert sent a warm and moving letter to Lord Robert Seymour. The misery of losing Minney was more than she could express, she told him. No person could feel for Minney as much love as she did, or 'be actuated by such real love and affection'. She was 'so totally wrapped up [in] and devoted' to Minney, that if she lost her, it would break her heart. She asked him to imagine how wretched she was at the 'dread' of having Minney taken from her. There was 'no one earthly thing' she would not be willing to do in order to secure her 'darling child' to her. She was 'quite certain' that no mother could feel more for her 'greatest favourite' than

she did for Minney, 'added to which the many years of friendship and attachment that subsisted between' her and Minney's
parents was an 'additional claim' upon her feelings. She went
on:

> I have not the good fortune to be acquainted with Lord
> Henry but I have always heard so much from every
> Quarter *that* I trust he will not be deaf to my intreaties.
> Tell him he can have no idea of the anxiety of my mind
> and suffering and that it depends entirely upon him to
> make me happy or miserable for life.
>
>   Do, my dear Lord, interest yourself for me. You are a
> Father and can judge what one must suffer at having a
> beloved Babe that one doats upon to the greatest degree
> possible, torn from one. Let these feelings operate
> through you upon Lord Henry and let me have to bless
> you both and to thank both you and him which I shall do
> from the bottom of my heart.

Lord Thurlow in the meantime suggested that the Prince
consult Samuel Romilly, one of the busiest and most ambitious
lawyers at the Chancery Bar. Romilly, having considered the
case, advised that a Bill should be filed in the Court of Chancery by a friend of Lord Hugh acting on Minney's behalf. Mr
William Bentinck was then chosen as 'next friend' of the appellant, and during the summer of 1803 the case began.

The case for the respondents argued that it could never
have been Lady Horatia's intention that the Prince should
become a guardian to Minney. 'She might perhaps, naturally
enough, presuming upon his great condescension and most
gracious kindness, be desirous of bespeaking, in the most earnest manner, his protection and patronage', but the 'idea of
proposing to H.R.H. to be the guardian to an infant of two
years old and that a female infant, could never have entered
into her mind'. And even if it did, she had no 'right' to act
upon it. They deplored too the idea that a Protestant child
should be educated by a Catholic.

When the superior effect of example over precept is
considered what hopes can be entertained that any system
of education could prevail against the example of a
person whom every tie of gratitude and every feeling of
affection would make the object of the child's strongest
admiration and regard? Nay, however insupportable the
idea may be, that the Law should appoint a guardian for
the child of a Protestant parent who should educate it as
a Roman Catholic, yet it may well be doubted, if Mrs
Fitzherbert is to be the guardian, whether she had better
not be permitted to educate the Appellant to her own
religion. For how much must it endanger the conviction
of the importance of those truths which religion teaches,
if the person whom she sees most affectionately interested
about her temporal welfare appears to pay no attention to
her religious concerns?

Several affidavits were sworn by the Prince, Mrs Fitzherbert,
the Countess of Euston and even by the Bishop of Winchester, who stated that Minney had made 'great progress' in her
religious studies under the guidance of the Revd Mr Croft,
and 'promised, as far as a child of her age could promise, to
be a firm and steady member' of the Church of England. One
of the Prince's doctors, Sir Walter Farquhar, argued that sepa-
rating Minney from Mrs Fitzherbert might even be damaging
to her health, for 'bilious complaints', from which Minney suffered, are 'frequently brought on and always aggravated by
great anxiety'.

None the less, the Master in Chancery was not to be persuaded by the Prince and Mrs Fitzherbert's arguments, and
during February 1805 he approved Lord Euston and Lord Henry
Seymour as guardians of the child. The Prince took the case
to a higher court, but there too he was rebuffed. Nothing was
then left but an appeal to the House of Lords.

The Seymour case, or the 'Trial of Mrs Fitzherbert', as Edward
Jerningham succinctly phrased it, eventually came on in the
House on 10 June 1806, after an earlier date had been cancelled.

There then followed four days of intense and often bad-tempered lobbying. The Prince entreated all his friends to attend and made it clear that he would not forget the names of any peers who opposed him. Fortunately, on 14 June an acceptable compromise was at last offered under the terms of which Minney would remain with Mrs Fitzherbert, but Lord Hertford, alone, would be guardian. This was then put to the vote and carried without a division.

Naturally Mrs Fitzherbert was overjoyed. Having once threatened to run away with Minney, she was ecstatic at the prospect of keeping her in her care, and even the cries of outraged Protestantism could not entirely dampen her pleasure. Many people were also sympathetic, not least Edward Jerningham, who professed to be 'perfectly glad' that the Lords had voted effectively in favour of confirming Minney in her custody. Voicing some of Mrs Fitzherbert's own arguments, he said that taking her from Mrs Fitzherbert would have been Minney's 'actual Death'. 'And Mrs Fitzherbert, having manifested her unequivocal Intention of rearing her little orphan in the Established Doctrine, it would have been a cruel persecution for the Lords to have acted otherwise.'

Mrs Fitzherbert often took Minney to Brighton during these years, where she had a new house built adjoining the Pavilion by the Prince's architect, the fashionable orientalist William Porden. As always, she guarded her reputation jealously and only once, when the Prince fell violently ill during the first weeks of 1804, is she known to have passed some of her nights in the Pavilion. The Prince's illness was the result of three days' hard drinking with the alcoholic Duke of Norfolk and one of Lord North's sons, the indolent and eccentric Lord Guildford. However, he was well enough by the beginning of February for Mrs Fitzherbert to write a consolatory letter to the Duke of Kent who, having recently heard only bad news from Brighton, confessed to having felt 'quite broken-hearted' about his brother. 'Pray', he wrote to Mrs Fitzherbert, 'say everything most affectionate from me and that nothing could be more kind than the intent expressed, both by the Queen and all our sisters about him.' He also asked Mrs Fitzherbert to express his gratitude to the Prince's physician Sir Walter Farquhar for the care he had taken of the Prince on the occasion.

Mrs Fitzherbert too had her share of ill health during this year, some of which was doubtless borne of her frustration with the Prince, though to outsiders his 'attachment and attention' to her was still thought to be 'unbounded and surprising'. She was almost fifty now, with a mouth rather spoilt by a set of 'not good' false teeth, and extremely fat, and often she made a 'great display of a very white but not prettily formed' bosom. To one commentator, the diarist Mrs Calvert, she seemed frequently depressed.

> Her manners are good humored [she wrote] . . .
> unaffected and pleasing, but very absent, and I have often
> thought she was not happy, for she heaves such deep
> sighs sometimes in one of those fits of absence, that I
> have actually started. There does not seem to be any
> brilliancy about Mrs Fitzherbert, no agreeable talents, or
> powers of captivation, but captivation there must be about
> her, though I don't perceive it, as she has captivated His
> Royal Highness for so many years.

Mrs Fitzherbert generally did the honours of the house at the Pavilion, welcoming the Prince's guests and putting them at their ease, leaving him to make an impressive entrance later on during the evening. In the opinion of Thomas Creevey, the Whig MP, who spent several weeks at Brighton during the autumn of 1805, the Prince was often at his best on these occasions; never had he seen him happier; he was always 'merry and full of his jokes', considerate, kind and amusing. He heard the Prince discuss military tactics with a clearly bemused Lord Hutchinson, and was present when the Prince introduced Warren Hastings, 'the Nabob of Arcot' whom the Whigs had done so much to discredit, to an obviously embarrassed Sheridan.

Mrs Fitzherbert, Creevey averred, was 'always the Prince's best friend': She kept a continual eye on his interests and persuaded the Prince to adopt a number of stratagems to avoid getting dead drunk again when the Duke of Norfolk arrived for his annual visit to the Pavilion. Creevey observed:

> I dined there . . . and letters were brought in each day after dinner to the Prince, which he affected to consider of great importance, and so went out to answer them, while the Duke of Clarence went on drinking with the Duke of Norfolk. But on the second day this joke was carried too far, and in the evening the Duke of Norfolk showed he was affronted. The Prince took me aside, and said 'Stay after everyone is gone to-night. The Jockey's got sulky,* and I must give him a broiled bone to get him in good humour again'. So of course I stayed, and at about one o'clock the Prince of Wales and the Duke of Clarence, the Duke of Norfolk and myself sat down to a supper of broiled bones, the result of which was that, having fallen asleep myself, I was awoke by the sound of the Duke of Norfolk's snoring. I found the Prince of Wales and the Duke of Clarence in a very animated discussion as to the particular shape and make of the wig worn by George II.

Mrs Fitzherbert, Creevey noted, 'always dined' at the Pavilion, usually in the company of 'one other lady – Lady Downshire very often, sometimes Lady Clare or Lady Berkshire' and, occasionally, her relative the Dowager Lady Sefton. Once he saw Sheridan arrive dressed as a police officer to arrest the Dowager for playing some 'unlawful game'; Mrs Fitzherbert was a 'great card-player, and played every night', while the Prince occupied himself in talking to his guests or in 'listening to and giving directions' to his orchestra.

When Creevey returned to London, Mrs Creevey remained behind, and sent him an amused and sometimes despairing

---

* 'The Jockey' was the Duke's nickname; one of his many weaknesses was his addiction to racing.

commentary: 'Oh, this wicked Pavillion! we were there till $\frac{1}{2}$ past one this morning . . . . The invitation did not come to us till 9 o'clock: we went in Lord Thurlow's carriage, and were in fear of being too late; but the Prince [who was drunk] did not come out of the dining-room till 11.' Till then, their 'only companions' were Lady Downshire and Mr and Miss Johnstone, though 'the former' was 'very goodnatured and amiable'. The Prince introduced her to McMahon, 'talked a great deal' about Mrs Fitzherbert, and told her that Mrs Fitzherbert 'wished much' to see her. When the Prince had asked Mrs Fitzherbert 'When?', her answer was apparently, 'Not till *you* are gone, and I can see her *comfortably*.'

A few days later Mrs Fitzherbert gave Mrs Creevey a detailed sketch of a friend of Lord Berkeley, a distressed Russian woman, who had apparently fallen violently in love with Lord Whitworth when he was ambassador in St Petersburg. 'He was poor and handsome – she rich and in love with him, and tired of a magnificent husband to whom she had been married at 14 years old'; she '*kept*' Lord Whitworth, and 'spent immense sums in doing so and gratifying his extravagance'. But then Whitworth returned to England; the couple corresponded, and she decided to follow him. She got as far as Berlin before discovering that he was married to the Duchess of Dorset. 'She was raving mad for some time', was 'often nearly so now, but at other times most interesting and miserable'. She was now in England, where she was 'an eternal subject of remorse to Lord Whitworth', who was, in Mrs Fitzherbert's words a 'monster'.

When fifteen days after the event news finally arrived in London of the death of Nelson and the great victory of Trafalgar, Mrs Fitzherbert immediately sat down and penned a brief note to Mrs Creevey: 'Twenty out of three and thirty of the enemy's fleet' had been 'entirely destroyed' she wrote, 'no English ship being taken or sunk – Capts. Duff and Cook both kill'd, and the French Adl. Villeneuve taken prisoner.' She went on:

Poor Lord Nelson received his death by a shot of a
musket from the enemy's ship upon his shoulder, and
expir'd two hours after, but not till the ship struck and
afterwards sunk, which he had the consolation of hearing,
as well as his compleat victory, before he died. Excuse this
hurried scrawl: I am so nervous I scarce can hold my pen.

With their growing intimacy, Mrs Fitzherbert often spoke to
Mrs Creevey of her personal affairs, and gave her her opinions
of other compromised women. She was amazed at Fox's 'folly'
in marrying Mrs Armistead, at Lord Wellesley's in marrying
the American adventuress, Mrs Paterson, and was 'all for' Lady
Nelson and 'against' Lady Hamilton, who, she said, '(hero as
he was)' had 'overpower'd' Nelson and taken 'possession of
him quite by force'. However, she was not malicious. 'Poor
creature! I am sorry for her now, for I suppose she is in grief',
she added.* On one occasion Mrs Fitzherbert gave Mrs Creevey

---

* During January 1801 it was supposed, not least by Nelson, that Lady Hamilton was Mrs Fitzherbert's rival. Learning that Sir William Hamilton was to
invite the Prince to his house in Piccadilly to hear Lady Hamilton sing,
Nelson worked himself up into a passion:

> No good can come of it but every harm. You are too beautiful not to
> have enemies, and even one visit will stamp you as his *chère amie*, and we
> know he is dotingly fond of such women as yourself, and is without one
> spark of honour in these respects, and would leave you to bewail your
> folly [Oliver Warner, *A Portrait of Lord Nelson*, 1958, p. 251]. You have
> been taken in. But his words are so charming that, I am told, no person
> can withstand him. . . . Hush, hush, my poor heart, keep in my breast, be
> calm, Emma is true. . . . But no one, not even Emma could resist the
> serpent's flattering tongue. . . . What will they all say and think, that Emma
> is like other women . . . Forgive me. I know I am almost distracted [Walter
> Sichel, *Emma, Lady Hamilton*, 1907, p. 360].

If Emma could not help dining with the 'villain', she was to 'get rid' of him
as quickly as possible. 'Do not let him come downstairs with you or hand
you up,' Nelson wrote. If she did, and he learned of it, then he would
murder the Prince. He had heard that Lady Abercorn and a distant relative, Mrs Walpole, had been trying to organize a tryst and that a Mrs Nisbet
had been quoted as publicly asserting that Emma had 'hit' the Prince's
'fancy'. 'Rather let the lowest wretch that walks the street dine at [Sir William's]

her life story, dwelling 'particularly' on her relationship with the Prince. 'If she is as *true* as I think she is *wise*', remarked Mrs Creevey, 'she is an extraordinary person, and most worthy to be beloved.'

She spoke too of the Prince's connection with the Duchess of Devonshire, whose massive gambling debts, long a cause for her notoriety amongst her friends, had contributed to undermine her health. The Prince, she said, knew 'everything' – how the Duchess exacted money in the Prince's name, but accepted it from 'motives of compassion and old friendship'. 'In short, he tells Mrs F. all he sees and hears,' Mrs Creevey wrote, 'shews her all the Duchess's letters and notes, and she says she knows the Dss. hates her.' They talked too of the possibility of Mrs Fitzherbert's life being written: 'She said she supposed it would some time or other, but with thousands of lies; but she would be dead and it would not signify.' Mrs Creevey then urged her to write it herself. 'But she said it would break her heart.'

During the following summer, at about the same time that the Minney Seymour case was heard, Mrs Fitzherbert found herself drawn into a long-standing quarrel between the Prince and Nathaniel Jeffreys, a jeweller whom the Prince had effectively ruined, as he had been unable to pay for almost £60,000 worth of jewels he had ordered for his ill-fated wedding. In 1796 Jeffreys took the Prince to court, won his case, entered Parliament to avoid arrest, but, still unpaid, was declared bankrupt in 1797. In 1801 he published a statement of his dealings with the Prince, coupled with an outspoken vindication. Then in 1806 he brought out a pamphlet in which he attacked both the Prince and Mrs Fitzherbert. He told of an occasion when the Prince 'with very visible marks of agitation in his countenance

---

table,' Nelson seethed, 'than that unprincipalled Lyar. . . . Sir William never can admit him into his house nor can any friend advise him to it unless they are determined on your hitherto unimpeached character being ruined. No modest woman would suffer it. He is permitted to visit only people of *notorious ill fame*' (George, Prince of Wales, *Correspondence*, V, p. 283).

Fortunately for Nelson's peace of mind, the dinner was cancelled.

and manner' had begged him to lend him £1,600 to pay off
one of Mrs Fitzherbert's creditors. He assured him that he
would and brought the money to Carlton House on the following
morning:

> His Royal Highness was unbounded in his expressions of
> satisfaction at what I had so promptly accomplished; and
> in the afternoon on the same day, he came to my house
> in Piccadilly, and brought with him Mrs Fitzherbert, for
> the express purpose, as his Royal Highness condescendingly
> said, that she might herself thank me for the great and
> essential service I had that morning rendered to her by
> the relief my exertions had produced in the minds of his
> Royal Highness and Mrs Fitzherbert.

Jeffreys noted, however, a look of 'mortified pride' on Mrs
Fitzherbert's countenance. Jeffreys spoke too of his difficulty
in recouping a loan of £420 from the Prince, and, building on
the public's sympathy for Caroline, hinted that Mrs Fitzherbert
had engineered the breakdown of the marriage.

Naturally Mrs Fitzherbert was offended at Jeffreys's cavalier
portrayal of her character, yet rather than withdraw the pamphlet
Jeffreys published a public letter specifically designed to hurt
her further. The public, he wrote, felt 'EXTREME DISGUST' at
her conduct; she was treated like a queen, while Caroline was
snubbed, and they were tired of supporting her extravagance.
'When the Prince of Wales was married to the Princess', he
wrote, 'it was agreed that you should retire from that *intimacy
of friendship* you had so long enjoyed, and your houses in Pall-
Mall and at Brighton were given up accordingly.' 'Yet', he sneered,

> viewed in a *retrospective* light, the *necessity* of such a retreat,
> (accompanied as it was by a pension of several thousands
> per annum, payable quarterly at an eminent banker's, and
> a retention of the very valuable plate, jewels, &c. &c. given
> to you by the Prince,) did not, in the opinion of the world,
> add much good fame to your reputation.

Had she continued to keep away from the Prince, then the public would 'probably' never have 'disturbed' her. But then she had resumed her '*intimacy*' with the Prince, an 'establishment, upon a still larger scale,' was formed for her,

> a noble house in Park-lane, most magnificently fitted up, and superbly furnished; a large retinue of servants; carriages of various descriptions; a new Pavilion, built for your *separate* residence at Brighton; and the Prince more frequently in your society than ever. When, Madam, your friends pretend that your feelings are hurt, let me ask you, (and them) if you think the people of moral character in this country have no feelings! I am sure they must relinquish all claim to any, if they could view with indifference, such a departure from decency as this conduct exhibits in you, and not see, with anxiety and fear for the future, the probable result of such a dreadful infatuation; – not less dangerous to the future interest of the country, than any that was ever experienced at the profligate court of Versailles.

Although several pamphlets appeared defending Mrs Fitzherbert and the Prince, and casting Jeffreys as a foolish and embittered liar whose own vanity had brought about his ruin, the damage to Mrs Fitzherbert's reputation was lasting.

Lady Hertford

The Prince, in his early forties, found in Lady Hertford a woman who could be considered his ideal partner. She was both a confidante and a strict nursemaid, formidably intelligent and, in company at least, naturally guarded. Unlike Mrs Robinson, for instance, she did not boast of her conquest; she was neither impulsive nor, when it came to affairs of the heart, particularly sentimental. She was witty, but her wit was of the leaden variety, urbane, but laboured; she was domineering, but poised; ambitious, pompous and only occasionally spiteful.

She was always immaculately dressed, and, though two years older than the Prince, still beautiful in a way the Prince appreciated: maternal, severe and on a 'very large scale'. 'We may reasonably doubt,' wrote Nathaniel Wraxall, 'whether Diana de Poitiers, Ninon de L'Enclos, or Marion de L'Orme, three women who preserved their powers of captivating mankind even in the evening of life, could exhibit at her age finer remains of female grace than the Marchioness of Hertford.'

Few people liked her, however, and Mrs Calvert, who spotted her at a ball at Lady Headfort's in 1807, thought her 'without exception' the 'most forbidding, haughty, unpleasant-looking woman' she had ever seen, though that was partly because she felt sorry for Mrs Fitzherbert. The Whig Lord Holland's assessment of her was also unkind and to the point; Lady Hertford was, he wrote, 'timid . . . stately, formal, and insipid'.

By 1800, both Lady Hertford and her husband were firm Tories, though Lord Hertford had once occupied, as reversionary head of the powerful Hertford interest, a considerable position in the Whig Opposition. 'His person, elegantly formed, rose above the ordinary height . . . his manners were noble yet ingratiating', wrote Wraxall; and when he spoke on Irish affairs, his contributions were received as those of an authority. Yet he frequently overreached himself. Thomas Pelham 'always thought him pleasant and few people are better informed, but there is a want of energy in his character and a love of money that makes him insignificant and unpopular'.* The King was fond of him, however, as was the Prince, who, grateful for his contribution in securing his niece Minney Seymour to Mrs Fitzherbert, later helped to engineer his elevation to the Garter.

Lady Hertford entertained the Prince at Manchester House, her husband's lavishly decorated 'palace' in Manchester Square,† at Sudbourne in Suffolk and at Ragley Hall, the ancestral home of the Hertfords, near Alcester in Warwickshire. The Prince loved Ragley, both for its beauty and quiet. It was a paradise; and he was 'always' happy there. The company, which usually consisted of the Hertfords and their Seymour-Conway relatives, was entirely to his taste; he would enjoy 'perfect tranquillity, comfort and total banishment of all gêne' in the Marchioness's society. Indeed the company of his 'dear nurse' was delightful; and 'no house could be pleasanter'.

Of the Marchioness's relatives, the Prince was especially fond of her only son, the unpleasant, alcoholic and famously libidinous Lord Yarmouth. No man's manner was 'more pleasing', he unctuously told Lady Hertford; 'his style of conversation is

---

* According to the satirist William Combe, avarice was the hereditary taint of all the Hertfords. Lord Hertford had, Combe insinuated in his deeply unpleasant *The Diaboliad*, 'perplexed' his first wife (Lady Hertford's predecessor) to death because she wasn't rich enough; and even his beneficiaries (including William Combe) were 'proud' to show their 'ingratitude'. 'Without one Virtue than can grace a name;/ Without one Vice that e'er exalts to Fame;/ The despicable [Hertford] next appears,/ His bosom panting with his usual fears:/ He strives in vain, – and fruitless proves the art,/ To hide with vacant smile, the treacherous heart.'

† Today, Manchester House, or 'Hertford House' as it is now known, holds the Wallace Collection. Among the pictures are three portraits of Mary Robinson, including one by Thomas Gainsborough, a gift from the Prince of Wales to Lord Hertford.

most truly delightful, as his sense and his information and the accuracy of his judgment and of his discrimination is really quite wonderful, and he is indeed in point of talent very superior to all the young men of the rising generation'.

Doubtless, they had much to talk about, for Yarmouth, or 'Red Herrings' as he was usually known, shared the Prince's passion for French art, fine food, and unprincipled women. In 1798 he had alienated his parents by marrying 'Mie Mie', the spoilt and adventurous offspring of the Marchesa Fagniani and either George Selwyn or 'Old Q', the Prince's elderly and dissolute friend, the Duke of Queensbury.

In order to ingratiate himself with the Marchioness, during 1806 the Prince had successfully pressed Fox to negotiate Lord Yarmouth's release from France, where he had been held since the breakdown of the Treaty of Amiens. He then set himself the task of bringing about a reconciliation between Lord Yarmouth and his parents, who had hardly spoken to him since 1798. 'You know that family matters are very delicate ground', he wrote to Lady Hertford, 'and must be very cautiously trod upon, for obvious reasons, and particularly with a highminded, quick and penetrating disposition which he possesses; at any rate if I can do you no good you may depend that I will do no harm.' He helped Lady Hertford in other ways too, on one occasion advising his old friend Lady Downshire, who had discreetly placed all her family's political interests in his hands, against putting forward a Mr Carr as a candidate for the County of Antrim (where Lord Hertford owned a vast estate), for it would be 'positively interfering' with Lord Hertford's interests.

> I told her Ladyship 'most distinctly, that I must
> insist upon this proposal being without delay rejected,
> as I never would risk the occasioning Lord Hertford
> any disquietude, for that I felt so infinitely grateful
> to both you and to him for the very kind and firm
> support that you had so recently given me in a business
> of such importance to my happiness, independent
> of the intimacy and the sincere and affectionate regard

which had so long subsisted between us, that I never
could endure the idea of repaying such unbounded
kindness from you both by such foul and black
ingratitude.

Yet he wished the details of the arrangement to be kept 'quite
private', in case they got back to Lady Downshire, who might
otherwise accuse him of breaching her confidence. He also
lobbied for Lord Yarmouth's entry into the House of Lords,
though he was not successful.

The Prince looked to Lady Hertford for emotional support,
independent of her sexual appeal, especially during the first
months of their relationship, when, according to many observers,
his health was visibly deteriorating. An apothecary who attended
him in Doncaster during September 1806 found his pulse 'quite
thin, low and weak'. 'He thinks him seriously unwell', remarked
Lord Fitzwilliam to Lord Grenville on the 24th, though 'whether
he will be persuaded to manage himself, as he ought to do, is
more than I feel confidant of'. Fortunately, however, on this
occasion Lady Hertford was close at hand, and he was able to
call on her at her mother Lady Irvine's mansion at Temple
Newsam near Leeds. Still, even she could only offer a temporary respite from his afflictions, and he returned to London
feeling sicker than ever.

In obedience to Lady Hertford's 'kind injunction' to keep
her informed of his health, he wrote her a sympathy-begging
letter from Carlton House, stating that his condition had certainly not improved since last he had had the 'happiness' of
seeing her. Indeed, he was 'growing weaker' by the day, owing
he supposed to the inefficiency of his doctors and his continuing 'total loss of appetite'. He had nevertheless '*obey'd*' her
prescription for 'warm milk' and 'soda water', which he had
taken 'regularly' every morning and which henceforth he promised
her he would also repeat in the evening. 'I really am quite
asham'd at saying so much about myself, my best and dearest
friend', he wrote, but she was 'so positive' in the 'requisition' she
had made him and she had 'enjoined it in so peremptory a

manner', that she really only had herself to blame if he bored
her.

By December, he looked so bad that it was reported in London that one eminent doctor had said he had not long to live.
One rumour was that he was suffering from an 'Atrophy'; another that he was unable to allay an 'internal heat', for which
he took copious draughts of the '*strongest tea*', '*iced*' before he
would drink it. During the following March, his horrified tailor noticed that he was so 'reduced in his size' that the 'Cloaths
which He formerly wore' hung 'like great coats upon Him'
and that he looked 'very old and wrinkled, very much so considering his age'. 'His Domestics speak of it with much concern, fearing for their situations,' recorded the artist and diarist
Joseph Farington.

More cynical observers, however, knowing the Prince and
his behaviour well, thought that his condition was mostly sham,
detecting not a mortal illness in his symptoms, but a typically
melodramatic response to Lady Hertford's refusal to offer him
her undivided attention. To this end, wrote Lord Holland, he
'actually submitted to be bled two or three times in the course
of a night, when there was so little necessity for it that different surgeons were introduced for the purpose, unknown to
each other, lest they object to so unusual a loss of blood'.

Eventually the Prince improved, but it was only to fall seriously ill again during the following autumn when, returning
from Ragley, he complained to the Marchioness of the 'most
horrible and torturing spasmodick attacks' in his head, which
had not only prevented him from writing, but 'from the possibility even of doing anything, as the agony I suffer is hardly to
be credited'. He begged her to write to him more often than
she had hitherto done, especially as he could not bear the
'dreadfully painful' thought that he had been forgotten.

In the melancholy state both of my body and of my mind,
you must know how incalculably comforting when
deprived of your dear society, your letters must ever be to
me; do therefore listen to my entreaties, and sit you down

for half an hour, now and then, to tell me in the first
place how you do, and all those belonging to you, for
whom I feel the sincerest interest.

'Nothing' but having felt himself 'so complete an invalid', he
added, had prevented him from joining Lord Hertford, who
was shooting at Sudbourne.

Without Lady Hertford, the Prince became morbid and melancholy, hardly speaking to his friends, and sometimes sitting
dumb and tearful in Carlton House for hours at a time. She
was the one woman in whom he confided all his secrets, and
when absent she monopolized his thoughts.

Following the death of Lady Hertford's mother on 20 November, the Prince counselled the bereaved Marchioness to
abandon the 'sad and melancholy scenes' at Temple Newsam
and come directly to him in London.

Surely you cannot have forgotten the extreme consolation
you ever offer'd me, when born down and almost
overwhelm'd by sorrows and afflictions, and how truly,
should such experience teach us that we can judge much,
much better in any case than in our own, but above all in
that which involves the object to which one's best
affections are due from the first and most sublime feeling
of the human heart, a just sense of gratitude.

This letter went unanswered, prompting a frightened Lieutenant-Colonel Benjamin Bloomfield, one of the Prince's new
Gentleman-Attendants, to remark to Lord Hertford on 10
December that he had never seen the Prince in such a 'state
of lowness and depression'.

Sir Walter Farquhar, he reported, had tried 'every species
of medicine without producing the most trifling effect'; it was
'above a fortnight' since the Prince had left his 'wretched room';
and except for McMahon and himself he had never seen a
soul, 'and us but for a moment. . . . It is not in the power of
my pen to describe the sufferings of this House'. He regretted

that the Prince had not been well enough to join him at Sudbourne, where the 'quiet attentions' he would have received could not have failed to be 'serviceable'.

Five days later, the Prince was in a still worse condition. Not only had he refused to get up, but he was 'plung'd into a state of apathy and indifference towards himself'. Bloomfield was exceedingly alarmed:

> He scarcely speaks a word, and I am persuaded until your Lordship and Lady Hertford arrive, in whom he reposes such unbounded confidence, and that the load with which he is so dreadfully oppress'd, is remov'd by unburthening himself to friends he so much regards and esteems, and in whose counsels he places unlimited reliance, we must not dare to hope for an amelioration of his situation.

Some kind of crisis occurred when later that evening the Prince, having granted a mysterious visitor permission to speak to him in his bedroom, was found by Bloomfield in a 'state of agitation':

> He clasp'd his hands and, in quick steps, walk'd up and down his room as if rouz'd by some dreadful event, when he exclaim'd, 'Oh, my dear Bloomfield, a terrible catastrophe was near happening in my Family,' and in the greatest agony continued, 'If Lord and Lady Hertford were but here, the only persons to whom I can talk and confide. What is now to become of me; of wretched me, in this moment of accumulating difficulties and distress, is more than I can support.'

He then told Bloomfield that he had confided in Lady Hertford alone the details of a subject closely connected with the arrival of his visitor, and the 'privation of her consoling advice and counsel, particularly at this moment' was therefore of the 'most dreadful consequence'. Bloomfield was stunned. 'Good God, my dear Lord, what is to become of us?'

Fortunately for both Bloomfield and the Prince, this last enigmatical letter persuaded the Hertfords and within days they were on their way from Ragley to see him. The Prince's relief was palpable: 'Thank God they are coming ... now I shall be among friends who really do love me, and for whom I have the most unbounded affection, and in whom I place all my confidence. Now I shall be able to unburthen myself. Oh! this is a relief for poor me'.*

While the Prince slowly recuperated in the company of Lady Hertford, most people could only guess at the true nature of their relationship. They wondered if his new love affair was like his relationships with his other mistresses or whether it was merely platonic. Caroline thought Lady Hertford 'too formal' to please the Prince for very long and that it was 'only a *liaison* of vanity on her part', while a friend of Lady Charlotte Campbell, though admitting that Lady Hertford had many good qualities, did not suppose for a moment that the Prince 'possessed any power over her feelings'. Sir George Jackson, having carefully considered the matter, decided that Lady Hertford was probably 'as much in the dark' as he was, 'being scarcely able to believe that charms she had not been aware of possessing – at least for many a year – should now prove, as has been suggested to her, so irresistibly attractive to her visitor'.

The Prince's letters to Lady Hertford were the subject of particular rumours, as people wondered what it was the couple found write to about. 'She is near fifty and has been a grandmother more than twelve or fourteen years,' observed Lord Glenbervie. 'The Prince is not much younger.'

According to Lady Harriet Cavendish, the Prince was rarely out of bed and when he was he spent almost all his time in writing to her. 'I hope for her sake she is not obliged to devote as many [hours] to reading these royal productions', she

---

* What the Prince meant by his reference to an impending 'catastrophe' is not at all clear. Although, as the Prince's comment makes clear, Lady Hertford was in on the secret, she did not, at least for some days, divulge it to her husband. Bloomfield rather unconvincingly maintained that it had to do with the King's health which was once again giving cause for concern.

remarked, 'especially as George Lamb assures me it is all "damned stuff".' 'I really believe his Father's malady extends to him, only takes another turn,' wrote Lady Bessborough to Lord Leveson Gower. 'He writes day and night almost, and frets himself into a fever, and all to persuade la sua bella *Donnone to live with him – publickly*!! A quoi bon, except to make, *if* possible, a greater cry against him?'

Meanwhile, consistent with her reputation for caution, Lady Hertford was cool and aloof to Mrs Fitzherbert rather than openly defiant, preferring to observe a gradual decline in her influence with the Prince than a sudden and final separation. Thus, when the Prince was at Brighton she made it clear that while she had no objection to his spending part of his mornings at Mrs Fitzherbert's house, he was not to speak to her in the more formal environment of the Pavilion. For some time, she even refused to visit the Prince at Carlton House, unless her rival was present. Consequently, while Mrs Fitzherbert was forced to suffer the indignity of observing her rival publicly exalted, Lady Hertford was to some extent able to preserve her own reputation.

The Prince himself did little to help. When Bloomfield was rude to Mrs Fitzherbert, he turned his back; and, at best, he was weak and vascillating. Usually, he followed Lady Hertford's advice and simply ignored her; at other times he had fits of compunction when he remembered his vows and swore that she was still all-important to him.

In one letter to Mrs Fitzherbert, she was his 'only, only love'; his only 'pleasant' and 'interesting' occupation was in writing to her. He was a 'different animal a different being from any other in the whole creation' and 'every thought and every idea' of his 'existence' and of his 'life' could 'never leave' or 'quit' her for the 'smallest particle of an instant'. Yet, when Mrs Fitzherbert next saw the Prince she found him just as besotted with Lady Hertford as ever. On occasions, Mrs Fitzherbert remonstrated with the Prince.

His affair, she told him, had 'quite destroyed the entire comfort and happiness' of both their lives; it had 'so completely destroyed' hers, that neither her 'health' nor her 'spirits' could bear it any longer. What was she to think of the 'inconsistency' of his 'conduct', she asked him, when 'scarcely three weeks ago', he had 'voluntarily declared' to her that '*this sad affair* was quite at an end, and in less than a week afterwards the whole business was begun all over again?' She now desperately wanted a decision; he 'must decide' and 'that decision must be done immediately.... I beg your answer may be a written one, to avoid all unpleasant conversations upon a subject so heart-rending to one whose whole life has been dedicated to you, and whose affection for you none can surpass'.

The Prince again promised to reform, and again he relapsed, presenting Mrs Fitzherbert once more with an almost impossible situation. Finally, on 18 December 1809, she decided that she had had enough, and she turned down an invitation to visit him at the Pavilion:

> The very great incivilities I have received these two years
> just because I obeyed your orders in going there was too
> visible to everyone present and too poignantly felt by me
> to admit of my putting myself in a situation of again
> being treated with such indignity, for whatever may be
> thought of me by some individuals, it is well known Y.R.H.
> four-and-twenty years ago placed me in a situation so
> nearly connected with your own that I have a claim upon
> your protection.

She owed it to herself, she went on, not to be 'insulted' under his roof 'with impunity', especially as the behaviour of Lady Hertford and the 'arrogance and unjustifiable conduct' of Bloomfield had the 'appearance' of his 'sanction and support'. 'Something is due to my character and conduct, both of which will bear the strictest scrutiny, particularly with regard to everything that concerns Y.R.H., for after all that has passed between Y.R.H. and myself I did not think human nature could have borne what I have had to undergo.'

This time, there was no great display of emotion on the

Prince's part; he merely assured her that whatever she might
do, he would neither 'deviate from or forget' his deep 'affectionate feelings'; and most of his letter was about Minney. 'Always
with every possible kindness and good wishes towards you I
remain, my dear Maria, ever very sincerely yours,' he added.

Yet, while the Prince was obsessed with Lady Hertford, she
was not the only woman forcefully to capture his imagination.
Compulsively libidinous, he also had one eye on his old flame
Lady Bessborough. On one occasion, tracking her down to
her late sister Georgiana's magnificent villa at Chiswick, he
threw himself on his knees, clasped her round her neck and
showered her with kisses. 'I screamed with vexation and fright',
Lady Bessborough told her lover Lord Granville Leveson Gower:

> he continued sometimes struggling with me, sometimes
> sobbing and crying. . . . Then mixing abuse of you, vows of
> eternal love, entreaties and promises of what he would do
> – he would break with Mrs F and Ly H, I should *make my
> own terms*!! I should be his sole confidant, sole advisor –
> private or public – I should guide his politicks, Mr
> Canning should be Prime Minister (whether in this reign
> or the next did not appear);* then over and over and
> over again the same round of complaint, despair,
> entreaties, and promises, and always Mr Canning *à tout
> bout de change*, and whenever he mention'd him it was in
> the tenderest accent and attempting some liberty, that
> really, G., had not my heart been breaking I must have
> laugh'd out at the comicality of having [Canning] so
> coupled and so made use of – and then that immense,
> grotesque figure flouncing about half on the couch, half
> on the ground.

It took Lady Bessborough more than two hours to calm the
Prince down, following which he spent a further two hours
gossiping about Lord Leveson Gower. 'You know I am humble

* George Canning (1770–1827), the Tory MP; a particular friend of Lady
Bessborough; hated by the Prince, who disliked his intimacy with Caroline.

enough,' remarked Lady Bessborough, 'but I really felt revolted
and indignant at his disgusting folly.'

Still, in spite of these occasional lapses (and there were others),
no one really doubted that Lady Hertford was the central influence on the Prince's life during this period. She looked
after his health, she increasingly guided him in his choice of
friends and, most important of all, she dominated his politics.
Under her influence, he wavered in his once firm support for
Catholic Emancipation and progressively loosened what remained
of his connection with the Whigs. His canary-yellow carriage
was a common sight on the road between Pall Mall and Manchester House; and on some days he saw few other people
than the Hertfords.

When during November 1810 the King again fell desperately ill, thus heralding the Prince's long-awaited appointment
as Regent, she used their intimacy to argue the case against
bringing into office his old friends in a Whig-dominated government. The King might well recover, she argued, in which case
he was morally bound not to change the administration. Once
more, a Regency Bill was introduced, the Tory Prime Minister
Spencer Perceval fought tooth and nail in the House and, once
again, the Whigs spent many a happy hour in the delightfully
quixotic activity of forming their first cabinet. Grenville was to
become the new First Lord of the Treasury, Grey was to have
the Foreign Office, Lord Holland or George Ponsonby was to
be Home Secretary, George Tierney was to be Chancellor; while
something would also be found for the increasingly distrusted
Sheridan.

Unfortunately for the Whigs, however, the Queen gave forceful
support to Lady Hertford's view when, on 29 January 1811,
she sent the wavering Prince a letter, partly drafted by Perceval,
in which she implied that the King was now well enough to
hold an intelligent conversation. 'You will be glad to hear, my
dearest son', she wrote,

> that Mr Perceval has seen the King and communicated
> the state of the public business pending in the two

Houses of Parliament. His Majesty gave perfect attention to his report, and was particularly desirous to know how you had conducted yourself, which Mr Perceval answered to have been in the most respectful, most prudent, and affectionate manner.

This letter finally settled the Prince's mind; after all, he would keep the Tories in government. He wrote to Perceval on 4 February, stating 'at this precise juncture' his 'intention not to remove from their situations those whom he finds there as his Majesty's official servants' and adding, at the same time, that it was solely his concern for the effect any change of administration might have on his father's health, and not any positive merit in the ministers themselves, which had dictated his decision.

Accordingly, the Tories remained in power when, on the following day during a ceremony at Carlton House, the Prince was at last sworn in as Regent.

Clearly delighted, Lady Hertford held a large assembly on 22 March at Manchester House, to which the Regent and four of his brothers were invited. The Regent arrived just after midnight from a dinner at Lord Cholmondeley's, considerably the worse for wear but clearly changed by his new status. He was less voluble than usual, 'looked wretchedly', remarked one of the guests, Mary Berry, 'swollen up with a muddled complexion, and was besides extremely tipsy'.

With the Regency came new opportunities, so that when the Regent announced that he would be holding a grand fête at Carlton House in order to celebrate the beginning of his Regency, it was pretty widely believed that Lady Hertford was behind it, 'being anxious to be displayed thus publicly in an ostentatious state of vanity and influence'. Certainly, in a position of almost unparalleled influence, she decided who was and who was not to be included on the guest list.

The Prince was barely able to suppress his excitement at the prospect of the fête, and presented Lady Hertford with a dress. He also ordered one for Mrs Fitzherbert, but when she learned that now that the Prince was Regent, 'rank alone' would 'regulate the ceremonial' and she would not be invited to sit at his table, she furiously rejected it. They had an angry meeting; the Regent attempted to defend himself, but Mrs Fitzherbert refused to be placated. She was in any case in no doubt that Lady Hertford was behind this latest humiliation, and she wrote to the Prince on the following day:

> You, Sir, are not aware in your anxiety to fill your table with persons only of the highest rank, that, by excluding her who now addresses you merely for want of those titles that others possess, you are excluding the person who is not unjustly suspected by the world of possessing in silence unassumed and unsustained a rank given her by yourself above that of any other person present.

As she had 'never forfeited' her 'title' to the Regent's 'public as well as private consideration by any act' she wondered, ironically, to what could this new 'etiquette' be imputed?

> No one, my dear Sir, has proved themselves through life less solicitous than myself. But I cannot be indifferent to the fair, honorable appearance of consideration from you which I have hitherto possessed and which I feel I deserve, and for which reason I can never submit to appear in your house in any place or situation but in that where you yourself first placed me many years ago.

Henceforth Mrs Fitzherbert saw very little of the Prince; the final, embittered phase of their relationship had ended.

Meanwhile, with the restrictions imposed on the Regent's authority at the time of his original appointment due to end on 17 February 1812, much speculation was excited as to his intentions. Would he at long last bring in the Whigs or would he continue with some form of Tory administration? If he chose the latter, he could no longer use the King as an excuse, for by now it was clear that he would never recover. On the other hand, buttressed by Lady Hertford, he did not fully trust the

Whigs, and they disagreed on many important areas of policy.

For a while he toyed with the idea of a coalition government led by the Duke of Wellington's brother Lord Wellesley; then, rejecting that idea, he decided he would not have the Whigs at all; but for form's sake, and to avoid accusations of having deliberately rejected them, he would ask them to help form a government anyway. This mendacious offer was made to Lords Grey and Grenville in the form of a letter to the Duke of York, who had instructions to communicate its contents to Lord Grey. At the heart of the letter was the Regent's attitude to the war against Napoleon, a titanic struggle in which Great Britain had 'added most important acquisitions to her empire'.

> The national faith has been preserved inviolate towards our allies; [he wrote] and if character is strength, as applied to a nation, the increased and increasing reputation of his Majesty's arms will shew to the nations of the Continent how much they may still achieve when animated by a glorious spirit of resistance.

He then expressed the 'gratification' he would feel if 'some of those persons with whom the early habits' of his 'public life' were formed would 'strengthen' his hand by forming a part of the government. 'With such support, and aided by a vigorous and united Administration formed on the most liberal basis', he could then look forward 'with additional confidence to a prosperous issue of the most arduous contest in which Great Britain was ever engaged'.

As the Prince had expected, Lords Grey and Grenville angrily rejected his offer. 'Our differences of opinion are too many and too important', they wrote in their response to the Duke of York, 'to admit of such a union'. Consequently, the Regent sent for Perceval, who was confirmed as Prime Minister.

Naturally, most Whigs once again felt grossly betrayed by the Regent, and when on 17 February the restricted Regency expired, they burst out in a torrent of invective against him and the supposed authors of their rejection, the Duke of Cumberland, Lord Yarmouth and, of course, Lady Hertford. Soon *The Scourge*, a new and vicious monthly magazine, was on the attack as were the Whig *Morning Chronicle* and Leigh Hunt's radical *Examiner*. 'We all incurred the guilt, if not the odium, of charging his Royal Highness with ingratitude and perfidy,' wrote Lord Holland. 'We all encouraged every species of satire against him and his mistress.'*

Within days a caricaturist (possibly Williams) depicted Lady Hertford as the Philistine temptress Delilah 'depriveing SAMPSON [the Regent] of those LOCKS in which consisted his STRENGTH'. As Perceval her husband's nephew Castlereagh and Lord Yarmouth look on approvingly, she cuts a lock labelled Grenville, to add to a pile labelled Sheridan, Norfolk, Erskine, Holland and Moira. Fores obscenely depicted her giving birth to the 'Present Administration', and Cruikshank as the object of 'A Procession from Wales to Manchester Square. N.B. By Way of Yarmouth'. Yet, remarked the *Morning Chronicle*, 'when a woman

---

* Hunt's famous article in the *Examiner*, 22 March 1812, is worth quoting here, not only as a contemporary response to the Regent's politics, but also because it became the rallying cry of much Radical propaganda focusing on the Regent's private life. It originated in response to a 'vapid prose abjurgation' and a 'wretched poem, graced with epithets intended to be extravagantly flattering to the Prince', which had appeared in the *Morning Post* and was itself a response to an article in the *Morning Chronicle*.

> What Person unacquainted with the true state of the case would imagine, in reading these astounding eulogies, that the Glory of the People was the subject of millions of shrugs and reproaches! That this Protector of the Arts had named a wretched foreigner his Historical Painter in disparagement of his own countrymen! That this Maecenas of the Age had not patronized a single deserving writer. That this Breather of Eloquence could not say a few decent extempore words, if we are to judge at least from what he said to his regiment on its embarkation for Portugal! . . . That this Exciter of Desire (bravo, Messieurs of the *Post*), this Adonis of Loveliness, was a corpulent gentleman of fifty. In short, that this delightful, blissful, wise, pleasurable, honourable, virtuous, true, and immortal Prince, was a violator of his word, a libertine over head and ears in debt and disgrace, a despiser of domestic ties, the companion of gamblers and demi-reps, a man who has just closed half a century without one single claim to the gratitude of his country or the respect of posterity (Chester New, *The Life of Henry Brougham to 1830*, 1961, pp. 90–1).

forgets the just decorum of her sex so far as to exert a malignant influence over the Counsels of the State, the annals of
the Empire may teach her to expect sarcasm'.

In the Lords, during a speech on Lord Boringdon's motion
calling on the Regent to form 'an efficient Administration',
Lord Grey spoke of her as 'cursed and baleful', an 'unseen
and separate influence' which 'lurked behind the throne', which
had 'too long prevailed' and which was not

> less compatible with the constitution, than with the best
> interests of the country.... An influence of this odious
> character, [he went on] leading to consequences
> the most pestilent and disgusting, it would be the duty of
> parliament to brand by some signal mark of condemnation.
> It was his rooted and unalterable principle, a principle
> in which those with whom he had the honour to act fully
> participated, not to accept of office without coming
> to an understanding with parliament for the abolition of
> this destructive influence; which consolidated abuses
> into a system, and by preventing complaints from
> reaching the royal ear, buried all hopes of a redress of
> grievances.

While Lady Hertford was attacked for persuading the Regent to abandon the Whigs, she was also savaged as the source
of his change of attitude towards Catholic Emancipation. Now
that he was in her hands, Catholic Emancipation was said to
be a lost cause; and the same Lord Hutchinson who had discussed military tactics at Brighton in 1805, argued that the
Catholics had nothing more to expect of him.

Hutchinson's brother, Lord Donoughmore, went further, and
during a speech in the House on 21 April he launched a vicious
attack in which he described Lady Hertford as a 'matured enchantress'. Lord Holland recalled that 'the Regent was so exas-
perated at their language that he affected to lament that he
was not a private man and able to call one of [the brothers]
at least to account for a personal affront'.

There was trouble for Lady Hertford in Ireland too. During June, at an aggregate meeting of the Catholic Committee in Dublin, the reformer Daniel O'Connell, a brilliant and incantatory speaker, read a series of resolutions, moved by Lord Killeen, in which he stated that the 'promised boon of Catholic freedom' had been 'intercepted' by the 'fatal *witchery* of an unworthy secret influence'. To this 'impure source', he went on

> do we trace, but too distinctly, our baffled hopes and protracted servitude – the arrogant invasion of the undoubted right of petitioning; the acrimony of illegal state prosecutions; the surrender of Ireland to prolonged oppression and insult; and the many experiments, equally pitiful and perilous, recently practised upon the habitual passiveness of an ill-treated, but high-spirited people.

The 'feelings and interests of millions' had been 'coldly' sacrificed at the 'shrine of perishable power', and he congratulated Lords Grey and Grenville and the other Whigs who had 'stood aloof' from the 'allurements of intrigue'.

The Regent and Lady Hertford did all they could to defend themselves from this onslaught. McMahon suppressed and bribed, and Lady Hertford apparently wrote articles for the Revd Bate Dudley's *Morning Herald*. Most of the Regent's efforts backfired, however. For instance, when at a banquet at Carlton House on 22 February he used the occasion to launch a 'furious and unmeasured attack' on his erstwhile friends among the Whigs, Princess Charlotte, who hated Lady Hertford, burst into tears, thus leading directly to the lines by Byron which immortalize the occasion: the Regent was a 'disgrace', the 'realm' in 'decay': 'Ah happy! if each tear of thine/Could wash a father's fault away'.

Yet, if Lady Hertford and the Regent had little to celebrate at home, better news could at least be expected from abroad where, in the years leading up to Waterloo, the myth of French supremacy was decisively shattered. Like the many emigrées who lived in and around Manchester Square, giving it a sophisticated

cosmopolitan air and the name of *le quartier de Manchester*, Lady
Hertford hated Napoleon. She was therefore delighted when
at 1.30 on the morning of 15 December 1812, the Regent wrote
her a rapturous letter informing her that he had just received
the 'glorious intelligence' that Napoleon's army, battle-scarred
and in retreat from Moscow, had been 'completely routed'.
The Austrians had captured 20,000 prisoners and taken 200
cannon, and, had it not been for the 'fleetness of his horse'
they would have captured 'Bony'.

> All this is accompanied with a personal message from the
> [Austrian] Emperor to me assuring me in the strongest
> and firmest language that no proposal whatsoever *from
> any quarter* shall induce him to listen to anything like a
> peace until he has exterminated Bonaparte, and can enter
> into one with us and our sanction, and such a one as to
> liberate *all Europe from the tyranny of this monster or
> that he and everyone in his country will be and shall be first
> exterminated.* . . . I am really almost quite out of my mind
> (in a certain way that cannot be express'd) with joy. . . .

The Regent went on, practically delirious at the prospect of
eventual victory. 'Pity my scrawl, recollect that I am dying to
see you.'

Lady Hertford also played an important role in the celebra-
tions which accompanied the news of the defeat and abdication
of Napoleon on 6 April 1814. She draped Manchester House
with a huge banner bravely announcing 'The Prince's Peace',
and entertained the crowned heads and dignitaries who subsequently crowded into London. Unfortunately, neither gesture
was appreciated. The mob smashed all her windows and Tsar
Alexander I, to whom she was introduced, merely muttered
that she was 'mighty old' before promptly ignoring her.

Equally disastrous was Lady Hertford's sole meeting with the
brilliant and scintillating Madame de Staël (or Mrs Stale as
she was sometimes called), the brave and extremely resourceful author of *Corinne* and *De la Littérature* who also spent some

time in London. When the two came unexpectedly face to face at an assembly at Lady Jersey's,* Lady Hertford immediately turned on Madame de Staël one of her most scornful looks, having already given out that she was determined not to receive her as she was 'an *athiest*' and an 'immoral woman'. Many of the Whig ladies were outraged by her behaviour, and Lady Elizabeth Foster, the new Duchess of Devonshire, confided to her journal, 'I do hate ill-nature, and to a foreigner, too.' Still, the Regent refused to be bowed down by Lady Hertford's rudeness, and when he met Madame de Staël they had a long and intelligent conversation.

Yet there was more good news for Lady Hertford, when following Napoleon's escape from St Helena and the so-called 'Hundred Days', the Regent received at Carlton House during the early hours of 22 June 1815 the first dispatch announcing Napoleon's final defeat at Waterloo. Naturally unable to contain his excitement, he immediately sat down and wrote to her.

He described Waterloo as the 'most glorious victory' that had 'perhaps ever yet been recorded in the pages of history'. The 'tyrant' Bonaparte had been destroyed 'after the most sanguinary battles ending the eighteenth at night; the carnage most shocking'. The allied loss, he reported, had been calculated at about ten thousand men, that of the French at about thirty thousand. 'The accounts state that nothing can surpass the conduct of our troops of every discription; or, of the undaunted heroism with which they resisted the most daring and persevering attacks of the enemy'. Unfortunately, many of his friends had been killed, Lord Uxbridge (soon to be created Marquis of Anglesey) had lost a leg, while the Prince of Orange had been 'dangerously wounded'.

Yet secured at last on Elba, Napoleon, if vanquished, was not entirely humbled. In a conversation with one English visitor, he remarked: 'They say that [the Regent] loves the mother of this Yarmouth, but you English, you love the old women.'

---

* Not the Prince's mistress, but her daughter-in-law, Sarah Sophia, Countess of Jersey (1785–1867).

With the return of peace to Europe, a kind of calm settled over Manchester House. Lady Hertford, ever calm and dignified, continued to offer the Regent her advice, and still the Regent was a regular visitor. He would typically arrive at some time during the late morning, then spend some hours tête-à-tête with the Marchioness, before returning to a much larger gathering in the evening. They would then play cards, listen to an amusing skit from one of Lady Hertford's protégés like the wit and practical joker Theodore Hook, or spend the evening deep in conversation with her 'great crony' Lady Castlereagh or one of the ambassadors' wives, who flocked to these sometimes heavy and rather dour occasions.

A high level of formality was always observed, and on one occasion the dandy Captain Gronow, was shocked to be told that the Regent was deeply offended on noticing that Gronow was not dressed in knee breeches, but in the then fashionable trousers. 'The "great man" ... is very surprised that you should have ventured to appear in his presence without knee breeches', remarked Horace Seymour, one of Lord Hertford's nephews. 'He considers it as a want of proper respect for him.'

Lady Hertford, 'who was known as "the Marchioness *par excellence*" was then the Queen of his thoughts', noted one visitor, the Comtesse de Boigne. 'She had been very beautiful, but was now past fifty, and looked it, in spite of her dressing and tiring. She had a frigid bearing, a pompous mode of speech, was pedantically accurate in her choice of words, with a manner both calm and cold.' She was a 'great lady in every sense of the word' and she 'exerted a great influence' over him.

There was nothing secretive about these visits; they were loudly mocked by the Whigs, and Sir George Jackson was probably not the only observer to remark on the drollery of seeing the occupants of the houses round Manchester Square at their windows, whenever the Regent's yellow chariot came into view. Some doubtless thought of the deserted Caroline, while others perhaps remembered Tom Moore's celebrated lines extracted from the 'Diary of a Politician':

Through M[a]nch[e]st[e]r Square took a canter just
now–
Met the *old yellow chariot*, and made a low bow.
This I did, of course, thinking 'twas loyal and civil,
But got such a look – oh 'twas black as the devil!
How unlucky! – *incog.* he was travelling about,
And I, like a noodle, must go find him out.

Mem. – when next by the old yellow chariot I ride,
To remember there *is* nothing princely inside.

With her long experience of her son's affairs, even the Queen
seems to have recognized that Lady Hertford was necessary to
him. Yet while she herself had no compunction about receiving her, she would not allow the ageing princesses the same
privilege. They could, for instance, see Lady Hertford in company in London, but under no circumstances were they to be
alone with her at the Pavilion. As for the Regent, both the
Queen and Princess Mary thought it preferable that he should
meet Lady Hertford at Brighton (where she now had a house
connected to the Pavilion by a covered way) than that he should
'*always*' be living with her at Ragley.

While Lady Hertford was there to share the Regent's happier
and more relaxed moments, she was also there to participate
in the many personal sorrows that crowded his life in the years
leading up to his accession. On 6 November 1817 he suffered
a severe loss when Princess Charlotte died following a long
and excruciating labour. Latterly, after a difficult and unset-
tled adolescence, she had felt much happier with her lot in
life, and she and the Regent had enjoyed much better relations. Her marriage to Prince Leopold of Saxe-Saalfeld had
been a great success, their wedding on 2 May 1816 a grand,
and, unusually for the Regent, largely decorous occasion.

Unfortunately, the Regent happened to be convalescing at
Sudbourne when he first heard that Charlotte was gravely ill,
giving scope to the uncharitable accusation that he would rather
neglect his sick daughter than part from Lady Hertford. In

fact, he left for London immediately he was told, and did not stop travelling until he arrived at Carlton House several hours later, wretched and exhausted. The best advice then was that although Charlotte's baby was stillborn, the mother herself was not considered to be at immediate risk. Shortly after the Regent had gone to bed, however, he was awakened by the Duke of York and Lord Bathurst with the devastating news that Charlotte too had died.

One commentator, Mrs Trench, caught the public mood on the occasion when she wrote to a friend that 'no description in the papers' could 'exaggerate the public sympathy and the public sorrow. . . . The nation would have resigned all the rest of her family to have saved her'. Why was no relative at hand to supervise the birth of the 'expected heir', remarked her correspondent, Mrs Leadbeater. 'Yet I cannot think – I cannot bear to think – there were any unfair doings.'

The Regent himself went into a state of shock and, having paid his respects to the bodies of Charlotte and her son at Claremont, he locked himself up in a room at Carlton House and took to his bed. 'All his thoughts and conversation turn upon the late sad event,' remarked the writer and Secretary to the Admiralty, John Wilson Croker.

The Regent was ill for some time afterwards, suffering from a 'sort of mishmash, Solomongrundy, Olla podrida' of illnesses, which included a 'good deal of rheumatism, as much of cold, with a little touch of bile to boot, not a very pleasant mixture on the whole, and composed of as unpleasant ingredients as can be well thought of or imagin'd'.

The Regent kept Lady Hertford informed about the health of the Queen, who had also been ailing for some time. Physically frail, she had difficulty catching her breath, a condition that was not helped by her frequent fits of anger. She died on 17 November 1818 at Kew, instigating another period of widespread, though somewhat less genuine, mourning. Many people had not forgiven her for her perceived encouragement of Lady Jersey.

Once more the Regent was plunged into a depression; he

rarely left Carlton House, until his doctors persuaded him to go to Brighton, where he arrived on 8 December dressed in the 'strict incognito of grief'.

The Regent suffered a further bereavement when little more than a year later the Duke of Kent, the 'strongest of the strong' and a real 'Hercules of a man', died, aged just fifty-three, having inadvertently exposed himself to the cold air after a bracing climb up Peak Hill in Devonshire. He had hoped to survive all his brothers; now he left behind him a grieving widow and an infant daughter, Victoria.

Sorely missed (at least by the Whigs), the Duke was barely cold in his seven-foot coffin, before news arrived from Windsor that the sad old King himself had at last died, at just after half past eight on the evening of 29 January 1820, a blind, almost deaf, quite possibly mad, and thoroughly helpless figure.

Two days later, George, Prince Regent of the United Kingdom of Great Britain, was proclaimed King; yet rather than enjoy that day's spectacle he felt ill. He was copiously bled, but his lungs were inflamed and this heralded an attack of pleurisy. Not for the first time, many people thought that he might die. 'Heavens', wrote the witty and frequently malicious Madame de Lieven to Prince Metternich, 'Shakespeare's tragedies would pale before such a catastrophe. Father and son, in the past, have been buried together. But two kings! I hope this one will recover.'

Lady Hertford had other things upon her mind: for some time now, the new King had not been behaving towards her as affectionately as he had in the past. Indeed, the sight of her buxom figure no longer seemed to offer him the solace it once had done; he seemed bored in her presence, and unwilling to discuss the once heavenly charms of Ragley.

Thus, as the country celebrated or mourned the passing of George III, Lady Hertford grieved over the end of a beautiful relationship. 'She talks of nothing now but unhappy constancy and love,' remarked Madame de Lieven, who had received a visit from her on 29 January 1820. Indeed, in view of Lady Hertford's character, it really was an 'odd subject'.

Lady Conyngham

The courtesan Harriette Wilson knew all about Elizabeth, Lady Conyngham. She had a cache of her letters to a former lover, and had kept a close watch on her career as it prospered in London. Lady Conyngham herself, a greedy, shrewd, sometimes kind-hearted, beautiful, and extremely fat mother of forty-nine had long given out that she would make a conquest of the King, and during the final weeks of 1819, when he was still Regent, she achieved her ambition. 'I never saw anyone in such high spirits as he was at St Carlos's Ball,' wrote the observant Lady Cowper on Christmas Day 1819, 'quite merry and good-humoured as in old times – the scowl quite gone and all sunshine and prosperity, and this I am told is the present disposition – all powerful Love again rules his destiny. . . . Ly Conyngham has carried the day completely, and they say the other is quite dished.'

Born in 1770, Lady Conyngham was the daughter of an extremely rich merchant banker called Joseph Denison, a Nonconformist whose rags-to-riches story neatly illustrates the rewards of luck and 'continuous working and scraping'. Having arrived in London virtually illiterate and penniless, he soon became clerk to a wealthy Irish Catholic who, in a neat reversal of roles, later became clerk to him. Denison's first wife died without issue, and in 1768 he married Elizabeth Butler, a merchant's daughter, who bore him three children: William (later a powerful Whig MP and banker); Maria, who married Sir Robert Lawley (created Baron Wenlock in 1831) and Elizabeth, who in 1794 married Francis Pierrepoint Burton, Viscount Conyngham of Mount-Charles in the peerage of Ireland.

Shortly before her marriage, Lady Conyngham had fallen desperately in love with the extraordinarily handsome John Ponsonby, and would have married him had not his father, the irascible Lord Ponsonby, refused to consent. 'She adored him beyond all that could be imagined of love and devotion' runs Harriette Wilson's breathless account, and such were her sufferings that her parents 'trembled for her reason'. The two later enjoyed an affair which lasted until 1802, when Ponsonby became besotted with Lady Jersey. Possibly there were other lovers too, for the Tory politician Charles Arbuthnot, who knew Elizabeth well in her early years, later told his wife that he still remembered 'some of her tricks'. One lover may have been the future Tsar Nicholas I, who visited London in 1816, when he was still a Grand Duke.

Lady Conyngham had known the King well since she and Lord Conyngham had first regularly formed part of the King's circle in 1812. The couple were friendly with the Hertfords, and though not very active in politics, Lord Conyngham was known to be personally ambitious. In 1816, thanks to his wife's increasing influence, he was created Viscount Slane, Earl of Mount-Charles and Marquis Conyngham. Though mocked for his complaisancy, like all the King's mistresses' husbands, he was proud of his new-found status.

Naturally, the couple had ambitions for their children too, and were happy to see the King become inordinately fond of Elizabeth, Maria and their youngest son, Lord Francis or 'Frank' Conyngham. Lord Francis rapidly took the place in the King's affections once occupied by Lord Yarmouth. The two girls he showered with presents, adopting a winningly flirtatious tone, by turns cajoling and playful.

Not every member of Lady Conyngham's family shared her enthusiasm for the King however; her eldest son, the sickly Earl of Mount-Charles, was distant, and her brother was positively hostile. William Denison hated the gossip and hated the sneers. Years later, he looked to Mrs Michelangelo Taylor, 'broken-hearted' by the affair: 'not that even now he can suppose

there is anything criminal between persons of their age', but
'he never goes into society without hearing allusions too plain
to be misunderstood; and he lives in daily fear and expectation of the subject coming before Parliament'. Denison begged
his sister to go abroad in order to protect his name; she responded with 'bursts of passion and defiance'.

Lady Conyngham's effect on the King was transforming and
immediate. He threw money and jewels at her, became
furious with the Duke of York as a possible rival and declared that he had never been so much in love. At Carlton
House, the enamoured couple spent night after night holding
hands on a sofa, 'whispering and kissing' in the company of
Lord Conyngham and Mrs Fitzherbert's sister Lady Haggerston.
There were private parties at the King's secluded *cottage ornée*
at Windsor and a long holiday at Brighton, where Lady
Conyngham sailed about 'in great Glory' from her house in
Marlborough Row with her daughter Lady Elizabeth. She soon
established herself effectively as 'Mistress' of the Pavilion, giving orders to the King's servants, and even taking precedence
over the princesses.

'All the members of her family are continually there,' wrote
the diarist Charles Greville, if exaggeratedly, on 2 May 1821.

> She dines there everyday; before the King comes into the
> room she and Lady Elizabeth join him in another room,
> and he always walks in with one on each arm. . . . The
> other night Lady Bath was coming to the Pavilion. After
> dinner Lady C. called to Sir William Keppel and said, 'Sir
> William, do desire them to light up the Saloon.' . . . When
> the King came in she said to him, 'Sir, I told them to
> light the Saloon, as Lady Bath is coming this evening.'
> The King seized her by the arm and said with the greatest
> tenderness, 'Thank you, thank you, My Dear; you always
> do what is right; you cannot please me so much as by
> doing everything that you please, everything to show that
> you are Mistress here.'

No one thought Lady Conyngham's relationship with the King would last long however; it was hoped that she was too foolish to keep hold of him, and many people simply could not accept that a man of the King's age and position could fall in love. '*Le Prince Regent d'Angleterre, agé de soixante-cinq ans*', ran one early dispatch from one of the foreign embassies, '*a quitté la Marquise de Hertford, agée de soixante-cinq ans, pour devenir amoureux fou de la Marquise de Cunningham, agée de cinquante ans.*' The Tory Mrs Arbuthnot remarked: 'Pretty ideas foreign powers must have of our gracious sovereign!!' Others wondered at the King's presumption: the Austrian Ambassador's Secretary, Philipp von Neumann, who saw Lady Conyngham sitting side by side with the King at a concert at the Hanoverian Minister's, found it a 'curious sight in such a century as ours to see a King exhibiting in public his weaknesses', at a time when the 'dignity of sovereignty' was attacked on 'all sides'.

Unlike Lady Hertford, Lady Conyngham was ostensibly sympathetic to the Whig Opposition and, when fear of the consequences did not get the better of her, strongly in favour of Catholic Emancipation. She used her influence with the King to put pressure on the ministers to soften some of the more Draconian features of the criminal code, and encouraged him in his rudeness to his ministers. On one occasion, Madame de Lieven, the scheming wife of the Russian Ambassador, found her surrounded by a large pile of books on theology and explanations of the oath that English kings traditionally made at their coronations. 'He concludes that this oath obliges him to maintain the exclusion of the Catholics from all public offices and civil rights. She wants to persuade him of the contrary.'

To Wellington, who was Master-General of the Ordnance, Lady Conyngham boasted: 'I know your colleagues say that I am stupid; I will show them that I am not a fool.' She read all the King's official papers, intrigued with the King's Machiavellian Private Secretary, her husband's close friend Sir William Knighton, and stated that she would use her influence to bring down the Government.

Naturally, Lady Conyngham's ascendancy was resented by the Tories, and not least by the Duke of Wellington, who had entered politics for idealistic reasons and was sickened to see the Government's prospects in the hands of Lady Conyngham. Like most Tories, he found her vain and trifling; he was snobbish about her background, shocked by her apparent duplicitousness, and alternately bored or irritated by her conversation. He interpreted the mainspring of her relationship with the King as 'patronage and patronage alone': 'that was why she mingled in everything she could, and it was entirely owing to the necessary interference of the Government on one or two points', and the 'offense' given by the Foreign Secretary's wife Lady Castlereagh, who had not invited her to one of her parties, 'that her present animosity to the Government proceeded, and the consequent difficulties with the King'. Yet Wellington also recognized that although she spoke of the Government's 'dismissal' as the 'only thing one can do', in reality she was 'terribly afraid of it'.

If she did succeed in bringing down the Government, the Opposition would come in; they would dissolve Parliament, the new Parliament would be a Radical one; and the road would then be clear for a Radical Government, which would, as a matter of principle, bring down the monarchy. 'God knows where it will all end,' the Duke wrote in one despairing letter to Madame de Lieven. 'I consider a change of Ministry effected under such auspices would be the last word in disgrace and misfortune for the country.'

To Lady Conyngham's tearful charge that the ministers treated the King appallingly, Wellington replied that 'there was not one [of them] who would not do any thing for him'; that 'they felt how peculiarly he was situated from having lived a great deal in the world and from having many friends looking to *him personally* for promotion and favours'; and that 'they were always anxious to further his views on such points'; but that the King could not make promises alone, but 'could only act through the medium of his responsible advisers'. Mrs Arbuthnot, to whom the Duke gave this account of their conversation, reported: 'She had nothing to say to this except that the King was more disposed to oblige them than they to do any thing for him, and boasted that [the King] had *sacrificed his own feelings.*'

One question of patronage that particularly soured Lady Conyngham's relationship with the Government was her attempt to use her influence with the King to have Lord Francis's former tutor, an obscure Hampshire curate called Charles Sumner, advanced to a vacant canonry at Windsor. The position was not entirely in the King's gift, and the Government was furious.

'I feel it my duty to state for His Majesty's consideration that the Stalls at Windsor have been, with scarcely any exception, hitherto given to some clergyman of known character and merit, who had already filled some conspicuous situation in the Church, or to persons of family and connexion', Lord Liverpool, the Prime Minister, wrote frostily to Bloomfield. Castlereagh stated that Sumner's appointment would not only be 'embarrassing to the King's service and best interests', but it would likely give rise to

reflections unnecessarily *prejudicial* to all the parties who may take an interest in Mr Sumner's being properly taken care of. . . . The circumstance of Mr Sumner's having been to Brighton and being there pointedly assured of His Majesty's gracious intentions, will not I trust make any alteration in the state of the question because were it otherwise, this circumstance, for obvious reasons, would only form an additional objection to the thing itself, – the admission *privately to kiss hands* being, in our system and in these times, a proceeding which might give rise to the most serious observations both in and out of Parliament.

The Home Secretary Viscount Sidmouth was more direct; Lady Conyngham would 'ever rue the day' if through her 'generous feelings' towards him Sumner obtained 'such a distinction and reward'.

The King, however, pressed by Lady Conyngham, was adamant. He wrote back to Liverpool, stating that in view of
Sumner's 'strict piety, exemplary conduct and great learning',
the 'absence of Church preferment' did not on this occasion
provide a 'just ground of objection'. There the matter stood
for some days, with Bloomfield maniacally commuting between
London and Brighton, and the Government close to resignation.

Fortunately, Sumner stepped nobly into the breach, writing
to Bloomfield that he 'should be very unworthy of so high a
favour' were he to 'suffer any private feeling to interfere with
arrangements which may be represented to His Majesty as more
advisable'. He would always think of the 'manner' in which
the King's offer had been conferred as the 'proudest and dearest
incident' of his life, but it would be 'far too dearly purchased
if its consequences have occasioned His Majesty the uneasiness of a single instant'. Thereupon he was offered a private
chaplaincy instead, and a further spin in the crisis was averted.

With the coronation set for July 1821, Lady Conyngham threw
herself into its organization, arranging accommodation for herself in a private box in Westminster Hall, where a grand banquet
was to be held, and making sure that the pages, who were to
support the King's magnificent twenty-seven-foot long train,
were chosen from the families of the Opposition. She even
approached some of these families herself, which led to some
unfortunate rebuffs: Lady Jersey refused to consider any request except a written one from the King (which was duly
sent); Lord Manvers send word that had he been asked by the
King he should have considered his son 'most highly honoured',
but he 'would not for an instant listen to such a proposal from
any woman whatever', and he rejected her offer with the 'utmost indignation'.

At the coronation itself, it was noted that the King behaved
'very indecently'. Mrs Arbuthnot observed that he was 'continually nodding and winking at Lady Conyngham and sigh-
ing and making eyes at her'. During the most 'most solemn
and religious part' of the service, he suddenly took a diamond
brooch from off his chest 'and looking at her, kissed it, on

which she took off her glove and kissed a ring she had on!!! Any body who could have seen his disgusting figure, with a wig the curls of which hung down his back, and quite bending beneath the weight of his robes and his 60 years would have been quite sick,' she added.

Yet most people were delighted with the ceremony.

> The great sight was truly beautiful both in the Hall and Abbey [noted Lady Cowper], perhaps more from the brilliancy of the Spectators than from the sight itself, but the whole thing was indeed very handsome in the Procession and the variety and beauty of the dresses had a very fine effect. Much of the ceremony in the Abbey was Monkish and twaddling and foolish and spun out, but the music and the applause had a grand effect.

When Caroline attempted to enter the Abbey, she was decidedly repulsed, the King having given strict instructions that she would have no part at the coronation. 'Even the Mob and Spectators hooted her away after she had been refused at every door and walked through the crowd with only Lady Anne [Hamilton] and jostled by all the lowest rabble.'*

A few weeks later, Lady Conyngham slipped out of London for Holyhead, where one of the royal yachts was waiting to carry her across the Irish Sea to Howth. She had previously instilled in the King's mind the idea that a brief tour of part of his Irish territories would improve his standing in Ireland, and now that the coronation was out of the way he was determined that nothing should stop him. As early as February 1821 he was 'full' of the intended visit, particularly as Lady Conyngham had insisted that part of his itinerary would include a few days

---

* Naturally, Lady Conyngham did not care for Caroline; and on the Queen's arrival in London on 5 June 1820 from the Continent, where she had been living in 'exile', she had become ill with anxiety. For a while Caroline's chief defence lawyer Brougham had toyed with the idea of calling her as a witness at the Queen's 'Trial' for adultery, which opened in the House of Lords on 17 August 1820, a fate from which she was saved partly by her connection with Lord Grey and the Opposition.

at her husband's ancestral home, Slane Castle in Meath. News of his proposed visit amused Mrs Arbuthnot. 'We hear he means to go and stay at Lord Conyngham's!' she confided to her journal, 'which will please the Irish vastly!!'

Unfortunately, a dramatic counterpoint occurred at Holyhead on 9 August, when the King was informed of the death of Caroline. Physically frail and depressed, she had witnessed a re-enactment of the coronation at Drury Lane, a torment which at last proved too much for her debilitated constitution. For nine days and nine nights, she lay in pain at Brandenburg House in Hammersmith, before finally succumbing to what her doctors officially described as an 'obstruction of the bowels, attended with inflammation'. Though the King was not very upset, he was, in Croker's words, 'affected'. The woman he most loathed was now dead, and he had plans to make for the future.

He agreed that the court would go into mourning for six weeks, but he thought that the people's grief should be entirely voluntary. To Lord Liverpool, he gave instructions for reclaiming from her executors any jewels that belonged to him; and he was particularly anxious that the body, as it was to be buried at Brunswick, should be conveyed out of the country as quietly as possible. He would not cancel his visit nor would he feign the appearance of being deeply moved. He would, however, spend his first five days in Ireland in retirement at the Viceregal Lodge in Phoenix Park, Dublin, as a mark of respect to Caroline.

While Lady Conyngham waited at Holyhead, the King put to sea on 12 August 1821, arriving at Howth six and half a hours later, apparently 'dead DRUNK', having 'partook most abundantly' of wine and whisky punch during his voyage. He was met by an enthusiastic crowd, and someone cut the shape of his 'sacred feet' out of a stone on the quayside. In an excellent temper, he shook hands with a fisherman called Pat Farrell, and when he saw the Earl of Kingston, he was widely reported to have shouted out, 'Kingston, Kingston, you black-whiskered, good-natured fellow! I am happy to see you in this friendly country!' 'The people clawed and pawed him all over, and called him his *Ethereal* Majesty,' noted the Countess of Glengall distastefully. 'They absolutely kiss his knees and feet, and he is enchanted with it all. Alas! poor degraded country!'

Lady Conyngham, meanwhile, showed 'but little in public'. On arrival, she too took up residence at Phoenix Park, then on about 18th August she left Dublin for Slane in order to prepare for the King's visit. Naturally, she kept the satirists busy, and day after day she was taunted by the King's enemies.

> When I think on the hours I have sat on your knee,
> And the roll and the leer of your bonny blue ee;
> On the cut of that beautiful wig that you wore,
> And the curl of those whiskers, which now are no more:
> When I think on your front which, despising the ways
> Of thin Dandies, was ready to burst through your stays,
> When I think on your leg that has suffered so much
> From the gout, love, – and Oh! when I think on your
> crutch,
> I rejoice in the thought of still lending a hand
> To enable you, G – – – E, on the *right leg* to stand;
> And I rail at the ties of mankind, and no wonder,
> To think that such turtles should e'er be asunder.

The King arrived at Slane Castle during the afternoon of 24th August, having dashed across country from Dublin. Unable to contain his desire to see Lady Conyngham, he had rudely interrupted a carefully organized public breakfast held in his honour by the Royal Dublin Society at Leinster House; General Bernard, one of the guests there, generously interpreted his obvious impatience as due to tiredness, but it was clear that the real reason was his desperation to see Lady Conyngham. 'He travelled at the rate of 10 Irish miles an hour,' recorded one commentator. 'None of his suite were able to keep up with him.' He was escorted by a troop of cavalry as far as Finglass – then, sensing nothing but warmth from the crowds of loudly cheering peasants who lined the roads, he dismissed half his bodyguard.

Lady Conyngham met him at the front of the Castle, 'dressed out as for a drawing-room. He saluted her, and they then retired alone to her apartments'. That night Slane and the surrounding neighbourhood were illuminated with bonfires in the King's honour. It seemed that even the 'hills and mountains' were in 'one continued blaze'.

On the following day, Lady Conyngham and one of her daughters 'without a guard of any kind' took the King to see the obelisk at Oldbridge, which marked the site of the Battle of the Boyne; then on the Sunday they accompanied him to Slane Church.

Once more, he was mobbed by cheering peasants, some of whom 'pressed so violently' against him that one of his suite called on the military to force them to disperse. 'Don't mind them,' the King then shouted gamely, 'the people intend no harm.' Henceforth, they were, however, kept at a much greater distance, whereas 'some of the respectable classes' were invited to come forward to kiss his royal hand.*

Undoubtedly the highlight of the visit was the sumptuous dinner held later that evening, at which the King, Lord and Lady Conyngham and their guests were regaled with sherry, claret and hot poteen punch. Croker, who was there, remarked that he had rarely seen the King in 'such excellent tone and spirits'. He spoke much about the impressiveness of the surrounding countryside, gawped continually at Lady Conyngham

---

* Some years earlier, Richard Parkinson, Lord Conyngham's 'partner' in the management of his Slane estate, wrote a candid description of these same peasants, in which he emphasized their fecklessness and total lack of honesty: 'Generally speaking', they are 'all thieves', he wrote; they 'prefer telling a lie to speaking the truth, even when the truth would answer to them a much better purpose.' He described their execrable living conditions, their pitiful diets and their poor health. Yet, he did not think that they were 'highly oppressed'; the 'fault' was 'wholly their own', for they were 'lazy'. *En masse*, they reminded him of the black slaves he'd encountered in America on George Washington's estate, who were apparently treated worse than any other slaves in the country. 'Finding the Irish to be of a similar disposition, I followed general Washington's example as nearly as I was able, and it answered my expectation' (Parkinson, *The English Practice of Agriculture*, London, 1806, pp. 176–81).

and described Slane itself as the 'most beautiful place in the world'.

Another of the guests that evening wrote a glowing account of the King's behaviour, telling his wife that within two minutes of the King's arrival, he succeeded in putting everyone at their ease. The King is a 'perfect master of Society as far as it can depend upon Art,' he observed. 'The French word enjoué was never so applicable to any man.'

> Upon subjects, he is pointed and even eloquent, but it is the eloquence of conversation and not at all declamatory, and the pleasantry with which he intermixes them is given with all the advantages of great quickness with natural humour, a wonderful memory, the opportunities he has had of hearing, witnessing and collecting all the good anecdotes of every kind, and a talent for mimickry quite surprising. He talks a vast deal, but I think not from natural garrulity, but because his rank makes it necessary for him to originate every subject, and perform a kind of solo to which what others say is little more than an accompaniment. He listens with great good breeding, however, assents in an encouraging manner when he agrees with you, and his contradictions, though politely given, are frank and peremptory. He is a perfect story-teller, and has the art which nothing but constant living in good company gives, of keeping out of view all the flat parts of a narrative, and only showing you the points of the picture upon which the light falls. His attentions are very seducing and impartial.

Less impressed however was Lord Burghersh, one of the King's aides-de-camp, who complained vehemently to Mrs Arbuthnot that during the visit the King never once spoke to him; that 'at Slane it was the most laughable thing that ever was'; that the King 'never drank wine without touching [Lady Conyngham's] glass with his holding her hand under the table all the time he was drinking!! and that the Princess Esterhazy [the

Austrian ambassador's wife] told him that before her *Le Roi ne se genoit pas* and was constantly kissing her'. Mrs Arbuthnot responded with the observation: 'The Esterhazys do not seem much pleased with their excursion, for the ladies in Ireland took no notice of Lady Conyngham and she had no associate but the Princess who does not seem to have fancied being *Madame Commode.*'

None the less, from Lady Conyngham's point of view, the visit was an unqualified success. For a while the King seemed to soften in his attitude to Catholic Emancipation; and as he left Slane Castle once more for Dublin it was clear to everyone that he would have dearly liked to stay longer. On his return to England, he met Lord and Lady Harcourt on the Portsmouth to London Road and they heard him remark on the 'very great change' Lady Conyngham had made in his 'moral habits and religious feelings'. When, some days later, he again left the country for an historic visit to Hanover (this time, without Lady Conyngham, who could not persuade even the Princess Esterhazy to accompany her), he could hardly contain his pleasure at the thought of seeing her upon his arrival back in England.

'I hear from Brighton the King is shut up in his harem,' wrote Lady Holland on 24 November 1821, 'no egress or ingress; not a mouse passes. The streets are dirty, the wind high, and all unpleasant. Lady Conyngham walks at nine on the Cliff to maintain her health and beauty.' She also noted that the King had given Lady Conyngham his portrait in miniature surrounded by diamonds; and that he seemed 'cheerful and happy, and good humoured with all the world'. According to Madame de Lieven, who was unable to resist the temptation of passing on the information to Mrs Arbuthnot, Lady Conyngham saw the King everyday at four o'clock in her room, at which time her husband, who after a long quarrel with the Government had now been appointed as Lord Steward, and Lady Elizabeth would tactfully leave them. The King, Mrs Arbuthnot remarked wistfully, has become 'much more authoritative and is often cross with her. Madme de Lieven thinks

the passion is on the decline and that, having been exceedingly embarrassed to get Ld Conyngham into the Household,
we shall soon have an equal *embarras* to get him out'.

In their less passionate moments, both Lady Conyngham and
the King were much preoccupied with the fate of the King's
de facto Private Secretary Sir Benjamin Bloomfield, whose determined grasp on the Privy Purse, and thus over the King's
generosity, had long provoked Lady Conyngham's ire. Though
outwardly 'very civil' to Bloomfield, she was pleased to encourage
her son to take over some of his functions, while the King
darkly plotted his downfall with the conspiratorial Sir William
Knighton.

Bloomfield, wrote Greville on 19 December,

> is no longer so necessary to the King as he was, for a
> short time ago he could not bear that Bloomfield should
> be absent, and *now* his absence is unfelt. Francis goes to
> the King every morning, usually breakfasts with him, and
> receives all his orders. . . . and it is understood that
> [Bloomfield] has made up his mind to resign his situation
> and leave the court. The King is still perfectly civil and
> good-humoured to him, but has withdrawn his confidence
> from him, and B is no longer his first Servant.

In a roundabout way, Bloomfield received a 'curious proof'
of Lady Conyngham's role in the affair. A French acquaintance told him that he had been informed by Lord Francis's
mistress that Lord Francis had spoken of his mother's '*goings
on*' with the King and of her desire to 'get rid' of him. Bloomfield
'thinks the King will go mad,' reported Mrs Arbuthnot, 'such
is his infatuation about Lady Conyngham'.

With Sir William Knighton's help, the King constructed a
letter to Lord Liverpool. Brushing aside any suggestion of personal antipathy, he pretended that his sole reason for wanting
to abolish Bloomfield's post was that it was no longer convenient to the Government.

As the Government is now, I hope, fixed on a settled and
firm basis, I am desirous that we should have no
impediment or interruption to our permanent tranquillity,
if it can possibly be avoided. With this view it has
occurred to me . . . that perhaps it might be desirable to
get rid of the office of Private Secretary.

Yet, rather than make some provision for Bloomfield himself
he wanted the Government to take care of it.

Your Lordship must be aware that my feelings are
naturally tender and delicate, and therefore must be
embarrassed by a question of this kind, and the
Government will therefore feel, I am sure, that they owe it
to me to take this necessary measure on themselves, and
thus relieve me, by providing most amply for Sr Benj.,
from all the natural and innumerable inconveniences of
misrepresentation &c. &c. &c. which must otherwise
devolve upon me, and to which such a question will
otherwise naturally be open.

Fortunately Liverpool took the hint, drafting a letter for the
King which was then sent on to the despondent Bloomfield.
    Liverpool told Bloomfield that while the King 'rendered the
fullest justice' to his 'attachment, zeal and integrity'; and though
it was not from 'any preference to any other individual, nor
from want of any personal confidence', he had none the less
decided to restore the office of private secretary 'as nearly as
possible' to what it was when held by his father's Private Secretary, Sir Herbert Taylor; 'to limit the functions of the situation to the arrangement of his papers, the copying of his letters
and the occasionally writing what he may think proper to dic-
tate, and afterwards sign'; and that 'in future no communication should be made to the King upon publick affairs except
through his ministers, unless in those cases where the individuals making them are entitled to apply directly to the King'.
Liverpool tendered to Bloomfield the Governership of Ceylon,

'in consideration of [his] long, meritorious and faithful services', and the King added the further suggestion of a Red Ribbon and an Irish peerage.

Bloomfield, however, was reluctant to accept this offer; he recognized his value as one of the King's once most trusted servants, and he wanted a British Peerage; failing that, he would remain in England in the enjoyment of his present salaries, 'his pension and the Park at Hampton Court'. Having formerly executed 'all' the King's 'dirty work, such as buying up caricatures and the newspapers to keep his own and Ly Conyngham's name out of them', he set a high price on his loyalty. So when Liverpool met him in March, after twenty-four hours' consideration he resolutely declined the proffered Governership of Ceylon.

At this stage, Wellington intervened with Bloomfield personally, hypocritically assuring him of the King's 'continued kind feelings towards him', tantalizing him with his 'eventual prospects of an Irish Peerage and of admission to the Bedchamber', and urging him to accept the governership, 'making use of all the topics' which the King had already suggested, and 'such others as suggested themselves to his own mind, and arose out of the conversation'. Bloomfield, however, refused to budge.

Finally, the King lost his temper. He decided to do to Bloomfield 'what he formerly did by the Queen', wrote Mrs Arbuthnot pertinently, 'namely to drive him out of society. He is furious with anybody that is commonly civil to him and takes it as a censure passed upon him and a cabal against him. Nothing can be more unjust or shew more plainly that the King feels himself in the wrong'.

On 21 March, the King wrote an angry letter to Lord Liverpool, confirming his bestowal on Sir Benjamin of the Red Ribbon, proposing he should retire upon his full salary as Private Secretary and that he should 'retain his situation of Privy Purse in my family until the opportunity arises for his further elevation, by a mission'.

Finally, I wish you to state, that when the inordinate
power of the late office of Private Secretary is
restrospectively look'd at, I am bound to say, that the
Government have acted wisely, and honestly for the
character of all parties, when they recommended its
abolition; but I must however be plain, and therefore
have no hesitation in saying, that my ready acquiescence
in the measure was entirely influenced, by the embarassment and painful distress I suffer'd, in consequence of
Sr B—n B—d's unhappy, uncertain and oppressive
temper; and likewise the change that had been gradually
taking place for the last two years, in his general
demeanour.

In order to bring this last comment home, the King desired
that Lord Liverpool should read the letter to Bloomfield.

Bloomfield's response was philosophical: though naturally
'indignant' and in poor health, he did not let it spoil his chance
of further advancement, though he did, at least initially, draw
the line at going to Brighton to receive the ribbon from the
King in case it brought him into contact with Lady Conyngham.
Shortly afterwards, he was given a sinecure of £650 per annum,
then made Minister at Stockholm, where he became a great
favourite of the French adventurer Bernadotte, and converted
to Wesleyism.

Henceforward, the road was free for the King – presumably
with Lady Conyngham's blessing – to appoint the egregious
Sir William Knighton to Bloomfield's vacated post, on the as-
sumption that now that Bloomfield was out of the way the
same objections to the office no longer held. In victory, Lady
Conyngham could afford to be generous; soon even Bloomfield
was back on good terms with his royal master, 'the most en-
lightened and most benevolent Monarch that ever sat upon
the British throne'.

Meanwhile, Lady Conyngham was still unable to resist the
temptation to exercise a 'little petty spite' whenever the opportunity arose. In spite of at least one independent effort to

patch up the quarrel between her and Lady Castlereagh,* she repeatedly declined Lady Castlereagh's offers of a reconciliation. During May the King told her that he would be inviting her to an official dinner at Carlton House for the Prince and Princess of Denmark, who were visiting England. Lady Conyngham immediately voiced her displeasure, advising the King that she would not come to the dinner if Lady Castlereagh was to be invited. With admirable logic, the King replied that he could not then have the dinner; for he could not have the Prince and Princess without the Foreign Secretary, who could not possibly be invited without his wife.

Lady Conyngham insisted. The King submitted; but he sent her to see Madame de Lieven to see if she could 'arbitrate between them'. 'I summoned all my eloquence' wrote Madame de Lieven to Metternich:

> I pointed out to her that an official dinner, given by the King to a foreign Prince and to the Ambassadors, from which the Minister for Foreign Affairs was excluded would be in the worst possible taste; that not to invite Lady Castlereagh would be to offer a personal insult to her husband; that the advances she had been making for a year to Lady Conyngham were enough to atone for her past rudeness; that, moreover, she owed it to the King not to make difficulties with his Minister. I added that, finally, all the credit would be hers, and begged her as a favour to promise to let him have the Castlereaghs.

Still Lady Conyngham remained obdurate; and only after a long 'battle' was she finally won over.

Lady Conyngham also quarrelled with Lady Hertford who, together with her old friend the Dowager Duchess of Richmond, deliberately overlooked Lady Conyngham's undoubted

---

* Actually Lady Londonderry. On 11 April 1821 Castlereagh succeeded his father as second Marquis of Londonderry. To avoid confusion, I have, however, continued to use Castlereagh. Wherever relevant, quotations have been silently altered accordingly.

claim to become one of the 'patronesses' of a planned Hibernian Ball for the relief of suffering in Ireland. Lady Conyngham's response was to organize a rival ball 'under the auspices of a *new* set of ladies, that is, the old set, with the omission of the Duchess of Richmond and Lady Hertford'.

Mrs Arbuthnot, who went along to the Ball with Wellington and her husband, wrote:

> The [Opera] House was beautifully done up, the centre boxes to the top of the house were turned into a large sort of tent beautifully decorated for the King, and on each side were boxes for the Lady Patronesses and the Foreign ambassadors. . . . Everybody was in full dress and it was a most brilliant spectacle. . . . The whole *coup d'œil* was such as no country but our own could [provide] for the magnificence of the dresses and the beauty of the women.

Naturally, Lady Hertford was furious, 'incensed at this practical retort from her successful rival'.

So perhaps was Castlereagh. The attempted snub over the dinner for the Prince and Princess of Denmark fresh in his mind, he was still painfully alive to every one of Lady Conyngham's 'tracessaries'. He therefore decided to approach Madame de Lieven for some kind of explanation for Lady Conyngham's conduct.

> You have shown me my position, our position, clearly [he remarked]. Things cannot go on like this. We cannot put up with a Lady Conyngham who is powerful enough to offer us such affronts. . . . From now on, I shall be nothing more than His Majesty's very humble servant – we shall see how long these relations will last. If they do not last, I shall resign. I have done enough for my country and my master to be independent in that respect; and nothing can stop me.

Madame de Lieven attempted to calm him, immediately expressing her surprise that he could be so moved by what was, after all, just a 'women's quarrel'. But it was more than that to Castlereagh; in his anguished and overwrought state of mind, it was also a matter of 'honour' and 'pride'.

A few hours after their conversation, Castlereagh sent his brother Lord Stewart to see Madame de Lieven, and Stewart confirmed that upon the subject of Lady Conyngham, Castlereagh was adamant. Castlereagh was 'disgusted with everything'; and had long felt unable to trust his colleagues; now, thanks to this latest quarrel, he was close to breaking point. Stewart had 'never seen a man in such a state'; and he begged Madame de Lieven to get from Lady Conyngham an 'open declaration of hostility' rather than 'leave things as they are'.

Unfortunately, Lady Conyngham had other things on her mind besides a broken-hearted Foreign Secretary. Guided by Madame de Lieven, who hoped to meet her lover Metternich, she was determined to persuade the King to spend part of the summer of 1822 in Florence and Vienna. Lady Conyngham exercised all her powers of influence over the King, but she did not succeed in her endeavours. The King decided he would visit Scotland instead.

With the King set fair for Scotland, Lady Conyngham took the opportunity of planning a holiday by the coast for herself and her daughter Elizabeth, who had been unwell for some months. She considered both Worthing and Hastings, but it came to nothing, for on 12 August news arrived in London that Castlereagh had committed suicide.

For some time, a number of prominent people had been receiving threatening letters from an obscure man named Jennings and the thought of these letters coupled with the public's gluttonous interest in the events surrounding the exposure of the Bishop of Clogher as a homosexual, seems finally to have overbalanced Castlereagh's reason.

It became clear to the King on 9 August that something was very wrong with Castlereagh. Entering the King's study at Carlton House, Castlereagh seized the King by the arm and asked him if he'd heard the 'terrible news'; that he was a 'fugitive from justice'; and that he was accused of the 'same crime' as the Bishop of Clogher? 'I have ordered my saddle horses,' he said. 'I am going to fly to Portsmouth, and from there to the ends of the earth.'

'The King took him by both hands and begged him to compose himself,' recorded a horrified Madame de Lieven. 'They were alone. Castlereagh began again; he accused himself of every crime, he threatened the King, and then kissed his hands and wept; for half an hour, he alternated between madness and repentance.' Upon leaving Carlton House, Castlereagh met the Duke of Wellington, who listened to the paranoid ravings of the distraught Foreign Secretary and became equally alarmed.

Shortly afterwards Castlereagh left for his country house at North Cray in Kent. Upon his arrival he asked for the key to his pistol box, which was naturally denied him; he was immediately cupped and sent to bed. Madame de Lieven recorded that 'He sweated a great deal but he was not delirious; his pulse was fairly steady all the time.... He saw nobody' but Lady Castlereagh and his physician Dr Charles Bankhead.

Two days later, while his family were at church,

> he remained alone with his doctor and talked a great deal about public opinion. He asked what people thought of him, and whether they accused him of any crimes. The doctor begged him to be calm and not to talk of such things, as they excited him.... Presently he grew calmer.

On the following morning, however, while in his dressing-room he stabbed himself in the neck with a small penknife. Bankhead 'found him standing up, his eyes fixed. He cried, "*Let met all in your arms, it is all over*".'

The King was in Edinburgh when he first heard the news of Castlereagh's death, but Lady Conyngham, not having felt well enough to leave for her holiday, was still in London. The King had already told her of his conversation with Castlereagh, so, although she had never seriously entertained the idea that he would kill himself, the news of his death did not strike her as entirely surprising. She had spent part of 11 August trying to arrange a meeting with Madame de Lieven in order to talk to her about the Foreign Secretary's condition; and Madame de Lieven was with her on the 12th when the first unconfirmed reports of his suicide arrived. 'Castlereagh is dead,' is all Lord Francis Conyngham at first said. 'Good God', said Lady Conyngham, 'he has killed himself.' 'But no, Mother, he had an apoplectic fit.' No, Lady Conyngham repeated, 'He has killed himself; he was mad.' All thought of travel was now pushed to one side, and Lady Conyngham went to stay with her brother at Denbies, where she awaited the King's return to London.

The King's choice for the vacant foreign secretaryship fell on the Duke of Wellington, but Lord Liverpool was determined to offer the post to Queen Caroline's erstwhile confidant, the ambitious and mercurial George Canning. Without Canning's support, Liverpool did not think his Government could survive; yet the King and Lady Conyngham were reluctant to accept a Liverpool-led government with Canning.

When Lady Conyngham learned that Canning had been offered the post of foreign secretary, she let out a 'cry of alarm', drawing forth from the King the comment: 'Very well, if you like I will not appoint him; I will change the Government and put in the Whigs'. There was a further 'cry of alarm' for, as Madame de Lieven remarked, in spite of her friendship with the Opposition, she did not have the 'necessary courage'. Canning went some way to conciliate her by offering to Lord Francis the post of Under-Secretary of State in the Foreign Office, an offer which Lady Conyngham admitted to Madame de Lieven she would be a 'fool' not to take advantage of. Nevertheless, though she was prepared to offer Canning some support in April 1827 when he briefly became Prime Minister, their relations remained wary.

Meanwhile, Lady Conyngham was beginning to lose her hold over the King. In the earlier part of their relationship he had been totally besotted, but he was no longer so blinded by love that he was unable to recognize her imperfections. Sometimes,

he was angered by her bad temper and irritability, and he had
no illusions about her avariciousness. 'You see how she takes
advantage of her position to push her family,' he once told
Madame de Lieven. 'Oh, she knows very well when she is well
off.' He even perpetrated the occasional joke at Lady Conyngham's expense, and sometimes there were violent arguments.*

In the King's circle, Lady Conyngham was 'regnante'; and
even so practised a courtier as Lord Cowper almost blundered
into addressing her as 'your Majesty'. She was ignored by the
King's sisters, but that was just a matter of form, and though it
gave 'mortal offense' to the King, it did not affect her unduly.
Although she was bored and she often spoke about leaving
the King, she was too well rewarded to take the step lightly.
'What a pity now if all this were to end' she once remarked to
Madame de Lieven, after showing her round her 'fairy's boudoir'
of a drawing-room, 'for you must admit that it is charming.'

Among the King's most splendid presents were several valu-
able jewels, including the so-called Stuart Sapphire, which had
once belonged to the Cardinal Duke of York, the second son
of the Chevalier de St George or 'James III', the 'Old Pre-
tender'. He had sold it to the King who, in a 'fit of parental
fondness', had given it to Princess Charlotte. For Christmas
1824 he gave Lady Conyngham a 'magnificent cross, seized
from the expiring body of a murdered bishop in the island of
Scio', a richly embossed almanac and a 'gold melon, which
upon being touched by a spring falls into compartments like
the quarters of an orange, each containing different perfumes. . . .
I returned like Aladdin after the cave, only empty-handed,'
wrote Lady Harriet Granville, who was privileged to get a look
at these gifts. Her mouth watered, she told the Duke of
Devonshire, and the visit made her 'almost wish for a situation'.

* During October 1822, Madame de Lieven told Wellington that the King
had called Lady Conyngham a *'Bécasse, avaricious* &c'. Yet, he remarked,
the King's 'complaints' were those of an *'Amant malheureux.* . . . He threat-
ens however to leave her; and says there are many ready and desirous of
stepping into her shoes! For God's sake who are they?' (*Wellington and His
Friends*, p. 34).

Typically, Lady Conyngham and the King spent most of their days when not in London or Brighton (which Lady Conyngham in any case did not like) at the Royal Lodge at Windsor. If the weather was fine, the King would drive Lady Conyngham around the Park in his pony phaeton or take her fishing, a favourite pastime, on Virginia Water. There would be few guests, except for the members of the so-called 'Cottage Cabinet', principally Lady Conyngham's family, the Esterhazys and the Lievens. 'The utmost care' was always taken to 'prevent intrusion', reminisced the Hon. Grantly F. Berkeley, who held a position at the Castle; tourists were deliberately discouraged; while even the local clergy and some 'retired functionaries' who still lived in Windsor Castle, had their keys to the grounds taken from them, solely because 'some person' was seen to point at Lady Conyngham. Yet, although the couple's privacy was respected by the officers of the King's household, their behaviour was also an 'inexhaustable source of secret amusement. . . . Now the happy pair were talked of as Romeo and Juliet, then as Oberon and Titania; sometimes they were Hamlet and Ophelia, at others Ferdinand and Miranda, and – alas! for the devotion of courtiers! – not unfrequently they were referred to as Falstaff and Dame Quickly'.

Wellington, a frequent guest, wrote in September 1824: 'Literally speaking, I saw nobody excepting our own Company and two Men who, attracted by the Musick on the water, came down to the Bank to see and were driven off by the Keepers, in the same manner as the people of Constantinople are driven from the sight of the Grand Signor!' Repeatedly, he complained to Mrs Arbuthnot of Lady Conyngham's 'Nonsense' and 'vulgarity'. Angered by Lady Conyngham's rudeness to the King, he told her that 'having made the King's house a desert and having estranged him from all his own friends that it was now her duty to sacrifice herself a little to please him'. If she was bored, then it was her 'own fault'; she had only to 'speak the word' to have '20 people or 100 everyday' with them. 'As to her *character*, if she had thought of that two or three years ago it might have been very well, but that now every body knew her position and that she might depend upon it she would get much more abuse by abandoning the King now than she ever could do by remaining with him'. Wellington's speech made no impression, however, as Mrs Arbuthnot observed, for Lady Conyngham still 'persisted' in threatening to leave the King.

Following the death of her son, the Earl of Mount-Charles, at the end of 1824, her opportunity arose but, characteristically, she was unable to persevere in her resolution to provoke a permanent separation. She refused to write to the King, who took sulkily to his bed; yet, having wrested from the King the concession that she would be free to dine alone in her own apartments whenever she wished, by the end of March she was back with him at Windsor.

On the other hand, though he obviously still needed Lady Conyngham, the King was not above the occasional dalliance. Though frail, frequently bad-tempered and often in an alcoholic or drug-induced stupor, he still retained his eye for an attractive woman. During the spring and early summer of 1826, for instance, he convinced himself that he was totally in love with Madame de Lieven, and that the Duke of Wellington was his rival. He became jealous whenever he found Madame de Lieven and Wellington together, was 'very much more formal' with all the Conynghams, and used 'all sorts of little intrigues to force' Madame de Lieven to visit him. Finally, he sent a royal command.

> He began by talking about the affairs of Europe, then proceeded to the relations of his Ministers amongst themselves, and to those of the Opposition with Mr Canning; that went on for a good time; and then he came to his own affairs; and here is the strange confession he made to me. His mistress bores him; she is a fool. . . . He has been in love with me for thirteen years. He has never dared to tell me; he hoped I should find it out for myself. Today, an inner voice told him that I alone could guide him. Our minds are alike; our views agree; my tastes will he his: 'In a word, Heaven made us for one another'.

Madame de Lieven confessed that they were indeed in many ways similar; that they were more like 'cousins' than friends. 'Well, yes, that's true, that's true', said the King. 'But you are satisfied too exclusively with the spiritual side; I can't be content with that – I am really and truly in love with you, very much in love.'

Madame de Lieven rose to leave; the King then opened his bedroom door and asked her to look at a portrait facing his bed, which turned out to be a sketch of herself by Sir Thomas Lawrence. 'What do you think of this strange scene?' Madame de Lieven asked Metternich. 'I intend to avoid a quarrel with my new cousin. It will be easier because he is lying.'

A far more immediate threat to Lady Conyngham's peace of mind came not from Madame de Lieven, but from one of the King's former acquaintances, the beautiful and impecunious Harriette Wilson. Having what might be described as a proprietorial interest in all the Conynghams, through her affairs with Lord Francis Conyngham and Lady Conyngham's former lover Lord John Ponsonby, she had decided to blackmail Lady Conyngham. Initially she had demanded a small *douceur* in return for withdrawing Lady Conyngham's name from her notorious *Memoirs* of 1825, but inevitably she had become greedier. Later that year, she wrote to Ponsonby, threatening to publish some of Lady Conyngham's letters to him, which had somehow fallen into her hands, unless she was given a large sum of money. Lady Conyngham was unsure how to proceed and the King was frantic, when a satisfactory solution to their problem was proposed by Canning.

He hit on the excellent idea of offering Ponsonby a diplomatic appointment in Buenos Aires to get him as far away as possible; at the same time he bought up the letters with some money from the Secret Service Fund. However, it transpired that Harriette Wilson had had a spy employed at Carlton House, who, the King wrote, for 'upwards' of five years had been '*inventing, accumulating, and putting by to make use of when it might suit his purpose*' a '*mass of lies and horrors*' against himself, the '*whole Royal establishment, every individual connected with it*' as well as his '*best and dearest friends*', which of course included Lady Conyngham. When the spy's existence was revealed to him, the King became almost apoplectic, and he was determined that Sir William Knighton should do something about it. It proved difficult to reach an agreement with Mrs Wilson, however, for having accepted one bribe, she wanted another for keeping the first bribe secret! She approached Lady Conyngham who again paid up, fearful of publicity. This was too much for Ponsonby, who heard about the situation when in Paris during November 1829 and immediately wrote a letter of remonstrance to Sir William Knighton. 'What can Lady Conyngham have to apprehend?' he wrote. 'She has her perfect innocence to support her, and, *if the accusations could be substantiated they go only to establish my infamy*. I alone could be branded.' Only his 'unbounded respect' for what he conceived to be Lady Conyngham's 'wishes' had hitherto prevented him from prosecuting Mrs Wilson. 'If innocent people shrink from facing slanderers they will never enjoy tranquillity and the morbid delicacy that induces them to do so will be the chief instrument in the hands of their persecutors wherewith to inflict renewed pains and deeper sufferings,' he counselled.

> My grief and indignation at being made the *means* by which this abandoned woman is able in her pursuit of gain to lacerate the feelings of a person whom I have known so well, and known only to respect the more, the more I did know her, is almost beyond my powers of endurance.

Lady Conyngham's fear of Mrs Wilson's menaces contributed to undermine her health, and during the autumn she took to her bed, where she prayed a lot in the confirmed belief that she was dying. 'Halford goes there [the Royal Lodge] every day,' Madame de Lieven reported on 17 November. 'The King is worried and upset.... She faints constantly.'

Meanwhile, Lady Conyngham had had more success with her favourite policy of Catholic Emancipation: during April

1829, it finally passed into law under a Wellington-led Government, in spite of the King's repeated objections to any measure of reform for the Catholics. Rumour followed rumour; Wellington threatened to resign, and, at one point, it was widely believed that the Duke of Cumberland, who had hurried back from Berlin, was to assemble a force of 20,000 Kentish men, who were to go down to Windsor to 'frighten' the King and Lady Conyngham. Wellington's response to this threat was robust; he would, he told Mrs Arbuthnot, 'send the Duke of Cumberland to the Tower as soon as look at him'.

Day after day, Lady Conyngham was attacked in the press. She was represented as a secret papist, and a tool of Rome. There were caricatures too. 'Speak freely thou *Cunning-one*, and by *St George*, I will give thee Absolution,' says a tonsured monk in *Converts in High Life; or, An Anticipation of the Catholic Emancipation*. '(Let me see) a *Faux-Pas*, is no *deadly* sin, and loving other men, it is our duty to love each other.'

Though frightened of the Duke of Cumberland, she took every opportunity to put the 'Catholic' point of view, and her arguments were skilfully bolstered by her former *protégé*, the erstwhile Revd Charles Sumner, now Bishop of Winchester. Like Wellington, she believed that if the Duke of Cumberland had not come over from Germany, the King's behaviour would not have been so difficult; 'all would have been quiet', she told Wellington, and 'all would be quiet when he went away' again. But Cumberland refused to leave, though he was deeply unpopular and the victim of outrageous rumours. Now that emancipation had been achieved, he turned his attention to bringing down the Duke of Wellington's Government.

While Lady Conyngham made a good recovery from her illness, appearing by March 1830 'so embellie in point of beauty that she looks twenty years younger', in the words of one courtier, there was no such rejuvenescence for the King.

He had always eaten and drunk to excess; now, aged sixty-seven and in poor health, he was suffering the consequences. There was a recurrence of his old urethral problem, which could not be alleviated by drugs; he was increasingly dropsical;

and most alarmingly, he suffered debilitating attacks of breath-
lessness. 'He gets black in the face and his pulse alters when
he has these attacks,' noted Mrs Arbuthnot. 'They took him
out airing ten days ago and, when he got to the Lodge, he was
so bad [his doctors] were frightened to death and thought he
would die.'

In his most perverse moods, the King's 'mode of living' was
'really beyond belief'. One day, he said to one his servants,
who was about to sit down to dinner, 'Now you are going to
dinner. Go down stairs and cut me off just such a piece of
beef as you would like to have yourself, cut from the part you
like the best yourself, and bring it me up.'

> One night he drank two glasses of hot ale and toast, three
> glasses of claret, some strawberries!! and a glass of brandy
> [noted Mrs Arbuthnot]. Last night they gave him some
> physic and, after it, he drank three glasses of port wine
> and a glass of brandy. No wonder he is likely to die! But
> they say he will have all these things and nobody can
> prevent him.

On the morning of 7 June, the King heard from Halford
that he was unlikely to recover; so he sent for the Bishop of
Chichester, and in the presence of Halford and Knighton he
altered his will, leaving all his plate and jewels to Lady
Conyngham. The King had been gratified to learn that she
had cried on being told how ill he was; now she burst into
tears again, quite overcome by the King's unexampled generosity.

Later that afternoon, she wrote to Wellington disclaiming
the bequest, a course of action which brought forth from the
Duke a brief encomium on her high-mindedness. This 'fit of
generosity' quickly passed, however, and soon she let it be known
that she did not see how she could not take what the King
had given her, for she had told all her family and it could not
be kept secret.

Consequently, Wellington confronted her and told her that
if she did accept the King's gift her decision would bring 'ut-

ter destruction upon her character'. He threatened to make her a present of the *Memoirs* of Louis XV's celebrated mistress Madame Du Barry, as a warning, advising her to

> recollect that, within 20 years of the death of Louis the Fifteenth, the French King was beheaded, the French monarchy destroyed, and Madame du Barri lost her ill-gotten wealth and her head, and the original cause of all was the profligacy and profuse avarice of Louis and his mistresses.

As Lady Conyngham flitted in and out of the King's room, piously sharing his prayers, rumours arose of convoys of loaded wagons making nightly journeys from the Castle. 'All Windsor knew this,' remarked Greville. 'Those servants of the King who were about his person had opportunities of hearing a great deal, for he used to talk of everybody before them, and without reserve or measure.'

The end came on 26 June 1830 at about a quarter past three in the morning. No one was present but Sir Henry Halford and Sir Wathen Waller, another of the King's physicians. To Waller the King is said to have remarked, 'My dear boy! this is Death!' Shortly after, he gave Halford his hand and expired 'with a very few short breathings'.

Epilogue

Mrs Robinson

There was no easy solution to Mrs Robinson's continuing financial problems, in spite of Charles James Fox's efforts to settle her remaining business with the Prince. By 1 July 1784, it was again said that she was too poor to puff herself in the newspapers, and at the beginning of August she joined Tarleton in 'exile' on the Continent. Naturally, her departure was dressed up as a search for health, but there was no doubt that the real reason was financial. During January 1785 she offered to execute any orders the Prince might have for her while she was in Paris, as she did not 'dare' to return to England.

From Paris she went to the South of France, then to Aix-la-Chapelle and Spa, before settling at St Amand in Flanders, from where she kept closely in touch with literary developments in England. For Sheridan, she wrote a comic opera (never performed) and, apparently, though her authorship was never publicly acknowledged, most of Tarleton's *History of the Campaigns of 1780 and 1781 in the Southern Provinces of North America.* On 5 December 1785 her father died while a serving officer in the Navy of Catherine the Great; six months later, her own death was erroneously reported in the London newspapers.

When she returned to England in January 1788, Mrs Robinson soon renewed her support for Fox by taking an active role campaigning for Lord John Townshend at the 1788 Westminster Election. Then, eschewing any more direct involvement she turned once more to literature. Under the pen name of

'Laura' she was one of the founding members of the 'School of Della Crusca', an influential trend in English poetry. Hyperbolically praised at first, the Della Cruscans were subsequently trashed by William Gifford, a critic and Tory apologist, and others. Gifford's venomous treatment of her work and his particularly vicious personal attacks on Mrs Robinson were never forgotten.

The French Revolution awoke the sympathy of people of varying political complexions, and Mrs Robinson was no exception. However, she revised her sympathies in light of the September Massacres and, more particularly, the Revolutionaries' treatment of the Royal Family. She did not blame the French, taking instead the standard Foxite Whig view that the Pitt government had, by its very intransigence, forced the Revolution into extremism. For Pitt, she had nothing but contempt, mocking him in a series of odes for the *Morning Post* as 'the virgin boy' (Pitt was famously celibate) and a 'demon of sin'. When Tarleton was elected as a Foxite MP for Liverpool, it was widely believed that she wrote his speeches for him.

The huge success of her *Poems* of 1791 (the first of a two-volume collected edition) led to her first novel, *Vancenza; or, the Dangers of Credulity*. Shamelessly puffed like all her work, it was none the less truly popular and by 1794 it had reached a fifth edition. She signposted her growing radicalism in the following passage:

> IGNORANCE only descends to bestow admiration upon the *gew-gaw* appendages of what is commonly called RANK: it fancies it beholds a thousand dazzling graces, dignifying and embellishing the varnished front of artificial consequence . . . but the ENLIGHTENED MIND thinks for *itself*; explores the precepts of uncontaminated truth; weighs, in the even scale of unbiased judgment, the rights and claims of INTELLECTUAL PRE-EMINENCE. (*Vancenza*, II, pp. 26–7)

In 1794, *Vancenza* was followed by *The Widow; or, a Picture of*

Modern Times, an uneven but sometimes brilliant attack on aristocratic morals; and by four other novels.

Still unable to economize, Mrs Robinson looked increasingly
to the stage in the hope that a successful play would help her
to support her lavish lifestyle. She wrote a comic opera (again
unperformed) for the Duke of Clarence's mistress Dorothea
Jordan, and *Nobody*, a comic afterpiece. Premiered at Drury
Lane on 29 November 1794, *Nobody* was howled down on its
third performance by the partisans of a fashionable clique, who
objected to Mrs Robinson's portrayal of female gamesters.

There was a palpable transition in her life when she met
the anarchist philosopher William Godwin in the spring of 1796.
The two enjoyed a sporadically close, but always touchy relationship. Godwin considered sincerity in personal relations of the
highest value; they often misunderstood one another, and were
frequently at loggerheads. Mrs Robinson accused Godwin of
neglect and of mistaking her for a 'fine lady'; he accused her
of hypocrisy and of capriciousness in friendships. Yet she always
admired Godwin and he was one of the few 'literary friends'
to attend her funeral.

She also met the writers Mary Hays, Amelia Opie and, of
supreme importance for her feminism, Mary Wollstonecraft.
Her own *Letter to the Women of England on the Injustice of Mental
Subordination* (later republished as *Thoughts on the Injustice of
Mental Subordination*) is best read as a coda to Hays's and
Wollstonecraft's arguments.

For a woman often censured for her self-obsessiveness, it
was only natural that she would turn to autobiography. Early
in 1798, having recently separated from Tarleton, she began
her *Memoirs*. Though sentimental and highly novelized, they
attest clearly to her state of mind, which had become increasingly morbid and demoralized due to financial problems and
ill health.

During the winter of 1799-1800 she met the poet Samuel
Taylor Coleridge, who told Southey: 'I never knew a human
Being with so *full* a mind – bad, good, and indifferent, I grant
you, but full, and overflowing.' (Coleridge, *Collected Letters*, edited

by E.L. Griggs, 6 vols, 1956–71, I, p. 562). Both were working for the *Morning Post,* and both were interested in the imaginative effects of opium. Mrs Robinson's *Lyrical Tales,* published in November 1800, are strongly influenced in content, style and format, by the *Lyrical Ballads.*
In an odd and patronizing letter, Coleridge once wrote to Mrs Robinson's daughter:

Others flattered her – I admired her indeed, as deeply as others – but I likewise esteemed her *much,* and yearned from my inmost soul to esteem her *altogether.* Flowers, they say, smell sweetest at eve; it was my Hope, my heart-felt wish, my Prayer, my Faith, that the latter age of your Mother would be illustrious and redemptory – that to the genius and generous Virtues of her youth she would add Judgement, and Thought – whatever was correct and dignified as a Poetess, and all that was matronly as Woman. Such, you best know, were her own aspirations. (Coleridge, *Collected Letters,* I, p. 904)

After a long period of illness, Mrs Robinson died at Englefield Green, near Windsor, on 26 December 1800. She is buried in the churchyard in Old Windsor.

Lady Jersey

Following their separation, Lady Jersey and the Prince were barely civil to one another. He eyed her 'askance' whenever he came across her; she made it her resolution to 'plague' him. On accidently meeting in the gallery of Henry Hope's house in Cavendish Square, they treated each other to looks of the 'utmost disdain'. 'Didn't I do well,' Lady Jersey remarked subsequently to the banker and poet Samuel Rogers. Following a later incident at the Opera House where, not instantly noticing the Prince, Lady Jersey did not make room for him to pass, the Prince sent her a note by Colonel McMahon desiring that henceforth she would '*not speak to him*'.

She remained a coquette well into her forties, and in 1800 Sarah Lady Lyttelton described her as 'still very beautiful, very full of affectation, and nothing can persuade her that she is more than thirty'. One of her targets was the handsome John Ponsonby, Lady Conyngham's lover, who in January 1803 married Lady Jersey's daughter Lady Frances Villiers.

Indeed, the affairs of her daughters were one of Lady Jersey's greatest passions. Lady Bessborough was much alarmed when she saw Lady Jersey pushing Lady Elizabeth Villiers together with her son Lord Duncannon. 'John admires her,' she wrote, 'and is of course flatter'd with the fuss they make of him, but I am sure has not a thought further than liking to talk to a very pretty Girl who marks a strong preference for him.' Lady Jersey, she added, mocked Ducannon for still being in 'apron strings' (Lord Granville Leveson Gower, *Private Correspondence*, I, p. 364).

In spite of her often cruel treatment of her husband, Lady Jersey was genuinely saddened when he died from a heart attack while out walking with his family in 1805. She told Lady Bessborough that she 'could form no Idea of what it was to be separated for ever in one moment from a person who had been one's constant companion for five and thirty years, and who, when all the world deserted her, continued to shew her undiminish'd and unremitting kindness' (*Private Correspondence*, II, p. 109). She was, however, ably comforted by her daughter-in-law Sarah, the new Countess of Jersey, who was herself something of a siren.

After her husband's death, Lady Jersey was often desperately short of money and during 1811, Colonel McMahon persuaded her to write to the Prince, putting in a request for a pension. She was reluctant to do this, but McMahon told her that it was the Prince's wish, for he was 'hurt' at reports that she was in an 'uncomfortable situation'. However, the request was ill received, leading Lady Jersey to remark to McMahon that she had now put herself 'in the disgraceful shape of a beggar!' (George IV, *Letters*, I, p. 216).

The Prince had suspected Lady Jersey of advising Princess Caroline, an accusation she forcefully refuted, claiming that she had had no contact with the Princess either 'directly or indirectly' since she had sent her her notorious letter of resignation.

If your Royal Highness recollects my character you will remember that to *advise* was never my taste, and if *truth* respecting me has reached your Royal Highnesses ears you will know that I have ever expressed myself with that dutyful respect, and attachment to your Royal Highnesses interests which I ought to feel (George IV, *Letters*, I, p. 240).

The pension, however, was not forthcoming.
Lady Jersey died at Cheltenham on 25 July 1821.

Mrs Fitzherbert

While Mrs Fitzherbert's refusal to attend the fête at Carlton House effectively brought to an end her public life with her husband, it did not of course conclude all her relations with the Regent. There was, for instance, the small matter of Minney Seymour, whom the Regent obviously still loved; and there was the question of Mrs Fitzherbert's income.

In 1808, her annuity had been raised from £3,000 to £6,000 on the understanding that the provisions of the Prince's will of 1796 would no longer be binding. However, since Mrs Fitzherbert had contracted large debts during her association with the Prince, which had yet to be paid off, this seemingly generous settlement did not prove satisfactory.

In 1814 she wrote: 'You will, I am sure, do me [the] justice to acknowledge that I never was an interested person; that I never which I certainly might have done solicited for, or benefited either my family or my friends at your expense.' Yet Minney's education was expensive, her own health was not good and 'comforts' at her 'time of life' and under her 'unfortunate circumstances' had 'become necessary'. She was, she added, 'very well informed' that his ear had been 'frequently assailed by malignant insinuation[s]' against her but she denied these, citing as 'no stronger proof' the fact that she had not made use of the compromising documents she had in her possession. 'Let me implore you, therefore, to answer this letter and to believe that, notwithstanding all your prejudices against me and all the misery and wretchedness you have entailed upon me, I most sincerely wish you every degree of happiness, health and prosperity.' (Sir Shane Leslie, *George the Fourth*, 1926, pp. 196–7).

Although there was no immediate response to this letter, Mrs Fitzherbert's income was raised to £8,000 per annum in 1820, and again to £10,000 before the King's death in 1830.

Both Mrs Fitzherbert and the King had wanted Minney Seymour to marry into the higher reaches of the aristocracy; they were therefore both disappointed when in 1825 she married Colonel George Dawson, an impoverished but handsome younger son of the first Earl of Portarlington. However, they were reconciled to Minney's decision, and on her marriage the King sent Minney a letter, begging her to 'be always good to my dear old friend, Mrs Fitzherbert'.

During the King's last illness, Mrs Fitzherbert wrote him a final letter. Although the King 'seized it with eagerness', he did not – perhaps because he was to ill to do so – answer it. He did, however, insist that a miniature of her by Richard Cosway should be placed round his neck. It was buried with him.

With the accession of William IV, Mrs Fitzherbert's position became more secure. The new King honoured her with a 'personal communication' at her own house, before she paid him a visit at the Pavilion. On placing her collected papers and his brother's will in the King's hands, he was 'moved to tears' on their perusal. 'He asked her what amends he could make her, and offered to make her a Duchess.' Her reply was that 'she had borne through life the name of Mrs Fitzherbert; that she had never disgraced it, and did not wish to change it.' William did, however, insist on her wearing the royal livery (Langdale, *Memoirs*, pp. 137–8).

In spite of ill health, Mrs Fitzherbert remained active well into old age, travelling widely. In 1835, for instance, she paid a visit to Aix-la-Chapelle and Paris. For Brighton she retained a particular affection, keeping a house there as well as one in London.

She died on 27 March 1837, and was buried in St John the Baptist's Church at Brighton.

Lady Hertford

However much Lady Conyngham and the King would have liked to be rid of Lady Hertford, until the retirement of her husband from the position of Lord Chamberlain in July 1821, Lady Hertford still had access to the court. The King abused her to his friends and was furious with anyone who visited her. In 1821, he reminisced to Mrs Pole that Lady Hertford had always been 'finding fault and abusing him', whereas now that he was together with Lady Conyngham, he 'found himself well with every body' and 'every thing was smooth' (Mrs Arbuthnot's *Journal*, I, p. 79). Under these circumstances, many of Lady Hertford's friends deserted her, not wanting to risk the loss of favour at court.

Following the death of Lord Hertford, Mrs Fitzherbert spotted Lady Hertford at Brighton in 1824. She told Minney Seymour that though Lady Hertford 'inhabited one of the largest houses', she was 'quite alone and nobody saw her. She sent to Mrs de Crespigny to ask her to tea but that great lady sent an excuse saying she had Colonel Whalley and Mr Wall with her and could not have the honour. Think of Lady Hertford making up to Mrs de Crespigny!' (Mrs Fitzherbert, *Letters*, p. 172).

In 1825 Lady Hertford went to Paris, but was still out of sorts; 'seemed pleased' for a while at a dinner, but was 'very grand and abusing everything'. When Lady Harriet Granville, noting her ill temper, asked her why she had come, she was unable to give her an answer.

Yet she never lost her appetite for politics, and during the spring of 1829 she was much in the company of the Duke of Cumberland, who had hurried over from Berlin to do everything possible to oppose the Catholic Relief Bill. Sir William Knighton took the fanciful view during April that if the Duke 'stays in England ... he will oust Lady Conyngham and reinstate' her.

She wrote to the King on his deathbed, but he could not or would not reply.

She died in 1834.

Lady Conyngham

After the King's death and Lady Conyngham's rapid departure from Windsor, Lady Conyngham and her family were the subject of 'innumerable' rumours. They were said to have stolen from the late King pictures, furniture and jewels. Countess Brownlow recalled one story that Lady Conyngham was actually discovered trying to take from the dead King's neck a key which she supposed opened a closet containing a rich treasury of valuables. The Conynghams left Windsor 'without even showing the decent respect of appearing in mourning; their carriages loaded with packages of all shapes and sizes covered with matting, and containing, as Sir Frederick Watson (Master of the Household) believed, clocks, china, etc., purloined from different rooms, and which disappeared with them!' (Emma Sophia Cust, Countess Brownlow, *The Eve of Victorianism*, 1940, p. 137–8.)

The public were particularly concerned about the fate of Lady Conyngham's collection of jewels, many of which were rightly supposed to be crown property. On 27 November 1830, however, in accordance with a request from Lady Conyngham, these were placed in the hands of the jewellers Rundell and Bridge, who in turn handed them over to the late King's executors. The parcel contained an immense hoard, including 'Brilliants belonging to His late Majesty King George 3s Sword, ...

Brilliants supposed to have arisen from a Picture of Her late Majesty Queen Charlotte, A Badge of the Bath of King George 3d, Three Brilliant and Pearl Bows, [and] A Single Stone Brilliant Ring' (Mrs Arbuthnot's *Journal*, II, p. 444). The Stuart Sapphire, however, which Lady Conyngham had also returned, was not considered crown property, and King William gave orders that Lady Conyngham be allowed to keep it.

Subsequently, the Conyngham family left London for Paris where, in contrast to her reception in London, Lady Conyngham was much fêted and her beauty much admired. 'She is wonderful,' Lady Harriet Granville wrote, 'as fresh as a daisy, *bouche comme une rose*, in a light blue gauze hat with white feathers, a salmon-coloured gown made extremely high with long sleeves; she looked infinitely handsomer than when in a satin frock, swaddled in jewels.' Lady Conyngham's husband, she added, had 'grown larger and meeker' (Harriet Countess Granville, *Letters*, 2 vols, 1894, II, pp. 107–08).

After Lord Conyngham's death on 28 December 1832, Lady Conyngham became increasingly pious and reclusive. She seems to have regretted her former life with the King, and retired to her estate at Bifrons near Canterbury. There, according to her granddaughter Lady Treowen, looking 'very different . . . from all those regrettably coarse and scandalous caricatures', she occupied herself in charitable works (Osbert Sitwell, *Left Hand, Right Hand!* 1945, p. 72).

In 1837 she donated to Patrixbourne Church a remarkable collection of Swiss stained glass, and in 1849 and again in 1857 she paid for the church's restoration. She died on 11 October 1861, aged ninety-one, and is buried inside the church, where there is a monument to her and her husband.

Appendix

The Illegitimate Children of George IV

The question of George IV's illegitimate children naturally falls into three categories: those children the King himself tacitly or unambiguously acknowledged; children he is said to have fathered on Mrs Fitzherbert; and children he is believed to have fathered on other women.

The first category is headed by George Seymour Crole, a sometime major in the 41st Foot. The King is known to have fathered him on Elizabeth Fox, otherwise known as Mrs Crole, the former mistress of Lord Egremont. Born on 23 August 1799 and described by his mother as a 'very gentlemanlike young man quiet and unpresuming', he was given a passing nod by the King in 1823 when, during a discussion of the provisions of his will with Lord Eldon, he mentioned that he 'thought himself bound' to leave him a legacy of £30,000. Like Mrs Robinson, Mrs Crole was awarded an annuity of £500, at about the time of her son's birth; until 1823, this was listed in the Privy Purse Pension Book as a payment to Charles Bicknell, the King's solicitor. Crole himself received numerous handouts, including the substantial sum of £10,000 paid to him on 12 August 1831 by Knighton and the Duke of Wellington, who were acting as the late King's executors. In 1832 he retired from the army, to settle at Chatham where, 'widely respected', he apparently 'gained a reputation for being a generous if somewhat eccentric character'. He died on 13 June 1863 and was buried in Highgate Cemetery (Lydia Collins, 'George

Seymour Crole – A Son of King George IV', *The Genealogists Magazine*, Sept. 1984, pp. 228–35).

The other child that the King is thought to have acknowledged was called William Francis. The putative son of an adventuress called Mrs Davies, he was born in 1806 and educated at a school in Parsons Green. His 'mother' received an annuity of £400, from the Privy Purse, which at her death in 1817 was converted to an annuity of £200 paid to her son. Unfortunately, in 1820 doubts were raised about his parentage and in 1823 this pension was discontinued. There is no further information about him; neither he nor Crole is thought to have had children (Collins, pp. 232–3).

Mrs Fitzherbert, at least on paper, never denied having had George IV's children. When invited to do so by her relative Lord Stourton, she 'smilingly objected on the score of delicacy'. However, though much work has been done by, among others, the late Jim Foord-Kelcey (who seems to have believed himself a descendant of the King and Mrs Fitzherbert (see *Mrs Fitzherbert and Sons*, 1991), no one has satisfactorily proved that Mrs Fitzherbert had any children by the King, so the case must remain open.

More or less compelling cases have been made for Mary Anne Smythe, who lived with Mrs Fitzherbert from about 1812, as one of her adopted daughters (Leslie, *Mrs Fitzherbert*, pp. 390–4); for James Ord, a Catholic, who was educated in America (Hibbert, *George IV Prince of Wales*, p. 63n); for Mrs Jane Bowman, Mills or Atkinson, who was born in 1801 (Joanna Richardson, *The Disastrous Marriage*, 1960, pp. 242–3); and for a Mrs Sophia Elizabeth Guelph Sims, a 'well dressed female of respectable appearance', who in June 1839 is reported to have waited upon the Lord Mayor 'for the purpose of soliciting his Lordship's assistance in proving that she was the daughter of Mrs Fitzherbert by George IV, in order that she might obtain, not honours and distinctions, but a sum of money which was left for her maintenance and education'. The Lord Mayor was unimpressed:

'What proof is there that there was any child at all
resulting from what you call the union, but what
everybody knew could be no union at all? . . . What! were
you born without [Mrs Fitzherbert's] knowledge?'

   'Mrs Guelph Sims [said] – She supposed that her child
was stillborn, and was never told to the contrary.'

   'If George IV knew it, I am sure that he would have
made provision for you. . . . I can only tell you that the
Lord Mayor cannot do it' (Mrs Fitzherbert, *Letters*, p. 75).

There is a similar lack of proof regarding children in the
third category, including George Lamb (Prince of Wales, *Correspondence*, VI, p. 377n); Georgiana Augusta Frederica Seymour
(see p. 31); and Lady Jersey's son (see p. 88). The evidence,
such as it is, is no more than circumstantial, as none of these
children, as far as we know, was ever acknowledged by the
King.

When Georgiana was first shown to the King, he is said to
have remarked, 'To convince me that this is my girl they must
first prove that black is white' (Horace Bleakley, *Ladies Fair
and Frail*, 1909, p. 219). In pursuit of this doubtlessly quixotic
object, her mother Grace Dalrymple Eliot is said to have whitened
the infant's eyebrows. Nevertheless, Georgiana later became
quite a celebrated personage; in 1808 she married a son of
the third Duke of Portland, Lord Charles William Bentinck.

Sources

Mrs Robinson

Mary Hamilton's *Letters and Diaries* (1925), 88; The Duchess of Devonshire's *Correspondence*, 289 (for the Duchess on the Prince's appearance and character); 291 (for Lord George Cavendish's discovery of the Prince and Mrs Armistead) and 292 (for the Prince's illness in 1781; Horace Walpole's *Last Journals* (2 vols, 1910), II: 360 and 361 (for the Prince's crude reference to the Princess Royal and for the incident at Lord Chesterfield's house); John King's *Letters from Perdita to a certain Israelite* (1781), ii; *Authentic Memoirs, Memorandum's and Confessions. Taken from the Journal of the Predatorial Majesty, the King of the Swindlers* (n.d.), 111; Fortescue's edition of George III's *Correspondence* (6 vols, 1927–8), vol. V, 269–70 (for the King's letter to Lord North and his reply); Lord Glenbervie's *Diaries* (2 vols, 1928), II: 6 (for Lord North's opinion of the Prince's letters); *A Poetical Epistle from Florizel to Perdita* (1781), 8 and 17 (for Mrs Robinson's 'ministerial' politics); The Countess of Ilchester's *Life and Letters of Lady Sarah Lennox* (2 vols, 1901), II: 25–6 (for the Napier quotation); The Duc de Lauzun's *Memoirs* (1928), 211; *The Festival of Wit* (1783), 76 (for George Selwyn's quip) and 129 (for Fox's justification for spending so much time with Mrs Robinson); *The Vis-A-Vis of Berkley-Square* (1783), 24 (for Mrs Robinson's carriage); M.J. Levy's edition of Mrs Robinson's *Memoirs* (1994), 20–1 (for Mrs Robinson's and her brother's appearance as children); 23–4 (for Nicholas Darby's 'wild and romantic' scheme); 32–3 (for his response to the knowledge that Hester Darby had opened a school); 37 (for Mrs Robinson and Garrick); 39 (for Hester Darby on Thomas Robinson); 54 and 58–60 (for Mrs Robinson, Lyttelton and the 'Harriet Wilmot' incident); 80–1 (for Mrs Robinson and the Duchess of Devonshire); 88

(for Mrs Robinson's début); 101–6 and 110–19 (for Mrs Robinson
and the Prince) and 121–2 (for Mrs Robinson and the Duc de Chartres); George IV's *Correspondence* (as Prince of Wales), I: 34–5; 54–6;
60; 65–9 and 72; The Capel Manuscripts, FH/IX/2, 3, 7, 8, 10, 16
and 23 (for Lord Malden's negotiations with Lieutenant-Colonel
Hotham for the return of the Prince's letters to Mrs Robinson); the
Morning Post, 11 and 13 December 1776; 12 February 1780; 7 October
1780 (for Thomas Robinson and the 'fillette'), 16 November 1780
(for the anonymous friend's letter to the newspapers, begging restraint
in their coverage of Mrs Robinson); 16 December 1780; 3 August
1781, 7 August 1782 (for the contrasting behaviour of Fox and Pitt);
21 September 1782 and 13 July 1784; the *Morning Herald*, 5 January
1781; 24 January 1781 (for the description of Mrs Armistead as the
'*High Priestess of Patriotism*'); 3 May 1781 (for the reference to Mrs
Robinson's 'elegant villa'); 4 August 1781; 3 September 1782 (for
the Biblical parody on Fox) and 16 June 1783 (for the reference to
Mrs Robinson's carriage as the 'aggregate of a few stakes' at Brooks's);
and the *Morning Chronicle*, 11 December 1776.

Mrs Fitzherbert

Langdale's *Memoirs*, 30; 113–14; 118–19 and 123–5; Malcolm Elwin's
The Noels and the Milbankes (1967), 254; *English Historical Documents*
(1953), vol. VIII, 107 (for the Royal Marriage Act); The Duchess of
Devonshire's *Correspondence*, 86–8 (for the Duchess's recollections of
the Prince's suicide attempt and Mrs Fitzherbert's letter to her) and
104 (for the Duchess's attitude to Mrs Fitzherbert, following her
'marriage'); Leslie's *Mrs Fitzherbert*, 24 (for the reference to the Prince's
letter to Mrs Fitzherbert of 17 July 1784); 31 (for Mrs Fitzherbert's
commonplace book) and 87 (for the Attorney General on Lord George
Gordon); Lord Malmesbury's *Diaries and Correspondence* (4 vols, 1844),
II: 122–3; 125 and 127; Hibbert's *George IV Prince of Wales*, 51 (for
Lady Anne Lindsay on Mrs Fitzherbert); 68 (for Mrs Fitzherbert's
response to Fox's speech); 70 (for Edmund Malone's letter to Lord
Charlemont) and 130 (for the Duke of Gloucester on the Prince's
disenchantment with Mrs Fitzherbert); Lord Holland's *Memoirs of the
Whig Party* (2 vols, 1852, 54), II: 126 (for the Prince's behaviour at
Mrs Armistead's house); 127–37 (for Fox's letter to the Prince on
the reports of his marriage, and the Prince's reply) and 140 (for the

Prince's response to Charles Grey's refusal to make a speech in the Commons relative to Mrs Fitzherbert); John Gabriel Stedman's *Journal* (1962), 306; Thomas Sedgewick Whalley's *Journals and Correspondence* (2 vols, 1863), I: 419 (for Mrs Siddons on Mrs Fitzherbert); *The Heber Letters* (1950), 34; Historical Manuscripts Commission *Rutland MSS* 14th Report, 432 (for Robert Hobart's description of the reports of Mrs Fitzherbert's marriage as a 'lie'); *The Jerningham Letters* (2 vols, 1896), I: 33 and 49; Reginald Blunt's *Mrs Montagu* (2 vols, n.d.), II: 207 (for Mrs Fitzherbert's 'shabby' carriage); Nathaniel Wraxall's *Memoirs* (5 vols, 1884), IV: 449 (for Alderman Newnham) and V, 357–8 (for the Prince and Mrs Crouch); Bernard Pool's edition of *The Croker Papers* (1967), 42 (for the Prince's first acquaintance with Mrs Fitzherbert) and 81 (for the Prince's dismissal of rumours of his marriage as 'nonsense'); *The Gentleman's Magazine* (May 1787), 451 (for Mrs Fitzherbert and Lord George Gordon); John Horne Tooke's *Letter to a Friend* (1787), 37 and 39–41; Hester Thrale's *Thraliana* (2 vols, 1942), II: 724; Philip Wither's *History of the Royal Malady* (n.d.), 29; and the same author's *Alfred to the Bishop of London* (1789), 5–6 and 9 and *Nemesis; or, A Letter to Alfred* (n.d.), 14–15; George IV's *Correspondence* (as Prince of Wales), I: 148–9; 150–2; 155–9; 164; 189; 199–201; 228–9; 231–2; 236; 240 and II: 442 and 444; and Wilkins's *Mrs Fitzherbert*, I: 221 (for the reminiscence of Mrs Fitzherbert in Brighton); 249 (for Lord Harcourt on the Prince's friends' suggestion that the Prince was distancing himself from Mrs Fitzherbert); 274 (for Thomas Raikes on Mrs Fitzherbert) and 310 (for the Prince's letter to Mrs Fitzherbert cancelling their dinner appointment in 1795).

Additionally, the speeches on the Prince and Mrs Fitzherbert in 1787 and 1789 are taken from Wilkins.

Lady Jersey

Nathaniel Wraxall's *Memoirs* (5 vols, 1884), V: 36; Robert Huish's *Memoirs of George IV* (2 vols, 1830), I: 263; Historical Manuscripts Commission *Carlisle MSS*, 15th Report, App. VI, 575 and Hibbert's *George IV Prince of Wales*, 131 (for Lady Jersey and the Prince in 1782); Earl Stanhope's *Pitt* (4 vols, 1861, 62), II: App. xx (for George III's letter to Pitt announcing his son's determination to marry); Lord Malmesbury's *Diaries and Correspondence* (4 vols, 1844), III: 182–4 and

210–11; Charlotte Bury's *Diary* (2 vols, 1908), I: 38–9 (for Caroline's recollections of her wedding night); Brian Connell's *Portrait of a Whig Peer* (1957), 318–19 (for Lady Palmerston on the Prince and Lady Jersey's cruelty); Hester Thrale's *Thraliana* (2 vols, 1942), II: 928 and 963; Reginald Blunt's *Mrs Montagu* (2 vols, n.d.), II: 317; Holme's *Caroline*, 39 (for the *Morning Chronicle* on the date of Charlotte's birth); Lewis Bettany's *Edward Jerningham and His Friends* (1919), 235; 241 and 244–8; Lord Colchester's *Diary and Correspondence* (3 vols, 1861), I: 37 (for Lady Jersey at the Queen's card parties); the Duke of Leeds's *Political Memoranda* (1884), 221 (for Caroline's reception at the Opera House); D.M. Stuart's *Dearest Bess* (1955), 74 (for James Hare's remark on Lady Jersey); Lord Granville Leveson Gower's *Private Correspondence* (2 vols, 1917), I: 123 (for Lady Jersey's behaviour after her dismissal as a lady of the bedchamber), 220 (for the Prince and Miss Fox) and 221 (for Lord Harcourt's disillusionment with Lady Jersey); The Duchess of Devonshire's *Correspondence*, 217 (for Lady Jersey's planned 'éclaircissement') and 219 (for the 'stuffed mawkin'); *A Review with suitable Remarks and Reflections . . . relative to a late Domestic Fracas* (n.d.), 6–7 (for the *Sun* on Lady Jersey's theft of Caroline's letters); *The Times*, 20 July 1796 (for Lady Jersey's letter to Dr Randolph and his response); British Library Add mss 27915 f. 26 (for Lady Jersey's resignation letter); *The Correspondence between the Earl and Countess of Jersey, and the Rev. Dr Randolph* (1796), 2; *The Jerningham Letters* (2 vols, 1896), I: 137 and Samuel Rogers's *Table Talk* (1952), 218 (for the Prince's attempts to finish with Lady Jersey), I.M. Davis's *The Harlot and the Statesman* (1986), 129 (for Fox's letter to Mrs Armistead, counselling her to be wary of the Prince); George IV's *Correspondence* (as Prince of Wales), III: 9; 11; 15–16; 28; 71–2; 98; 122; 130; 159–61; 168–74; 177–9; 181; 184–5; 187; 191; 194–5; 197–8 and 207; and Chatsworth MS C.128.1 (for Lady Jersey's comment on Lady Melbourne).

Mrs Fitzherbert Again

Langdale's *Memoirs*, 127 (for Mrs Fitzherbert's response to the Prince's marriage to Caroline) and 129 (for the Revd Nassau's embassy to Rome and Mrs Fitzherbert's and the Prince's reconciliation); Leslie's *Mrs Fitzherbert*, 135; 146 and 148 (for the Seymours' thoughts on Mrs Fitzherbert's proposed reunion with the Prince); *The Jerningham Letters*

(2 vols, 1896), 1: 160 and 274 (for Edward Jerningham on the Seymour case); Lady Holland's *Journal* (2 vols, 1908), II: 49 (for Madame de Coigny's description of Mrs Fitzherbert's relationship with the Prince as 'like a rondeau'); Mrs Fitzherbert's *Letters*, 13–14 (for the Respondents on the threat to Minney's religious education); 21 (for Minney's progress in the Church of England's catechism); 23 (for Sir W. Farquhar on the threat to Minney's health of removing her from Mrs Fitzherbert); 25 (for Mrs Fitzherbert's meeting with Lady Horatia Seymour, on her return to England); 123 (for Mrs Fitzherbert's letter to Coutts); 125–7 (for Mrs Fitzherbert's letter to Lord Robert Seymour) and 128 (for the Duke of Kent's letter to Mrs Fitzherbert); Hibbert's *George IV Prince of Wales*, 173 (for Mrs Fitzherbert's comment to Lady Anne Lindsay on her life with the Prince); Mrs Calvert's *Unpublished Journals* (1911), 16–17; *The Creevey Papers*, 48–51; 57; 65–7 and 69–71; Nathaniel Jeffrey's *Review of the Conduct of the Prince of Wales, . . . to which is added A Letter to Mrs Fitzherbert* (1806), 11; 13–15 and 74–5; and George IV's *Correspondence* (as Prince of Wales), III: 133–8, 452–3 and 478; IV: 9; 12–13; 16–17; 31; 48–50 and 314–16.

Lady Hertford

Nathaniel Wraxall's *Memoirs* (5 vols, 1884), IV: 137 and 138; Mrs Calvert's *Unpublished Journals* (1911), 80; Lord Holland's *Memoirs of the Whig Party* (2 vols, 1852, 54), II: 69 and 72 (for Lady Hertford's character); and the same author's *Further Memoirs of the Whig Party* (1905), 122 and 124 (for the Whig's satire on the Prince and its consequences); *The Creevey Papers*, 189 and D.M. Stuart's *Dearest Bess* (1955), 198 (for Lady Hertford and Madame de Staël); Charlotte Bury's *Diary* (2 vols, 1908), I: 24 (for Caroline's opinion of Lady Hertford) and II: 222; Sir George Jackson's *Diaries and Letters* (2 vols, 1872), II: 245; Lord Glenbervie's *Diaries* (2 vols, 1928), II: 5; Lady Harriet Cavendish's *Letters* (1940), 258–9; Lord Granville Leveson Gower's *Private Correspondence* (2 vols, 1911), II: 297–8 (for Lady Bessborough on the Prince's letters to Lady Hertford) and II: 349–50 (for the same writer's account of the Prince's attempted seduction of her); Langdale's *Memoirs*, 132 (for Mrs Fitzherbert's 'trials'); Wilkins's *Mrs Fitzherbert*, II: 109–10 (for Mrs Fitzherbert's letter to the Prince calling on him to decide between her and Lady Hertford); Hibbert's *George IV Prince of Wales*, 256 (for the Prince's letter

to Mrs Fitzherbert telling her she was his 'only, only love'); Mary
Berry's *Journal and Correspondence* (3 vols, 1865), II: 471; Cobbett's
Parliamentary Register (Vol. XXII), 85 (for Lord Grey's description of
Lady Hertford as a 'cursed and baleful influence'); Michael Roberts's
The Whig Party (1965), 96 (for Lord Donoughmore's description of
Lady Hertford as a 'matured enchantress'); Henry Gratton's *Memoirs*
(5 vols, 1839–46), IV: 484–5 (for the so-called 'witchery' resolutions);
Sir Shane Leslie's *George the Fourth* (1926), 190–1 (for Mrs Fitzherbert's
letter to the Prince refusing his invitation to the Pavilion) and 193–4
(for Mrs Fitzherbert's final break with the Prince); and the same
author's *Mrs Fitzherbert*, 185 (for the Prince's response to Mrs
Fitzherbert's 'Pavilion' letter); Bernard Falk's *'Old Q's' Daughter* (1951),
88 (for Napoleon on the Prince's preference for older women); John
Raymond's edition of Gronow's *Reminiscences and Recollections* (1964),
191–2; The Comtesse de Boigne's *Memoirs* (3 vols, 1907–08), II: 133;
Godley's edition of Tom Moore's *Poetical Works* (1910), 168; Joanna
Richardson's *George IV* (1966), 85 (for the Prince's health in 1806–
07) and 168–9 (for Mrs Trench and Mrs Leadbeater on the death
of Princess Charlotte); Madame de Lieven's *Private Letters*, 3–5; George
IV's *Correspondence* (as Prince of Wales), V: 459 and 470–1; VI: 21–3;
93–4; 220–1; 225–6; 232–4 and VIII: 406–07 and 420–1; and George
IV's *Letters*, II: 223.

Lady Conyngham

Mrs Arbuthnot's *Journal*, I: 8 (for the foreign dispatch); 16; 77; 97–
8 (for Wellington's conversation with Lady Conyngham on the King's
relationship with his ministers); 108–09; 117–18; 131; 138; 147; 154;
163–5; 243 (for Lady Conyngham's worries about her 'character');
II: 254 (for the rumour that Cumberland would attempt to 'frighten'
the King); 351; 352 (for the King's deteriorating health) and 363
(for Wellington's intention to give Lady Conyngham a copy of Madame
du Barry's *Memoirs*); Madame de Lieven's *Private Letters*, 38; 98–9
(for Lady Conyngham's interest in the Catholics); 139–40 (for Madame de Lieven's attempt to arbitrate between Lady Conyngham and
Lady Castlereagh); 141–2 (for Castlereagh's despair of Lady
Conyngham); 154–5 (for the account of Castlereagh's suicide); 166;
176; 182 (for Lady Conyngham's drawing-room); and 304–05 (for
the King's attempt to seduce Madame de Lieven); George IV's *Let-*

ters, II: 425; 430–3; III: 178–9(for Harriette Wilson's spy) and 466 (for Ponsonby's letter to Sir William Knighton); Lady Palmerston's *Letters* (1957), 23; 31; 79 and 86–7 (for the King's coronation), 114; Sitwell's *Left Hand, Right Hand!* (1945), 56 (for Joseph Denison's industry); Harriette Wilson's *Memoirs* (1929), 72; *The Creevey Papers,* 371–2 (for the King in Ireland, and 490 (for Mrs Michelangelo Taylor's account of William Denison's dislike of his sister's relationship with the King); Fulford's edition of *The Greville Memoirs* (1963), 3–4; 6 and 49; Philip von Neumann's *Diary* (2 vols, 1928), I: 61; Wellington's *Letters,* 67; 295 and 297 (for Lady Conyngham's determination to bring down the Government) and 298; Pool's edition of *The Croker Papers* (1967), 60; and 71 (for the Hibernian Ball); Hibbert's *George IV Regent and King,* 209 (for the King in Ireland) and 355 (for Sir William Waller on the King's death); *The Dublin Mail* (1821), 19–20 (for Lady Conyngham's satirical 'letter' to the King); The Duke of Buckingham and Chandos's *Memoirs of the Court of George IV* (2 vols, 1859), I: 200 and 202; *The Royal Visit* (1821), 97–8 (for the King's journey to Slane Castle); *Mr Gregory's Letter-Box* (1981), 100–02 (for the material on the King's conversation at Slane Castle); Lady Holland's *Elizabeth Lady Holland to her Son* (1946), 7; Harriet Countess Granville's *Letters* (2 vols, 1894), I: 243 (for Lady Conyngham's jewels); The Hon. G.F. Berkeley's *Life and Recollections* (4 vols, 1865–6), III: 100 and 102; *The Lieven-Palmerston Correspondence* (1943), 9; Joseph Jekyll's *Correspondence* (1894), 226; Carola Oman's *The Gascoyne Heiress* (1968), 176; and *The Times,* 9 July 1830 (for the restrictions on entering the park at Windsor).

Select Bibliography

Arbuthnot, Harriet, *The Journal of Mrs Arbuthnot 1820–1832*, edited by F. Bamford and the Duke of Wellington (2 vols, 1950). High politics and gossip from the King's accession to just before the First Reform Act.

Cavendish, Georgiana, *Georgiana. Extracts from the Correspondence of Georgiana, Duchess of Devonshire*, edited by the Earl of Bessborough (1955). Whig society at its fashionable apex.

Colley, Linda, *Britons* (1992). Excellent on Anti-Catholicism.

Farington, Joseph, *The Diary of Joseph Farington*, edited by K. Garlick, A. Macintyre and K. Cave (16 vols, 1978–84). Hugely enjoyable; anecdotal and undiscriminating.

Fulford, Roger, *Royal Dukes* (1933). The standard popular account of George IV's brothers.

George IV, *Correspondence 1770–1812* (8 vols, 1963–71) and *Letters 1812–1830* (3 vols, 1938), both edited by A. Aspinall. Exemplary scholarship, but marred by some suppressions.

George, M.D., *English Political Caricature* (2 vols, 1959). Informed and informative.

Gibbs, Lewis, *Sheridan* (1947). Engaging.

Hibbert, Christopher, *George IV Prince of Wales* and *George IV Regent and King* (1972 and 1973). Much the best life of the King; accurate and skilfully narrated.

Hill, Draper, *Fashionable Contrasts* (1966) and *The Satirical Etchings of James Gillray* (1976). Gillray's mordant view of eighteenth-century society.

Hobhouse, Christopher, *Fox* (1934). Still the best popular life of the Whig statesman.

Holme, Thea, *Caroline* (1979). A solid account of one of history's great eccentrics.

Langdale, Charles, *Memoirs of Mrs Fitzherbert* (1856). Important for Lord Stourton's account of Mrs Fitzherbert's reminiscences.

Leslie, Sir Shane, *Mrs Fitzherbert* (1939). Kaleidoscopic and entertaining; a companion volume to the same author's *The Letters of Mrs Fitzherbert* (1940).

Lieven, Dorothea, *The Private Letters of Princess Lieven to Prince Metternich 1820–1826*, edited by P. Quennell (Albemarle Library edition, 1948). Self-conscious, amusing and malicious.

Masters, Brian, *Georgiana Duchess of Devonshire* (1981). Enjoyable and thought-provoking.

Maxwell, Sir Herbert (ed.), *The Creevey Papers* (1905). A Whig MP's extraordinary collection of letters and diaries.

Penny, Nicholas (ed.), *Reynolds* (1986). A wide-ranging critical account of the consummate painter-flatterer.

Priestley, J.B., *The Prince of Pleasure and his Regency* (1969). Lively and well illustrated.

Robinson, Mary, *Perdita: The Memoirs of Mary Robinson*, edited by M.J. Levy (1994). An informative and sometimes moving apologia.

Wellington, First Duke of, *Wellington and His Friends*, edited by the Seventh Duke of Wellington (1965). Social and political correspondence.

Wilkins, W.H., *Mrs Fitzherbert and George IV* (2 vols, 1905). Groundbreaking.

Unless otherwise indicated, all quotations from letters from or to members of the royal family are taken from Arthur Aspinall's editions of the King's *Correspondence* and *Letters*.

Index

Act of Settlement (1701), 45, 69, 71
Alexander I, Tsar, 146
Arbuthnot, Charles, 153, 170
Arbuthnot, Harriet, 155, 156–7, 158–9, 160, 163–4, 165, 167, 170, 175–6, 179, 180
Armistead, Elizabeth, 28, 29, 30, 31, 41, 50, 78, 102, 124
Aston, Mrs, 81

Bankhead, Dr Charles, 172
Bedford, Duke of, 70, 83
Bellois, Marquis de, 49, 72
Bentinck, Lord Charles, 194
Berkeley, Hon. Grantly, 175
Bessborough, Lady, 77, 136, 138–9, 186
Bicknell, Charles, 192
Bloomfield, Lt.-Col. Benjamin, 133–5, 135n., 136–7, 157–8, 165–8
Boigne, Comtesse de, 148
Bouverie, Hon. Edward, 46
Bowman, Jane, 193
Brereton, William, 20
Bridgeman, Orlando, 56, 65
Broderip, Edmund, 14
Brougham, Henry, 159n.
Brownlow, Countess, 190
Brunswick, Duchess of, 81, 91, 97
Brunswick, Duke of, 80
Burghersh, Lord, 163
Burt, Revd Robert, 56
Butler, Hon. Elizabeth, 65, 111

Butler, Elizabeth (*Lady Conyngham's mother*), 152
Byron, Lord, 78, 145

Calvert, Mrs, 121, 128
Campbell, Lady Augusta, 33
Canning, George, 138, 138n., 173, 176, 177
Canterbury, Archbishop of, 67, 84
Carlisle, Earl of, 78, 85
Carnarvon, Countess of, 81
Caroline, Princess (*later Queen*), viii, 79–95, 97–101, 104, 106, 107–8, 113, 126, 135, 148, 159, 159n., 160, 167, 187
Castlereagh, Lady, 148, 156, 169, 169n., 172
Castlereagh, Lord, 143, 157, 169, 169n., 170–3
Catherine II, Tsarina, 68, 182
Catholic Emancipation, 54n., 115, 139, 144–5, 155, 164, 178–9, 190
Cavendish, Lord George, 28
Cavendish, Lady Harriet, 135–6
Charlotte, Princess, 87–8, 89, 92, 105, 106, 108, 116, 145, 149–50, 174
Charlotte, Princess Royal, 22
Charlotte, Queen, vii, 30, 32–3, 57, 79–80, 82, 83, 85, 86, 87–8, 92, 94, 94n., 97, 101–2, 113, 120, 139–40, 149, 150
Chartres, Duc de, see *d'Orléans, Duc*
Chichester, Bishop of, 180
Cholmondeley, Countess of, 81, 90, 92

Cholmondeley, Earl of, 87, 92, 140
Clarence, William, Duke of, 76, 122, 188–9, 191
Clarges, Lady, 42
Clermont, Lady, 104
Clogher, Bishop of, 171–2
Coleridge, Samuel Taylor, 184–5
Combe, William, 129n.
Conyngham, Elizabeth, Marchioness of, viii, 152–65, 167–81, 189, 190–1
Conyngham, Lady Elizabeth, 153, 154, 164, 171
Conyngham, Lord Francis, 153, 165, 173, 177
Conyngham, Henry, Marquis of, 152–3, 160, 162, 164, 165, 191
Conyngham, Lady Maria, 153
Cosway, Richard, 54, 188
Coutts, Thomas, 114
Cowper, Lady, 152, 159
Creevey, Mrs, 122–5
Creevey, Thomas, 121–2
Croft, Revd, 119
Croker, John Wilson, 45, 150, 160, 162
Crole, Mrs, 102, 192
Crole, George Seymour, 192–3
Crouch, Anna Maria, 75–6
Cumberland, Anne, Duchess of, 53, 70
Cumberland, Ernest, Duke of, 108, 111, 143, 179, 190
Cumberland, Henry, Duke of, 26, 27, 29, 30, 53, 70

Darby, George, 17
Darby, Hester, 14, 15, 16, 17
Darby, Nicholas, 14–16, 182
Davies, Mrs, 193
Dawson, Col. George, 188
Denison, Joseph, 152
Denison, Maria, 152
Denison, William, 152, 153–4, 173
Devonshire, Elizabeth, Duchess of, 147
Devonshire, Georgiana, Duchess of, 19–20, 42–3, 46–9, 52, 53, 54, 57, 125

Devonshire, William, 5th Duke of, 53
Devonshire, William, 6th Duke of, 174
Donoughmore, Lord, 144
d'Orléans, Duc, 31, 39, 59, 72
Dorset, Duchess of, 123
Dorset, Duke of, 33
Downshire, Lady, 122, 123, 130–1

Egremont, Lord, 102, 192
Eldon, Lord, 192
Eliot, Grace Dalrymple, 31, 194
Elizabeth, Princess, 108
Elliot, Sir Gilbert, 87
Errington, Henry, 53, 56, 104, 113
Erskine, Thomas (*later Lord*), 72, 96, 143
Esterhazy, Princess, 163–4
Euston, Countess of, 119
Euston, Earl of, 116–17, 119

Farquhar, Sir Walter, 119, 121, 133
Fawkener, William Augustus, 78
Fitzgerald, George Robert, 18
Fitzherbert, Maria Anne, vii, viii, 44–50, 52–7, 59–76, 77, 79, 80, 83, 84, 89, 104–27, 128, 129, 136–8, 140–1, 187–9, 192–4
Fitzherbert, Thomas, 44, 45, 54n.
Fortescue, Charlotte, 42
Fox, Charles James, 29, 40–2, 52, 54–5, 60–5, 68–9, 70, 71, 73, 74, 86, 95, 102, 115, 124, 130, 182
Fox, Elizabeth, see *Crole, Mrs*
Francis I, Emperor of Austria, 146
Francis, William, 193

Gainsborough, Thomas, 129n.
Garrick, David, 16, 20
George II, 45, 104, 122
George III, vii, 22, 25–6, 30, 31, 34, 35, 37, 38, 46, 50–1, 57, 58, 59, 60, 61, 63, 64, 65, 70–1, 74, 79, 84, 86, 92, 93–4, 96–7, 99, 104, 106, 112, 129, 135n., 139–40, 141, 151

Gleorge IV, vii–viii, 13, 21–43, 44–76, 77–97, 99–103, 104–27, 128–40, 141–51, 152–81, 182, 185–8, 189–90, 192–4
Gifford, William, 183
Gillray, James, 74
Gloucester, William Henry, Duke of, 26, 30, 75
Godwin, William, 184
Gordon, Lord George, 67–8
Granville, Lady Harriet, 174, 189, 191
Grenville, Lord, 131, 139, 142, 143, 145
Greville, Charles, 154, 165, 181
Grey, Charles (*later Lord*), 65–6, 70, 74, 86, 139, 142, 144, 145, 159n.
Gronow, Captain, 148

Halford, Sir Henry, 178, 180–1
Hamilton, Emma, Lady, 124, 124n.
Hamilton, Mary, 14
Hamilton, Sir William, 124n.
Harcourt, Lady, 75, 164
Harcourt, Lord, 96, 164
Harcourt, Mrs, 82
Hardenburg, Count von, 31–3
Hardenburg, Countess von, 31–3
Hare, James, 95
Harris, Sir James, see *Malmesbury, Earl of*
Harris, Thomas, 16, 18
Hastings, Warren, 121
Hays, Mary, 184
Heber, Revd Reginald, 56–7
Hertford, Francis, 1st Marquis of, 60
Hertford, Francis, 2nd Marquis of, 80, 117, 120, 128–9, 129n., 130, 133–5, 189
Hertford, Isabella, Marchioness of, viii, 128–41, 143–51, 169–70, 189–90
Hodges, Mrs, 42
Holland, Lady, 164
Holland, Lord, 128, 132, 139, 143, 144
Hook, Theodore, 148
Hotham, Lt.-Col. George, 34–7, 50, 51, 58

Hotham, Sir Richard, 101
Hulse, Lt.-Col. Samuel (*later General*), 32, 87
Hunt, Leigh, 143, 143n.
Hussey, John, 16
Hutchinson, Lord, 121, 144

Irvine, Lady, 131, 133

Jebb, Sir Richard, 30, 32
Jeffreys, Nathaniel, 125–7
Jerningham, Edward, 75, 100, 101, 103, 119, 120
Jerningham, Lady, 57, 113
Jersey, Frances, Countess of, viii, 42, 76, 77–91, 93–103, 104, 106, 108, 110, 150, 153, 185–7
Jersey, George, 4th Earl of, 78, 81, 86, 87, 96–7, 98, 103, 186
Jersey, Sarah, Countess of, 147, 147n., 158, 186
Johnes, Revd Samuel, 55–6
Jordan, Dorothea, 184

Keate, Thomas, 46, 47, 48
Kent, Edward, Duke of, 120–1, 151
King, John, 18, 34, 34n.
Knighton, Sir William, 155, 165, 168, 178, 180, 190, 192

Lake, Lt.-Col. Gerard (*later General*), 26, 30, 34, 50, 87
Lamb, George, 136, 194
Lamballe, Princess de, 70
Lambton, Lady Anne, 95
Lauzun, Duc de, 39
Lawrence, Sir Thomas, 177
Leeds, Duke of, 94
Leigh, Mrs, 15
Leveson-Gower, Lord Granville, 102, 136, 138
Lieven, Madame de, 151, 155, 156, 164–5, 169, 170–1, 172, 173, 174, 174n., 176–7
Lindsay, Lady Anne, 45, 52, 53, 115
Liverpool, Lord, 157–8, 160, 165–8, 173
London, Bishop of, 72

Lorrington, Meribah, 15
Loughborough, Lord, 70–1, 104
Louis XV, King of France, 45, 181
Louis XVI, King of France, 94
Lyttelton, Lord, 18–19, 34n.

McMahon, Col. John, 102, 108–9,
  123, 133, 145, 186
Madan, Revd Martin, 27
Malden, Lord, 13, 21, 22, 23, 24,
  27, 33, 34, 35–7, 39, 40
Marie-Antoinette, Queen of France,
  39, 67–8, 70
Mary, Princess, 109, 149
Melbourne, Lady, 42–3, 47, 77
Metternich, Prince, 151, 169, 171,
  177
Meyer, Jeremiah, 22
Moira, Earl of, 96, 99, 106, 143
Moore, Dr John, see *Canterbury,
  Archbishop of*
Moore, Tom, 148–9
More sisters, 14
Mount-Charles, Earl of, 153, 176
Mount Edgecumbe, Countess of, 77

Napoleon I, Emperor of France,
  142, 146, 147
Nassau, Revd William, 113
Nelson, Lord, 123–4, 124n.
Newnham, Alderman Nathaniel,
  59–61, 66
Nicholas I, Tsar, 153
Norfolk, Duke of, 120, 122, 122n.,
  143
North, Lord, 38, 41, 55
Northington, 1st Earl of, 14–15
Northington, 2nd Earl of, 34n.

O'Connell, Daniel, 145
Onslow, Lord, 46, 47, 48
Opie, Amelia, 184
Ord, James, 193

Paget, Arthur, 109, 114
Palliser, Sir Hugh, 14
Palmerston, Lady, 85
Parkinson, Richard, 162n.

Payne, Captain John, 71, 75–6,
  80–1, 82, 91, 106, 108, 117
Pelham, Mrs, 81, 86
Perceval, Spencer, 139–40, 142, 143
Pitt, William, 40, 59–63, 65, 66, 68,
  70, 79, 86, 115, 183
Ponsonby, John, 153, 177–8, 186
Porden, William, 120

Queensbury, Duke of, 130

Raikes, Thomas, 75
Randolph, Revd Dr, 97, 98
Reynolds, Sir Joshua, 40
Richmond, Duchess of, 169–70
Robespierre, Maximilien, 85, 85n.
Robinson, Maria Elizabeth, 19, 185
Robinson, Mary, vii, viii, 13–30,
  32–42, 44, 74, 128, 129n., 182–5,
  192
Rogers, Samuel, 185
Rolle, John, 61, 62, 63, 64, 66, 73–4
Romilly, Samuel, 118
Romney, George, 33
Rosenhagen, Revd Philip, 55
Royal Marriage Act (1772), 45, 55,
  71, 74
Rutland, Duchess of, 109–10, 111

Salisbury, Lady, 42
Sefton, Lady, 57, 122
Selwyn, George, 40, 130
Seymour, Georgiana, 31, 194
Seymour, Lord Henry, 116–19
Seymour, Horace, 148
Seymour, Lady Horatia, 80, 111,
  115–16, 118
Seymour, Lord Hugh, 80–1, 111,
  115–16
Seymour, Minney, 115–20, 129,
  138, 187–8, 189
Seymour, Lord Robert, 117–18
Shelburne, Lord, 40, 41
Sheridan, Elizabeth, 67
Sheridan, Richard Brinsley, 20, 21,
  60, 61–2, 66–7, 71, 74, 121, 122,
  139, 143, 182
Siddons, Sarah, 56

Sidmouth, Viscount, 157
Sims, Sophia Elizabeth, 193–4
Smith, William, 13
Smythe, John, 56, 113
Smythe, Mary, 44, 45, 110, 111
Smythe, Mary Anne, 193
Smythe, Walter (*Mrs Fitzherbert's father*), 44, 45, 59
Smythe, Walter, 68
Southampton, Lord, 32, 35, 37, 46, 47, 51, 57, 58
Staël, Madame de, 146–7
Stedman, John Gabriel, 56
Stewart, Lord, 171
Sumner, Charles (*later Bishop of Winchester*), 157–8, 179

Talbot, Countess of, 69
Tarleton, Col. Banastre, 40, 41, 42, 182, 183, 184
Thrale, Mrs, 71, 85–6
Thurlow, Lord, 117, 118, 123
Tooke, John Horne, 67–9, 71, 95

Victoria, Princess, 151
Villiers, —— (*Lady Jersey's infant son*), 88, 96, 194

Villiers, Lady Elizabeth, 186
Villiers, Lady Frances, 186

Waldegrave, Lady, 115
Waller, Sir Wathen, 181
Washington, George, 162n.
Weld, Edward, 45
Wellesley, Lord, 124, 142
Wellington, Duke of, 155, 156, 167, 170, 172, 173, 174n., 175–6, 179, 180–1, 192
Weltje, Louis, 71
Whitworth, Lord, 123
William IV, see *Clarence, Duke of*
Willis, Col. Henry Norton, 103
Willoughby, Lady, 90
Wilmot, Harriet, 18–19
Wilson, Harriette, 152, 153, 177–8
Winchester, Bishop of, 117, 119
Withers, Revd Philip, 71–2
Wollstonecraft, Mary, 184
Wraxall, Sir Nathaniel, 78, 128, 129

Yarmouth, Lord, 129–30, 131, 143, 153
York, Frederick, Duke of, 22, 23, 26, 30, 33, 46, 70, 71, 142, 150, 154